MOON

TULUM

GARY CHANDLER & LIZA PRADO

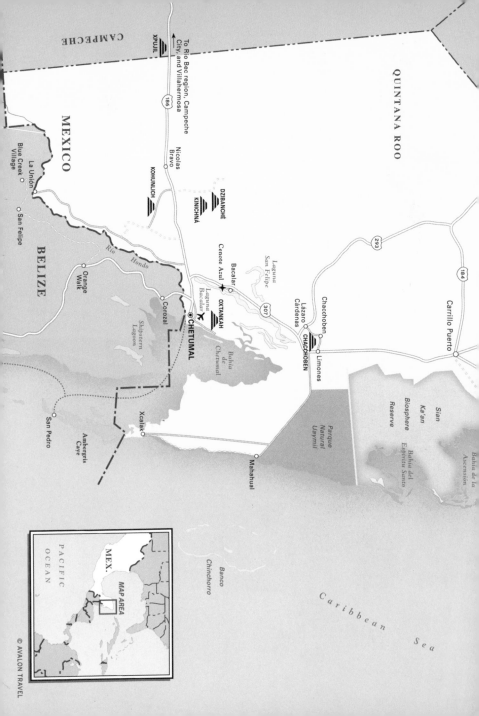

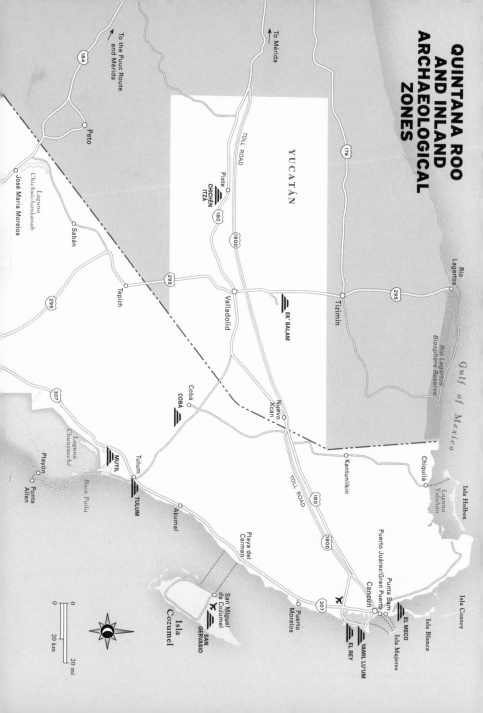

QUINTANA ROO AND INLAND ARCHAEOLOGICAL ZONES

To the Puuc Route and Mérida

To Mérida

184

Peto

Laguna Chichuchankanab

José María Morelos

Sabán

295

Tepich

295

307

Playón

Punta Allen

Laguna Chunyaxché

Boca Paila

MUYIL

Tulum

TULUM

Akumal

YUCATÁN

TOLL ROAD

Pisté

CHICHÉN ITZÁ

180

180D

Valladolid

EK' BALAM

Cobá

COBÁ

Nuevo Xcan

Kantunilkin

TOLL ROAD

180

180D

176

Río Lagartos

Tizimín

295

Río Lagartos Biosphere Reserve

Gulf of Mexico

Chiquilá

Isla Holbox

Laguna Yalahau

Isla Contoy

Isla Blanca

EL MECO

Isla Mujeres

Punta Sam

Puerto Juárez/Gran Puerto

Cancún

YAMIL LU'UM

EL REY

307

Puerto Morelos

Playa del Carmen

SAN MIGUEL de Cozumel

SAN GERVASIO

Isla Cozumel

0 20 km
0 20 mi

Contents

DISCOVER
Tulum

The secret is out about Tulum. It has the makings of a favorite getaway: idyllic beaches, oceanfront *cabañas,* and ancient Maya ruins perched on a cliff overlooking the turquoise sea— all without a mega-development in sight. Farther south, the Costa Maya remains relatively undeveloped, while the inland archaeological sites such as Chichén Itzá never fail to impress.

Equally unexpected are the area's numerous natural and ecological attractions. You can dive and snorkel in the longest underground river system in the world and kayak through mangrove forests and lagoons. At Cobá archaeological site, you can climb the second-highest Maya pyramid, *and* see parrots and toucans, *and* bike from temple to temple on wide forest paths, all in the same visit.

So what sort of trip will it be? Sunbathing by the pool, swimming and snorkeling in cenotes, or exploring the Maya ruins? With luck, you'll do a little of each. In the process, you may discover that Tulum and the Costa Maya are more than they seem. They are places to love, laugh at, be surprised by, and above all, to experience and explore.

Clockwise from top left: beach in Tulum; Cobá's main pyramid; *chac-mool* figure at Chichén Itzá; Cenote Sagrado Azul; stone carvings at the Temple of Kukulkán in Chichén Itzá; Mahahual's main beach.

Planning Your Trip

Where to Go

Tulum and the Costa Maya

Tulum is justly famous for its stunning beaches, eco-chic bungalows, and namesake **Maya ruin**, with a dramatic view of the Caribbean. An hour from Tulum, **Cobá** boasts the second-tallest Maya pyramid and a lovely forest setting teeming with birds. Directly south of Tulum is the pristine **Sian Ka'an Biosphere Reserve** and beyond that the isolated towns of the **Costa Maya**. There's a lovely freshwater lagoon, **Laguna**

Bacalar, a short distance from **Chetumal**, the busy state capital and gateway to Belize.

Chichén Itzá

Several fascinating Maya ruins are within easy reach of Tulum. **Chichén Itzá** is one of the most impressive and recognizable of all Maya ruins, and just two hours from Tulum. Even closer, **Ek' Balam** is small but has a spectacular stucco frieze and relatively few visitors.

Know Before You Go

When to Go

Considering weather, prices, and crowds, the best times to visit the Yucatán Peninsula are from **late November to mid-December,** and from **mid-January to early May.** You'll avoid the intense heat from June to August, the rain (and possible hurricanes) in September and October, and the crowds and high prices around the winter holidays.

The big caveats with those periods are spring break (March/April) and Semana Santa (the week before Easter), when American and Canadian students, and then Mexican tourists, turn out in force and prices spike temporarily.

Be aware that certain attractions are only available (or recommendable) during specific months, such as visiting Chichén Itzá on the spring equinox. Even many year-round activities like sportfishing, kiteboarding, and bird-watching are better or worse according to the season.

Passports and Visas

American and Canadian travelers are required to have a valid passport to travel to and from

Mexico. **Tourist visas** are issued upon entry; you technically are allowed up to 180 days, but agents often issue just 30 or 60 days. If you want to stay longer, request the time when you present your passport. To extend your visa, visit the immigration office in Cancún.

Vaccinations

No special vaccines are required for travel to the Yucatán Peninsula, but it's a good idea to be up-to-date on the **standard travel immunizations,** including hepatitis A, MMR (measles-mumps-rubella), tetanus-diphtheria, and typhoid.

Transportation

Cancún International Airport (CUN) is far and away the most common and convenient entry point to the region. A handful of flights go directly to Chetumal, and there are plans (but nothing more) for a new airport outside Tulum; there also is an airport near Chichén Itzá, but it is used exclusively for charter flights. An excellent network of **buses, shuttles,** and **ferries** covers the

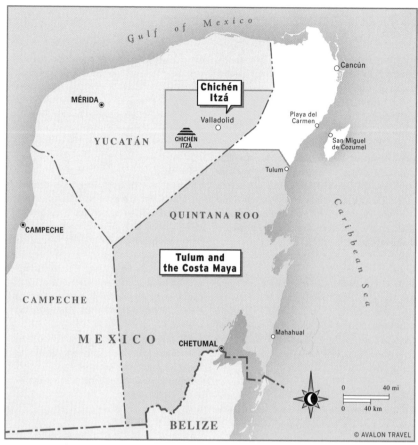

Gulf of Mexico

MÉRIDA

Chichén Itzá

Valladolid

YUCATÁN

CHICHÉN ITZÁ

Cancún

Playa del Carmen

San Miguel de Cozumel

Tulum

CAMPECHE

QUINTANA ROO

Tulum and the Costa Maya

Caribbean Sea

CAMPECHE

MEXICO

CHETUMAL

Mahahual

0   40 mi

0   40 km

BELIZE

© AVALON TRAVEL

entire region, though a rental car makes a world of difference in more remote areas.

What to Pack

Bring what you would to any beach destination: light cotton clothing, hat, sunscreen, sunglasses, flip-flops, etc. Beach buffs should bring two or even three swimsuits, plus snorkel gear if you've got it. Water shoes come in handy wherever the beach is rocky, while sneakers and bug repellent are musts for the Maya ruins. Finally, it's always smart to bring an extra pair of glasses or contacts, prescription medications, birth control, and a travel clock. If you do leave anything behind, no worries—there's a Walmart in all the major cities.

The Best of Tulum

With picturesque beaches, elegant restaurants, relaxing spas, and cozy accommodations, Tulum has all the makings of a perfect getaway.

Day 1

Fly into Cancún, and make your way by bus or taxi to Tulum. Settle into your beachside bungalow, complete with a hanging bed, mosquito net, and candles. If you want something a little more upscale, consider staying in a suite at one of the chic high-end hotels. Spend the remainder of the day on the beach. In the evening, head to Mezzanine or La Zebra for drinks, followed by dinner at Hechizo.

Day 2

Visit the Tulum ruins in the morning before the crowds arrive. Bring your swimsuit to enjoy the small beach there. Afterward, walk to gorgeous Playa Mar Caribe, just south of the ruins. Enjoy lunch at nearby Adelita Tulum. If you're up for it, head down the road for a drop-in yoga class at Yoga Shala Tulum in the late afternoon.

Day 3

Leave bright and early to get to the Maya ruins of Chichén Itzá before the crowds do. Spend the morning there, followed by lunch in the colonial city of Valladolid. From there, go swimming in nearby cenotes, or visit Ek' Balam, a much smaller ruin. Both Valladolid and Ek' Balam have good lodging options, if you want to turn this into an overnight trip.

Day 4

Choose between taking an organized eco-tour in the Sian Ka'an Biosphere Reserve, a sprawling coastal reserve south of Tulum that is home to an astounding array of wildlife, or do-it-yourself cenote hopping (four cenotes on the road to Cobá are just minutes away). If you're at a high-end hotel, book a beachside dinner—complete with a personalized menu—before starting your day. Also consider reserving a massage for your last day at the Yaan Wellness Energy Spa.

Day 5

Spend your last full day beachcombing on Tulum's southern beaches. Take a private paddleboarding lesson with Ocean Pro Kite. Afterwards relax on the beach and don't forget to go to your massage!

Best Diving and Snorkeling

For many travelers, the Yucatán's underwater treasures are as compelling as its terrestrial ones. The region includes the world's second-longest coral reef, the longest known underground river system, and the Northern Hemisphere's largest coral atoll. Below are some of the region's top spots to get underwater:

Tulum

Journey into the abyss! The Yucatán Peninsula is dotted with hundreds of eerily beautiful cenotes (freshwater caverns and sinkholes) offering out-of-this-world snorkeling and diving for novices and experts alike. Tulum's dive shops specialize in cenote dives and courses, while snorkelers can grab their gear and spend the day cenote hopping. Try the string of cenotes west of Tulum including Car Wash and Gran Cenote. Dos Ojos, near Tulum, also offers full-service guided tours for snorkelers and divers, in a gorgeous stalagmite-filled cavern.

Maya Ruins

Besides its incredible beaches and world-class resorts, Mexico's Caribbean coast is also home to (or within easy reach of) numerous ancient Maya ruins, including some of the most important archaeological sites in the country and the continent. A visit to one or more is well worth a day off the sand, even for committed beach hounds. (And at least one site—Tulum—has historical value *and* a pretty little beach. Sweet!)

- **Chichén Itzá,** with its iconic pyramid and massive ball court, is one of the New Seven Wonders of the World. Scores of tours head there from Cancún, but getting to the site early—by bus or rental car—lets you beat the crowds and enjoy this fascinating site at your own pace.

- **Ek' Balam** boasts one of the best-preserved stucco friezes in the Maya world and an all-embracing view from atop its main pyramid. A nearby cenote is great for cooling off.

- **Cobá** has an even better view from its main pyramid—at 42 meters (138 feet) high, it's the second tallest in the Yucatán Peninsula. Nestled in a forest near several small lakes, it's also a good place to spot birds and butterflies.

- **Tulum** is the subject of innumerable postcards, perched on a bluff overlooking the turquoise Caribbean Sea. Like Chichén Itzá, it's far more rewarding to skip the tour and make your way to Tulum early to enjoy the site before the throngs arrive.

Ek' Balam is a small but fascinating Maya ruin that boasts a remarkable stucco frieze.

- **Kohunlich,** in southern Quintana Roo, is the most remote of the ruins listed here and is best known for a series of imposing stucco masks. Nearby is a unique all-inclusive luxury resort with guided trips in the surrounding forest and lagoons.

The Costa Maya

Banco Chinchorro is the largest coral atoll on this side of the planet, and has spectacular diving and snorkeling. Getting there can be a bear—2-3 hours by boat each way—but the massive and pristine coral structure atoll is worth the time and expense. Dive shops in **Mahahual** or **Xcalak,** two small towns near the Belize border, offer Chinchorro trips. There's also fantastic snorkeling and diving right from the shore, including at night.

A Family Affair

The Yucatán Peninsula is an excellent family destination, with plenty to see and do for kids and parents alike. Here are some recommended spots:

- **Dos Ojos Cenote:** Great cenote snorkeling for all ages, either with a guide or on your own.

- **Chichén Itzá:** Impressive ruins with several family-friendly hotels nearby. The Ik Kil cenote just east of town is a sure hit.

- **Valladolid:** Charming midsize city, with three impressive cenotes nearby for swimming.

- **Cobá:** Renting bikes or bicycle taxis makes visiting these ruins especially fun for kids, while the thick forest provides cool shade and a chance to spot birds and insects.

- **Punta Laguna Spider Monkey Reserve:** A great family outing, where you'll spot not only spider and howler monkeys, but a slew of birds, tropical vegetation, and more.

one of the long-armed, long-tailed residents of Punta Laguna Spider Monkey Reserve

Ecoadventure

Lazing on a beach or contemplating museum displays is all right, but some travelers crave a little more action. The Yucatán has plenty to offer active travelers, including kiteboarding, fly-fishing, kayaking, and mountain biking. The only things this tour doesn't include are snorkeling and diving, which are covered in a list of their own.

Day 1

Ease into things by spending a day stand-up paddling (or SUPing). It's challenging but fairly easy to master, and especially rewarding in the area's warm clear water. **Tulum** and **Mahahual** are fine places to start.

Day 2

Kayaking is another low-key, easy-to-learn activity, and perfect for exploring the region's rich mangrove forests. The **Sian Ka'an Biosphere Reserve** and **Laguna Bacalar** both have fascinating kayak tours that include paddling through mangrove canals, spotting birds, and locating hidden beaches and lost Maya ruins.

Day 3

Today's the day for pushing yourself. Why not try kiteboarding? The sport has been growing in popularity along the Caribbean coast. **Tulum** has terrific kiteboarding, with plenty of options for travelers who want to learn or practice the sport.

Day 4

You may want to spend a second day kiteboarding—few people master it in a day! Otherwise, dig out your sneakers and sign up for a mountain bike tour. Both **Tulum** and **Laguna Bacalar** have fun and moderately challenging rides, pedaling

Cenote Hopping

All along the coast and well inland are dozens of cenotes—pools of shimmering blue water fed by a vast underground freshwater river system. Some look like large ponds, others are deep sinkholes, others occupy gaping caverns or have dramatic rock formations. Many cenotes are open to the public, and their cool clear water is perfect for swimming, snorkeling, and scuba diving. Facilities range from simple restrooms and snorkel rental to full-service "cenote parks" with guided tours. Some favorites include:

NEAR TULUM

- **Dos Ojos:** A cenote park with rentals, guides, and spectacular caverns.

- **Gran Cenote:** Lovely cavern with natural arches and stalactite formations; east of Tulum on the road to Cobá.

- **Car Wash:** Just past Gran Cenote, this innocuous-looking cenote has stunning rock formations below the surface.

INLAND AREAS

- **Cenote X'Canché:** A pretty 12-meter-deep (39-foot) cenote, a kilometer (0.6 mile) down a forest path from Ek' Balam ruins.

- **Cenote Choo-Ha:** One of four dramatic cenotes near Cobá, with a high domed ceiling and iridescent blue water.

- **Cenote Sagrado Azul:** Just three kilometers

The Yucatán Peninsula has hundreds of cenotes, from simple pools to spectacular caverns, like Cenote Choo-Ha outside Cobá.

(1.9 miles) from Chichén Itzá, this huge deep cenote can be crowded but is impressive all the same.

- **Cenote Yokdzonot:** Also nearby Chichén Itzá, this little-known gem is all the more rewarding for being operated by a cooperative of enterprising local women.

through the jungle to little-visited Maya ruins and remote beaches.

Day 5
You've gotta be getting tired by now. Spend the day fishing, either trolling in the ocean or fly-fishing in the region's vast coastal flats. **Sian Ka'an** and **Xcalak** are world-class fly-fishing

spots, brimming with tarpon, permit, bonefish, and snook.

Day 6
Bring your ecoadventure to a fitting close with a day on the beach. The beaches in **Tulum** and **Mahahual** have plenty to keep you active—swimming, snorkeling, SUPing, and more.

Tulum and the Costa Maya

Tulum has long been favored by travelers who cringe at the splashy resorts and package tourism found in Cancún (and increasingly the Riviera Maya). In that sense, Tulum is a fitting bridge between Quintana Roo's

booming northern section and its far-less-traveled south. Tulum has so far managed to avoid the impulse to fill the coast with ever-bigger resorts; prices have certainly gone up, but there are still no megadevelopments here, or even power lines for that matter. Its beaches and *cabañas* remain as idyllic as ever.

If Tulum is the anti-Cancún, you might call southern Quintana Roo, or the "Costa Maya," the non-Cancún. Though fairly close in distance, it's worlds apart by any other measure. Immediately south of Tulum is the massive Sian Ka'an Biosphere Reserve, one of the Yucatán's largest and richest preserves, whose bays, lagoons, mangrove stands, and inland forests support a vast array of plants and animals, from dolphins to jaguars; there's even a large Maya ruin and several smaller temples. Beyond Sian Ka'an is the Costa Maya, the sparsely populated stretch of coast reaching down to the Belize border;

the largest towns are Mahahual and Xcalak, with numerous small bed-and-breakfasts and seaside hotels in both (and a highly incongruous cruise ship port in Mahahual). Most of the beaches aren't postcard perfect like Tulum's, but the isolation—not to mention the far-less-expensive lodging—are hard to match. Inland and farther south is the multicolored Laguna Bacalar and several significant but all-but-forgotten Maya ruins. Chetumal, the state capital, isn't much of a destination itself but has some unexpectedly appealing areas nearby, and is the gateway to Belize.

Less than an hour from Tulum—and a great alternative to the overcrowded ruins there—is the ancient city of Cobá (42 kilometers/26 miles from Tulum), home of the second-tallest known Maya pyramid. Unlike many other ruins, Cobá is ensconced in a thick tropical forest that teems with birdlife, including parrots and toucans.

Previous: Tulum's scenic Maya ruins; Mahahual beach. **Above:** mural in Tulum.

Look for ★ to find recommended
sights, activities, dining, and lodging.

Highlights

★ **Tulum's Southern Beaches:** Mile after mile of powdery white sand, tranquil turquoise water, cozy bungalows peeking out from behind softly bending palm trees . . . these are the beaches you've been dreaming of (page 23).

★ **Cenotes near Tulum:** Sure the ocean reefs are gorgeous, but don't miss a chance to explore these eerie and unforgettable limestone caverns, bristling with stalagmites and stalactites, and filled with the crystalline water of the world's longest underground river system (page 24).

★ **Cobá Archaeological Zone:** Just an hour from Tulum are the terrific jungle-cloaked ruins of Cobá, where you can climb the Yucatán's second-highest pyramid and rent bikes to get from temple to temple (page 42).

★ **Cenotes near Cobá:** A visit to Cobá just got better, with the opening of three impressive cenotes a short distance from the ruins. Each is unique, but all are massive caverns, with stalactites above and easy-to-use stairs descending to the cool shimmering water below (page 47).

★ **Bahía de la Ascensión:** A huge protected expanse of calm ocean flats and tangled mangrove forests make this a world-class destination for bird-watchers and anglers (page 51).

★ **Banco Chinchorro:** A punishing two-hour boat ride across the open sea is rewarded

with spectacular diving on one of the world's largest coral atolls (page 59).

★ **Fuerte San Felipe Bacalar:** Housed in a stout star-shaped fort, this small-town museum has fascinating and innovative displays on piracy and the Caste War (page 71).

Tulum and the Costa Maya

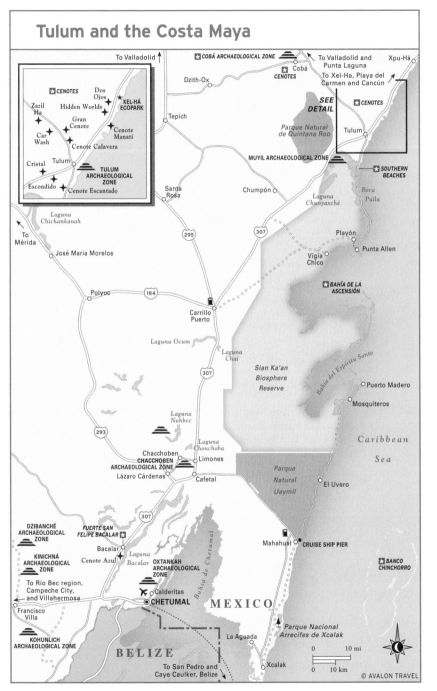

PLANNING YOUR TIME

Tulum is the first stop, of course, and for many people their main destination. From Tulum you can take day trips or short overnighters to the Sian Ka'an reserve and Cobá archaeological site, both fascinating. To venture any farther south you'll probably want a rental car, as bus service grows infrequent. Mahahual and Xcalak are certainly worth savoring; despite their isolation, there's plenty to do in both, including snorkeling, diving, kayaking, fishing, and, of course, just relaxing. Laguna Bacalar is worth a day or possibly two, to take a boat trip on the Caribbean-like water, swim in Cenote Azul, and visit the surprisingly good history museum in town. Chetumal is a logical stopover for those headed west toward the Río Bec region or crossing into Belize, and it has an interesting Maya museum.

Tulum

Tulum is the subject of a thousand postcards, and justly so. It's hard to know if the name is more closely associated with the ancient Maya ruins—perched dramatically on a cliff overlooking the Caribbean—or the idyllic beaches and oceanfront *cabañas* that have long been the jewel of the Riviera Maya. What's certain is that Tulum manages to capture both the ancient mystery and modern allure of Mexico's Riviera Maya.

Tulum has definitely grown and changed, with more changes on the way. The beach used to be a haven for backpackers and bohemians, with simple *cabañas* facing beautiful untouched beaches. The beaches are still beautiful, but the prices have long since gone through the *palapa* roof, catering more to urban escapists and upscale yoga groups. It's still a lovely place to stay, no matter who you are, just not as cheap as it used to be.

One consequence of the spike in prices on the beach is that the inland village of Tulum (aka Tulum Pueblo) has perked up significantly. Long a dumpy roadside town, it now has a growing number of hotels, B&Bs, and recommendable restaurants catering to independent travelers who have been priced out of the beachfront hotels. To be sure, a beachside *cabaña* will always be the most appealing place to stay in Tulum—and there are a handful of bargains still to be had—but staying in town is no longer the huge step down that it once was.

ORIENTATION

The name Tulum is used for three separate areas, which can be confusing. The first is Tulum archaeological zone, the scenic and popular Maya ruins. This is the first part of Tulum you encounter as you drive south from Cancún. A kilometer and a half (1 mile) farther south (and well inland) is the town of Tulum, known as Tulum Pueblo, where you'll find the bus terminal, supermarket, and numerous restaurants, hotels, Internet cafés, and other shops. The third area is Tulum's beachfront hotel zone, or Zona Hotelera. Located due east of Tulum Pueblo, the Zona Hotelera extends for almost 10 kilometers (6 miles) from the Maya ruins to the entrance of the Sian Ka'an Biosphere Reserve, with fantastic beaches and bungalow-style hotels virtually the entire way. There's a walking path, but no road, connecting the Tulum ruins to the upper end of Tulum's Zona Hotelera.

TULUM ARCHAEOLOGICAL ZONE

The Maya ruins of Tulum (8am-5pm daily, US$4.50) are one of Mexico's most scenic archaeological sites, built atop a 12-meter (40-foot) cliff rising abruptly from turquoise Caribbean waters. The structures don't compare in grandeur to those of Cobá, Uxmal, or elsewhere, but are interesting and significant nevertheless.

Tulum is the single most frequently visited

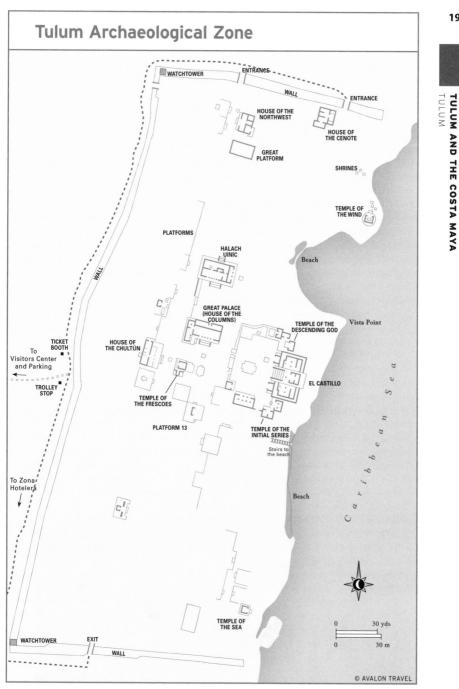

Tulum Archaeological Zone

WATCHTOWER

ENTRANCE

WALL

ENTRANCE

HOUSE OF THE NORTHWEST

HOUSE OF THE CENOTE

GREAT PLATFORM

SHRINES

TEMPLE OF THE WIND

Beach

PLATFORMS

HALACH UINIC

Vista Point

GREAT PALACE (HOUSE OF THE COLUMNS)

TEMPLE OF THE DESCENDING GOD

TICKET BOOTH

To Visitors Center and Parking

HOUSE OF THE CHULTÚN

EL CASTILLO

TROLLEY STOP

TEMPLE OF THE FRESCOES

Caribbean Sea

To Zona Hotelera

PLATFORM 13

TEMPLE OF THE INITIAL SERIES

Stairs to the beach

Beach

WATCHTOWER

EXIT

TEMPLE OF THE SEA

WALL

0   30 yds
0   30 m

© AVALON TRAVEL

Maya ruin in the Yucatán Peninsula, receiving thousands of visitors every day, most on package tours from nearby resorts. (In fact, it's second only to Teotihuacán, near Mexico City, as the country's most visited archaeological site.) For that reason, the first and most important piece of advice for independent travelers regarding Tulum is to *arrive early.* It used to be that the tour bus madness didn't begin until 11am, but it creeps earlier and earlier every year. Still, if you're there right at 8am, you'll have the ruins mostly to yourself for an hour or so—which is about all you need for this small site—before the hordes descend. Guides can be hired at the entrance for around US$50 for 1-4 people. Bring your swimsuit if you fancy a morning swim: This is the only Maya ruin with a great little beach right inside the archaeological zone.

History

Tulum was part of a series of Maya forts and trading outposts established along the Caribbean coast from the Gulf of Mexico as far south as present-day Honduras. Its original name was Zamá-Xamanzamá or simply Zamá (derived from *zamal,* or dawn) but was later called Tulum, Yucatec Maya for fortification or city wall, in reference to the thick stone barrier that encloses the city's main structures. Measuring 380 by 165 meters (1,250 by 540 feet), it's the largest fortified Maya site on the Quintana Roo coast (though small compared to most inland ruins).

Tulum's enviable patch of seashore was settled as early as 300 BC, but it remained little more than a village for most of its existence, overshadowed by the Maya city of Tankah a few kilometers to the north. Tulum gained prominence between the 12th and 16th centuries (the Late Post-Classic era), when mostly non-Maya immigrants repopulated the Yucatan Peninsula following the general Maya collapse several centuries prior. Tulum's strategic location and convenient beach landing made it a natural hub for traders, who plied the coast in massive canoes measuring up to 16 meters (52 feet) long, laden with honey, salt, wax, animal skins, vanilla, obsidian, amber, and other products.

It was during this Post-Classic boom period that most of Tulum's main structures were built. Although influenced by Mayapán (the reigning power at the time) and Central Mexican city-states, from which many of Tulum's new residents had emigrated, Tulum's structures mostly exemplify "east coast architecture," defined by austere designs with

House of the Cenote at the Tulum ruins

Rediscovering the Maya

The Maya ruins of the Yucatán Peninsula were all but unknown in the United States and Europe until well into the 19th century. Although Spanish explorers and colonizers had occupied the peninsula for more than two centuries, conflicts with local Maya and Catholic antipathy for all things pagan probably account for the Spaniards' lack of research or even apparent interest. To be fair, the immensity of the task was surely daunting—by the time the Spanish reached the Yucatán in the early 1500s, the majority of sites had been abandoned for at least 300 years, and in some cases double or triple that. Many were piles of rubble, and those still standing were mostly covered in vegetation. Just getting to the sites was a task in itself.

And so it was an American and an Englishman—diplomat **John Lloyd Stephens** and artist-architect **Frederick Catherwood**—who brought the Maya world to worldwide attention. Between 1839 and 1841, they conducted two major explorations of the Maya region, including present-day Yucatán, Chiapas, and Central America, visiting a total of 44 ruins. Stephens kept a detailed account of their travels, making many observations on the nature of Maya civilization that proved remarkably prescient. He correctly surmised that Maya writing contained detailed dynastic and historical accounts, and rejected the prevailing notion that Mesoamerican civilizations were descended from Egyptian or other Old World societies, declaring the mysterious ruins "a spectacle of a people skilled in architecture, sculpture, and possessing the culture and refinement attendant upon those, not derived from the Old World, but originating and growing here without models or masters like the plants and fruits of the soil, indigenous." Meanwhile, Catherwood made incredibly precise drawings of numerous structures, monuments, hieroglyphs, and scenes of peasant life. (Though they've been widely reprinted, you can see a rare collection of original Catherwood prints in Mérida, at the highly recommended museum-gallery Casa Catherwood.)

Stephens and Catherwood published their work in two volumes, both of which were instant sensations in the United States and Europe, awakening immense interest in ancient Maya civilization. Their books now are condensed into a single, very readable volume, *Incidents of Travel in Yucatán* (Hard Press, 2007), available in English and in many bookstores in the Yucatán. It is a fascinating read, not only for the historical value but also as a backdrop for your own travels throughout the region.

relatively little ornamentation and a predominantly horizontal orientation (compared to high-reaching pyramids elsewhere). Ironically, construction in these later eras tended to be rather shoddy, thanks in part to improvements in stucco coverings that meant the quality of underlying masonry was not as precise. Today, with the stucco eroded away, Tulum's temples appear more decayed than structures at other sites, even those built hundreds of years prior.

The Spanish got their first view of Tulum, and of mainland indigenous society, on May 7, 1518, when Juan de Grijalva's expedition along the Quintana Roo coast sailed past the then brightly colored fortress. The chaplain of the fleet famously described the city as "a village so large that Seville would not have appeared larger or better." Tulum remained an important city and port until the mid-1500s, when European-borne diseases decimated its population. The once-grand city was effectively abandoned and, for the next three centuries, slowly consumed by coastal vegetation. In 1840, Spanish explorers referred to an ancient walled city known as Tulum, the first recorded use of its current name; two years later the famous American/English team of John Lloyd Stephens and Frederick Catherwood visited Tulum, giving the world its first detailed description and illustrations of the dramatic seaside site. During the Caste War, Tulum was occupied by members of the Talking Cross cult, including the followers of a Maya priestess known as the Queen of Tulum.

House of the Cenote

The path from the ticket booth follows Tulum's wall around the northwest corner to two low corbel arch entryways. Using the second entrance (closest to the ocean), you'll first see the Casa del Cenote. The two-room structure, with a third chamber added later, is less impressive than the gaping maw of its namesake cenote. The water is not drinkable, thanks to saltwater intrusion, but that may not have been the case a half millennium ago; it's unlikely Tulum could have grown to its size and prominence without a major water source, not only for its own residents but passing traders as well. Cenotes were also considered apertures to Xibalba, or the underworld, and an elaborate tomb discovered in the floor of the House of the Cenote suggests it may have had a ceremonial function as well.

Temple of the Wind

Following the path, the next major structure is the Temple of the Wind, perched regally atop a rocky outcrop overlooking a picturesque sandy cove. If it looks familiar, that's because it appears on innumerable postcards, magazine photos, and tourist brochures. (The view is even better from a vista point behind El Castillo, and of course from the ocean.) The name derives from the unique circular base upon which the structure is built: In Central Mexican cosmology, the circle is associated with the god of the wind, and its presence here (and at other ruins, like San Gervasio on Isla Cozumel) is evidence of the strong influence that Central Mexican migrants/invaders had on Post-Classic Maya societies.

Temple of the Descending God

One of Tulum's more curious structures is the Temple of the Descending God, named for the upside-down winged figure above its doorway. Exactly who or what the figure represents is disputed among archaeologists—theories include Venus, the setting sun, the god of rain, even the god of bees (as honey was one of the coastal Maya's most widely traded products). Whatever the answer, it was clearly a deeply revered (or feared) deity, as the same image appears on several of Tulum's buildings, including the upper temple of Tulum's main pyramid. The Temple of the Descending God also is notable for its cartoonish off-kilter position, most likely the result of poor construction.

El Castillo

Tulum's largest and most imposing structure is The Castle, a 12-meter-high (40-foot) pyramid constructed on a rocky bluff of roughly the same height. Like many Maya structures, El Castillo was built in multiple phases. The first iteration was a low broad platform, still visible today, topped by a long palace fronted by a phalanx of stout columns. The second phase consisted of simply filling in the center portion of the original palace to create a base for a new and loftier temple on top. In the process, the builders created a vaulted passageway and inner chamber, in which a series of intriguing frescoes were housed; unfortunately, you're not allowed to climb onto the platform to see them. The upper temple (also off-limits) displays Central Mexican influence, including snakelike columns similar to those found at Chichén Itzá and grimacing Toltec masks on the corners. Above the center door is an image of the Descending God. Archaeologists believe a stone block at the top of the stairs may have been used for sacrifices.

Temple of the Frescoes

Though quite small, the Temple of the Frescoes is considered one of Tulum's most archaeologically significant structures. The name owes to the fading but remarkably detailed paintings on the structure's inner walls. In shades of blue, gray, and black, they depict various deities, including Chaac (the god of rain) and Ixchel (the goddess of the moon and fertility), and a profusion of symbolic imagery, including corn and flowers. On the temple's two facades are carved figures with elaborate headdresses and yet another image of the Descending God. The large grim-faced masks on the temple's corners are believed to represent Izamná, the Maya creator god.

Halach Uinic and the Great Palace

In front of El Castillo are the remains of two palatial structures: the House of the Halach Uinic and the Great Palace (also known as the House of the Columns). Halach Uinic is a Yucatec Maya term for king or ruler, and this structure seems to have been an elaborate shrine dedicated to Tulum's enigmatic Descending God. The building is severely deteriorated, but what remains suggests its facade was highly ornamented, perhaps even painted blue and red. Next door is the Great Palace, which likely served as residential quarters for Tulum's royal court.

Practicalities

Tulum's massive parking lot and strip-mall-like visitors complex ought to clue you in to the number of tourists that pass through here every day. (Did we mention to get here early?) You'll find a small museum and bookshop amid innumerable souvenir shops and fast-food restaurants. (If this is your first visit to a Maya ruin, don't be turned off by all the hubbub. Tulum is unique for its excessive and obnoxious commercialization; most sites have just a ticket booth and restrooms.)

The actual entrance and ticket booth are about one kilometer (0.6 mile) from the visitors center; it's a flat mild walk, but there are also **trolleys** that ferry guests back and forth for US$2.25 per person round-trip (kids under 10 ride free).

Getting There

The Tulum archaeological zone is a kilometer (0.6 mile) north of Tulum Pueblo on Highway 307. There are two entrances; the one farther south is newer and better, leading directly to the main parking lot (parking US$5.75). Arriving by bus or *combi,* be sure to ask the driver to let you off at *las ruínas* (the ruins) as opposed to the town. To return, flag down a bus or *combi* on the highway.

BEACHES AND CENOTES
Northern Beaches

The road from Tulum Pueblo hits the coast near the upper end of the Zona Hotelera, which stretches from the archaeological zone down to the entrance of the Sian Ka'an reserve, almost exactly 10 kilometers (6 miles). The area north of the Tulum/Zona Hotelera junction has two easy-to-reach beach areas that are ideal for people staying in town.

Playa El Paraíso (Carr. Tulum-Punta Allen, 2 kilometers/1.2 miles north of junction, cell tel. 984/113-7089, www.elparaisohoteltulum.com, 8am-11pm daily) is a popular beach club on a scenic beach of the same name. Once little more than a bar and some hammocks, the beach club has grown popular with tour groups and has morphed into a bustling expanse of lounge chairs, beach beds, and umbrellas (US$5-20/day), with waiters weaving between them and the full restaurant and beach bar. It's busy but still scenic and relaxing.

Directly north of Playa El Paraíso is **Playa Mar Caribe** (Carr. Tulum-Punta Allen, 2.3 kilometers/1.4 miles north of junction), named after the rustic bungalows that have long fronted this portion of beach. Broad and unspoiled, this is a great place to come to lay out your towel on the soft white sand, which you share with a picturesque array of moored fishing boats. There are no services here, so be sure to bring snacks and plenty of water. Don't feel like carting lunch to the beach? Head to **Adelita Tulum** (tel. 984/116-7645, 10am-midnight, US$10-19), a laid-back restaurant on the beach just a few steps to the south.

★ Southern Beaches

Tulum's very best beaches—thick white sand, turquoise-blue water, gently bending palm trees—are toward the southern end of the Zona Hotelera. Not surprisingly, Tulum's finest hotels are in the same area, and there are no official public access points. That said, hotels rarely raise an eyebrow at the occasional nonguest cutting through to reach the beach. You can also grab breakfast or lunch at one of the hotel restaurants and cut down to the beach afterward; in some cases, you can even use the lounge chairs.

Aimed at an older crowd, **Ana y José Beach Club** (Carr. Tulum-Punta Allen, 2.4 kilometers/1.5 miles south of junction, no phone, www.anayjosebeachclub.com, 10am-6pm daily, free) is located about a kilometer north of the resort of the same name and is open to guests and nonguests alike. An airy, sand-floored dining area serves mostly seafood, including ceviche, shrimp cocktail, and grilled fish, at decent prices (US$6-14) and has a full bar (US$2-6). Chaise lounges and four-poster beach beds (US$5-20/day) are arranged a bit too close together, but they are comfy and relaxing nonetheless.

Ziggy Beach (Carr. Tulum-Punta Allen, 3.5 kilometers/2.1 miles south of junction, cell tel. 984/745-8023, www.beach-tulum.com, 9am-5pm daily, free) is a mellow beach club with rows of thick queen-size beach beds and lounge chairs plus hammocks strung from palm trees. They're free to use as long as you buy something from the restaurant bar. (Drinks often come with a complimentary round of chips and salsa, too). The beach, as expected, is as gorgeous here as pretty much anywhere along this coast.

A popular spot for weddings, **Ak'iin Beach Club** (Carr. Tulum-Punta Allen, 4 kilometers/2.4 miles south of junction, cell tel. 984/113-7293, www.akiintulum.com, 8:30am-5pm daily, free) is truly a beautiful spot. A wood plank walkway snakes through the leafy property before arriving at the white-sand beach. Along the way, guests pass the restaurant, a spacious high-roofed *palapa* structure, with a solid menu of Mexican and international dishes. There's also a two for one happy hour 5pm-7pm most days. Like neighboring beach clubs, use of the comfy beach couches, beds, and chairs are complimentary with the purchase of pretty much anything on the menu.

★ Cenotes

Dos Ojos (Hwy. 307 Km. 244, tel. 984/105-1048, www.divedosojos.com, 8am-5pm daily), or Two Eyes, is a reference to twin caverns that are the largest openings—but far from the only ones—into the labyrinthine river system that runs beneath the ground here. You can snorkel on your own (US$11.50), but you'll see a lot more on a guided snorkeling tour (US$46 pp, no reservations required); be sure to ask to visit the Bat Cave. After the tour, you're free to keep snorkeling on your own; in

one of Tulum's gorgeous southern beaches

fact, there are hammocks and benches, so you can bring food and drinks and make a day of it. Diving trips (US$120/two tanks, US$80/one tank, US$20/day for gear; maximum 4 divers/guide) should be arranged in advance. It's two kilometers (1.2 miles) from the entrance to the cenotes, so a rental car is handy. Discounts are available if you have your own gear. Cash only.

Once a bustling tourist attraction with a well-respected dive shop, **Hidden Worlds** (Hwy. 307 Km. 243, no phone, 9am-sunset daily) is now like most cenote businesses: a couple of people running the show from a simple *palapa*. Nevertheless, it remains a great introduction to underground snorkeling, with a gorgeous on-site cenote system. A 1.5-hour snorkeling tour runs US$35. (DIY snorkeling is not permitted—in fact, staffers drive visitors to the cenote entrance, deep in the jungle.)

One of the only cenotes in the Zona Hotelera that's open to the public, **Cenote Encantado** (aka Cenote Yax Chen, Carr. Tulum-Punta Allen Km. 10, 8am-sunset) is a winding channel of cool clear water with freshwater plants along the edges. Measuring about 300 meters (984 feet) in length, it's part of an intricate network of about 100 cenotes on the jungle side of Tulum. Three small hotels—Cabañas Xbalamque, Cenote Encantado, and Cenote El Encantado Cabañas—provide easy access (US$3.85 pp) as well as rent kayaks (US$4-7) and snorkel gear (US$4) to better explore it. Look for schools of tiny fish (and some say baby crocs) in the water as well as herons in the low-lying trees.

Other favorite cenotes include **Zazil Ha, Car Wash, Gran Cenote,** and **Calavera Cenote** (all west of Tulum on the road to Cobá); **Cristal** and **Escondido** (Hwy. 307 just south of Tulum); **Casa Cenote** (at Tankah Tres); and **Cenote Cristalino, Jardín del Edén,** and **Cenote Azul** (Hwy. 307 just north of Xpu-Há). All can be visited on a tour or by yourself, and most have snorkel gear for rent (US$6-8). Most are on private or *ejido* (collective) land and charge admission fees, usually US$4-7 for snorkelers and US$9-10 for divers. If you take a tour, ask if admission fees are included in the rate. Most cenotes are open 8am-5pm daily.

TOURS OF SIAN KA'AN BIOSPHERE RESERVE

Community Tours Sian Ka'an (Calle Osiris Sur near Calle Sol Ote, tel. 984/871-2202, www.siankaantours.org, 7am-7pm daily) is an excellent community-run agency offering

Despite being deep underground, most of the Riviera Maya's popular cenotes are quite accessible, with stairways and interior lighting.

a variety of tours (US$75-109, 3-7 hours) to the Sian Ka'an Biosphere, a 1.3-million-acre reserve of coastal and mangrove forests and wetlands, with pristine coral reefs and a huge variety of flora and fauna. Among the most popular outings are the "Muyil" route, which begins with a visit to the Muyil archaeological zone, then a boat tour of Muyil and Chunyaxche lagoons, including a chance to jump in and float down a long mangrove-edged canal; "Mayaking" in Sian Ka'an, a bird- and animal-spotting tour by kayak through the lagoons and mangroves; and a "Chicle" tour, where you learn about the practice of tapping *chicle* (gum) trees, from Maya times to today, followed by a swim in the lagoon.

Visit Sian Ka'an (Sian Ka'an Biosphere Reserve, Carr. Tulum-Punta Allen Km. 15.8, cell tel. 984/141-4245, www.visitsiankaan. com) offers many of the "standard" Sian Ka'an tours—boating, snorkeling, bird-watching, ruin exploration—but will run a tour with just two guests (there's a maximum of 6). Though pricier, it also offers customized tours of the reserve, tailored to your interests. All excursions include a typical Maya lunch plus snacks and drinks. Guides are enthusiastic and knowledgeable; all are bilingual.

ENTERTAINMENT AND SHOPPING
Entertainment
ZONA HOTELERA

The lounge bar at **La Zebra** (Carr. Tulum-Punta Allen, 4.8 kilometers/3 miles south of junction, cell tel. 984/800-1943, www.laze-bratulum.com, 8am-10pm Mon.-Sat., 8am-midnight Sun.) serves up shots and mixed drinks, including its signature Zebra margarita, made with pineapple and ginger and served on the rocks. On Sunday, it hosts a salsa party 8pm-midnight, with a free dance class at 6pm. Dinner reservations are recommended if you want to feast on pulled-pork tacos between sets.

Papaya Playa Project (Carr. Tulum-Punta Allen, 1.5 kilometers/1 mile south of junction, cell tel. 984/116-3774, www. papayaplayaproject.com, hours vary) has a regular lineup of live musical acts, plus full-moon parties, bongo drum sessions, and an overall counterculture vibe. Saturday is the main night, but look for schedules online or around town for upcoming events. Papaya Playa is actually a rustic-chic resort, hence all the *cabañas*, but is better known (and better liked, really) as a place to party. Most shows begin around 10pm; cover is US$5-10.

The upscale boutique resort **Mezzanine** (Carr. Tulum-Punta Allen, 1.3 kilometers/0.8 mile north of junction, cell tel. 984/131-1596, www.mezzaninetulum.com) is known as the go-to bar on Friday nights, with cool cocktails and a hip vibe on a relaxed beachfront patio.

Gitano (Carr. Tulum-Punta Allen, 3 kilometers/1.8 mile south of junction, cell tel. 984/188-2184, www.gitanotulum.mx, 6pm-12:30am) is a hipster jungle restaurant/bar, known for its mixologists, DJs, and dance floor. It's definitely a scene—down to the beautiful people inside and the velvet ropes keeping out the riffraff. That said, if you like mezcal, can clean up nicely, and want to run with the "it" crowd, this is a great option.

IN TOWN

El Curandero (Av. Tulum at Calle Beta, tel. 984/871-2414, www.curanderotulum.com, 7pm-2am daily) is the best of several local bars cut from the same cloth: small, mood lit, with great music and a relaxed, welcoming vibe. There's live music weekdays, electronica on Saturday, and movies on Thursday. Look for the crowd spilling out—and partying—right outside its doors.

Just off the main drag, **El Batey** (Calle Centauro Sur btwn Av. Tulum and Calle Andromeda Ote., no phone, 7am-2am Mon.-Sat., 7am-1am Sun.) is a hopping bar that features live jazz, blues, and Mexican *bohemia* groups most nights starting at 9pm. There's a leafy courtyard in the back where bands set up, an artsy little bar in front, and a VW bug converted into a mojito bar on the street in front (with drinks made with real sugar cane!).

Waye'Rest-Bar (Av. Tulum btwn Calles Beta and Osiris, tel. 984/806-4206, 7am-3am daily) is a bigger *palapa*-roofed place playing mostly reggae and *norteños* (Mexican music from the northern states). It doesn't have the hipster atmosphere of other bars in town, but its drinks are cheap and strong, making it a popular stop.

Shopping

Tulum's main drag is peppered with *artesanía* and knickknack shops. You'll find everything from T-shirts and magnets to high-end Maya replicas and custom-made jewelry. Consider window-shopping a bit—it won't take long to peruse most of the shops. A couple of standouts include:

MexicArte (Av. Tulum btwn Calles Alfa and Jupiter, tel. 984/871-2136, 10am-10pm daily) has a large selection of quality folk art, from green copper suns to carved wooden angels and masks. Cool T-shirts, jewelry, cards, and more also are sold. There's a sister shop of the same name in the Zona Hotelera (Punta Piedra, Carr. Tulum-Punta Allen, 1 kilometer/0.6 miles south of junction, same hours).

Casa Hernández (Av. Tulum at Calle Centauro, no phone, 9am-5pm daily except Thurs.) specializes in handcrafted pottery and ceramics, mostly from Puebla. Items range from mugs and picture frames to finely painted plates and dinner sets.

SPORTS AND RECREATION
Scuba Diving

The reef here is superb, but Tulum's diving claim to fame is the huge and easily accessible network of freshwater cenotes, caverns, and caves, offering truly one-of-a-kind dive environments. Divers with open-water certification can dive in cenotes (little or no overhead) and caverns (no more than 30 feet deep or 130 feet from an air pocket) without additional training. Full-cave diving requires advanced certification, which is also available at many of Tulum's shops. If you haven't dived in a while, definitely warm up with some open-water dives before doing a cenote or cavern trip. Buoyancy control is especially important in such environments because of the roof above and the sediment below, and is complicated by the fact that it's freshwater instead of saltwater, and entails gear you may not be accustomed to, namely thick wetsuits and a flashlight.

Prices for cenotes and caverns are fairly uniform from shop to shop: around

painted *calaveras*, a kind of *artesanía*

US$85-120 for one tank or US$120-165 for two. Be sure to ask whether gear and admission to the cenotes are included. Shops also offer multidive packages, cave and cavern certification courses, and hotel packages if you'll be staying awhile. As always, choose a shop and guide you feel comfortable with, not necessarily the least-expensive one.

If you plan on doing as much cave and cavern diving as possible, **Xibalba Dive Center** (Calle Andrómeda btwn Calles Libra and Geminis, tel. 984/871-2953, www.xibalbadivecenter.com, 9am-7pm daily) not only has an excellent record for safety and professionalism, but now has an on-site hotel with comfortable rooms, a small swimming pool, and space to dry, store, and repair gear. Good lodging and diving packages are available. Xibalba also fills its own tanks and offers free Nitrox to experienced clients. The shop's name, aptly enough, comes from the Yucatec Maya word for the underworld.

Koox Dive Center (Av. Tulum btwn Calles Beta and Osiris, tel. 984/141-5502, www.kooxdiving.com, 9am-sunset daily) is another reliable option for diving and snorkeling, on the reef and in cenotes.

Mot Mot Diving (Av. Tulum at Calle Beta, tel. 984/802-5442, www.motmotdiving.com, 8am-9pm daily) is recommended by several hotel owners.

Cenote Dive Center (Calle Centauro at Calle Andrómeda, cell tel. 984/876-3285, www.cenotedive.com, 8am-4pm Sun.-Fri.) offers a large variety of tours and courses, in Tulum and beyond.

In the Zona Hotelera, **Mexi-Divers** (Punta Piedra, Carr. Tulum-Punta Allen, 1.5 kilometers/0.9 mile south of junction, tel. 984/807-8805, www.mexidivers.com, 8:30am-5pm daily) is located opposite Zamas Hotel in the Punta Piedra area and has regularly scheduled snorkeling and diving trips, in the ocean and nearby cenotes.

Snorkeling

Like divers, snorkelers have an embarrassment of riches in Tulum, with great reef snorkeling and easy access to the eerie beauty of the area's many cenotes. **Dive shops in Tulum** offer snorkel trips of both sorts; prices vary considerably so be sure to ask which and how many reefs or cenotes you'll visit, for how long, and what's included (gear, entrance fees, transport, snacks, etc.). Reef trips cost US$30-45 visiting 1-3 different spots, while cenote trips run US$50-65; snorkel gear can also be rented.

Kiteboarding

Extreme Control (no storefront, tel. 984/745-4555, www.extremecontrol.net) is Tulum's longest-operating kiteboarding outfit, offering courses and rentals for all experience levels and in various languages. Classes are held on Tulum's southernmost beach at Rosa del Viento Hotel (Carr. Tulum-Punta Allen Km. 10) as well as at Caleta Tankah, just a short drive north of town. Private classes are US$75 per hour, or US$225-390 for 3-6-hour introductory packages, including equipment; group classes are somewhat less.

Mexican Caribbean Kitesurf & Paddlesurf (Ahau Tulum, Carr. Tulum-Punta Allen Km. 4.4, tel. 984/168-1023, www.mexicancaribbeankitesurf.com, 9am-5:30pm daily) is a friendly shop with IKO-certified instructors and top-of-the-line equipment. Private and group instruction is offered in 3-9-hour courses (US$165-405 group, US$240-600 private). Wave-kitesurfing—a hybrid of kiting and surfing—classes are also offered (US$55-80/hour).

A well-respected kiting shop, **Ocean Pro Kite** (Av. Tulum btwn Calles Centauro and Orion Sur, cell tel. 984/119-0328, www.oceanprokite.com, 9am-5pm daily) offers classes on 100 meters (300 feet) of empty (or near-empty) beach in front of the Villa Las Estrellas hotel (Carr. Tulum-Punta Allen Km. 8). Instruction is offered to beginners as well as experts. Ninety-minute private classes run US$100, group classes US$80. Packages and rentals are also available.

Morph Kiteboarding (Hotel Playa Azul, Carr. Tulum-Punta Allen Km. 7, cell tel. 984/114-9524, www.morphkiteboarding.com.

com, 9am-sunset daily) also offers classes to all levels of kiteboarders. Rates are for private classes, though group lessons can be arranged as well: US$235, US$390, and US$468 for three-, five-, and six-hour courses, respectively.

Stand-Up Paddling

Stand-up paddling, or "SUPing," has exploded in popularity, a challenging but relatively easy sport to learn, and especially well-suited to the calm clear waters found in much of the Riviera Maya. You can see a surprising amount of sealife doing SUP instead of kayaking, thanks simply to the improved vantage point.

Ocean Pro Kite (Av. Tulum btwn Calles Centauro and Orion Sur, cell tel. 984/119-0328, www.oceanprokite.com, 9am-5pm daily) offers SUP lessons for all levels, starting with safety and theory on the beach, graduating to kneeling paddling, then standing and catching waves. Private classes are US$40 per hour, while groups of two or three start at US$25 per person per hour. Classes typically are held in the Zona Hotelera at Villa Las Estrellas (Carr. Tulum-Punta Allen Km. 8). Gear and refreshments are included, and rentals are also available.

Mexican Caribbean Kitesurf & Paddlesurf (Ahau Tulum, Carr. Tulum-Punta Allen Km. 4.4, tel. 984/168-1023, www.mexicancaribbeankitesurf.com, 9am-5:30pm daily) offers paddleboarding and paddlesurfing classes (US$50/hour). Once the lesson is over, students are free to use the paddleboards for as long as they'd like. Several SUPing-snorkeling tours are also offered (US$80-90, 4 hours). Rentals are available, too, with free delivery.

Extreme Control (no storefront, tel. 984/745-4555, www.extremecontrol.net) offers SUPing lessons (US$70 private, US$50 pp 2 pax, US$40 pp 3+ pax; 2 hours) plus tours in area cenotes and on the oceanfront, including transport to and from Tulum, Akumal, and Tankah. Hourly and weekly paddleboard rentals are also available.

Ecoparks

Built around a huge natural inlet, **Xel-Há** (Hwy. 307, 9 kilometers/5.6 miles north of Tulum, toll-free Mex. tel. 800/009-3542, toll-free U.S./Can. tel. 855/326-2696, www.xel-ha.com, 9am-6pm daily, US$80 adult all-inclusive, US$40 child under 12, child under 5 free) is all about water—being in and around it. Activities include snorkeling, snuba, tubing,

For some, stand-up paddling is a family affair.

aquatic ziplines, and interactive programs with dolphins, manatees, and stingrays. Although it doesn't compare to snorkeling on the reef, there's a fair number of fish darting about, and it makes for a fun, easy intro for children and beginners. A buffet lunch and open bar are included. Check the website for online deals and combo packages with sister parks Xcaret and Xplor.

Bicycling

In town, **iBike Tulum** (Av. Cobá Sur at Calle Venus, tel. 984/802-5518, www.ibiketulum. com, 9am-5:30pm Mon.-Sat.) offers mountain bike tours through jungle trails to cenotes and dry caves. Prices vary depending on the tour; they typically last 4-5 hours and are limited to eight cyclists.

Spas

Set on the jungle side of the road, the luxurious **Yaan Wellness Energy Spa** (Carr. Tulum-Punta Allen Km. 10, tel. 984/179-1530, www.yaanwellness.com, 9:30am-9pm daily) offers a wide range of spa services. Massages, body treatments, facials, soaking baths— even energy healing and traditional *temascal* (pre-Hispanic sweat lodge) ceremonies. All treatments begin with a "Healing Water Circuit," which includes leisurely stops in the sauna, steam room, and hot and cold massage pools. Most services run around US$175-200 per hour—pricey for sure, but totally worthwhile.

Overlooking the beach at Azulik Hotel, **Maya Spa Wellness Center** (Carr. Tulum-Punta Allen Km. 5, toll-free Mex. tel. 800/681-9537, www.maya-spa.com, 8am-8pm daily) offers a variety of massages, facials, and body wraps in a gorgeous setting. Massages run US$80 to US$185 (45-90 minutes), while other treatments include body wraps (US$185, 90 minutes) and facials (US$90, 60 minutes).

Located at the Ana y José hotel, **Om...Spa** (Carr. Tulum-Punta Allen Km. 7, tel. 984/871-2477, www.anayjose.com, 9am-5pm daily) is a full-service spa set in a chic beachfront setting. Choose from a menu of massages ranging from Swedish and Thai to Reiki and Maya

(US$80-130, 60-90 minutes) and body treatments like exfoliations, facials, and body wraps (US$70-100, 60-80 minutes). Packages for individuals and couples are also available.

Yoga

Surrounded by lush vegetation, **Yoga Shala Tulum** (Carr. Tulum-Punta Allen Km. 7.4, cell tel. 984/141-8116, www.yogashalatulum. com, 8:30am-6pm Mon.-Fri., 10am-6pm Sat.-Sun.) offers a wide range of yoga instruction in its gorgeous open-air studio. Classes cost US$15 each or US$50 per week for unlimited classes. There also is an affordable hotel on-site. Look for it on the inland side of the Zona Hotelera road.

Yaan Wellness Energy Spa (Carr. Tulum-Punta Allen Km. 10, tel. 984/179-1530, www.yaanwellness.com, 9:30am-9pm daily) offers drop-in yoga classes—vinyasa and hatha, mostly—in its second-story open-air studio. Classes are at 10am and 5pm every day and run US$20 per person.

Maya Spa Wellness Center (Azulik Hotel, Carr. Tulum-Punta Allen Km. 5, toll-free Mex. tel. 800/681-9537, www.maya-spa. com, 8am-8pm daily) also offers hatha and vinyasa yoga sessions at 7am and 9am daily. Classes cost US$15 per person; private instruction is also available.

ACCOMMODATIONS

Chances are you've come to Tulum to stay in one of the famous beachside bungalow-type hotels. There are many to choose from, each slightly different but most sharing a laid-back atmosphere and terrific beaches. However, some travelers are surprised by just how rustic some accommodations are, even those charging hundreds of dollars per night. The root of the matter is that there are no power lines or freshwater wells serving the beach. Virtually all accommodations have salty water in the showers and sinks. Most have fans, but not all, and electricity may be limited to nighttime hours only. Air-conditioning is available in only a handful of places. At the same time, some hotels use generators to power their restaurants and reception, so it's worth asking for a room away from the generator; nothing is a bigger killjoy than a diesel motor pounding outside your window when the point of coming here was to enjoy the peace and quiet.

If staying on the beach is out of your budget (join the club!), staying in town is a perfectly good alternative. The options have improved significantly, with a crop of new bed-and-breakfasts and boutique hotels to go along with a burgeoning number of hostels and budget digs. The beach is just a short drive or bike ride away, and prices for food, Internet, and laundry are much lower.

Zona Hotelera
UNDER US$50

Fronting a winding cenote, ★ **Cenote Encantado** (Carr. Tulum-Punta Allen Km. 10, cell tel. 984/142-5930, www.cenoteencantado.com, US$15.50 pp tent) is, in some ways, a throwback to Tulum's beginnings: a haven for backpackers with boho spirit. The hotel is more like a camping village with 17 tents set up around the leafy property. Each has an airbed with sheets, a bedside table, a lamp and fan (there's electricity), Wi-Fi, even a rug. There's also a clean communal kitchen and a cozy wood-floor lounge for meditating, yoga classes (US$8-15), and just hanging out; both structures are breezy but enclosed with strong mosquito netting. Open-air showers and dry toilets round out the camping-plus experience. Use of bikes is complimentary—and a necessity, really, if you want to go to the beach. Admission to the cenote also is included, as are inflatable rafts and floaties (snorkel gear extra).

Next door, **Cabañas Xbalamque** (Carr. Tulum-Punta Allen Km. 10, cell tel. 984/140-3156, xbalamquetulum@gmail.com, US$45-65 s/d with shared bathroom) has eight simple *palapa*-roofed cabins on a palm-tree-laden property. Each has a decent bed with mosquito netting, big screened windows, and electricity (5:30pm-2am only). There's also an open-air kitchen with a gas-operated fridge to keep your perishables kicking, as well as a

comfortable lounge with Wi-Fi. Admission to Cenote Yax Chen (in the backyard) is included in the rate as is use of kayaks and snorkel gear.

Santa Fe (Carr. Tulum-Punta Allen, 2.5 kilometers/1.5 miles north of junction, tel. 984/136-5248, US$8 pp tent) is a beachfront restaurant (8am-6pm daily) that welcomes campers on its property. The facilities are very basic—wear your flip-flops in the shower—and there's no electricity after 10pm. Better to enjoy the night sky . . .

US$50-100

A private home turned yoga hotel, **Yoga Shala Tulum** (Carr. Tulum-Punta Allen Km. 7.5, cell tel. 984/141-8116, www.yogashalatulum.com, US$49/79 s/d with shared bath, US$99/109 s/d) offers simple but comfortable rooms on a jungly plot on the inland side of the Zona Hotelera. Rooms have whitewashed walls, polished cement floors, and good beds and linens, with a bit of boho flair, too. Outside is an impressive open-air yoga studio with a high *palapa* roof and gorgeous wood floors. There's also a restaurant on-site and Wi-Fi in the common areas.

Ahau Tulum (Carr. Tulum-Punta Allen Km. 4.4, cell tel. 984/802-5632, www.ahautulum.com, US$79 s/d) is not exclusively a budget place—it's got rooms that go for over US$400—but its guesthouse units (with shared bathrooms) and stick-built "Bali Huts" are among the cheapest digs on the beach. Gaps in the walls and bathrooms that never get truly clean are the price you pay to be on the sand for this cheap—a bargain for boho beach hounds.

US$100-200

Although sharing a bathroom for over US$150 a night doesn't seem quite right, **Coco Tulum** (Carr. Tulum-Punta Allen Km. 8, cell tel. 984/157-4830, www.cocotulum.com, US$155-180 s/d with shared bath, US$225-330 s/d) does the basics with style. Tidy *palapa*-roofed bungalows have cement floors, comfy beds, hanging bookshelves, fans, and sleek black exteriors with private patios. The

Tulum Town and Zona Hotelera

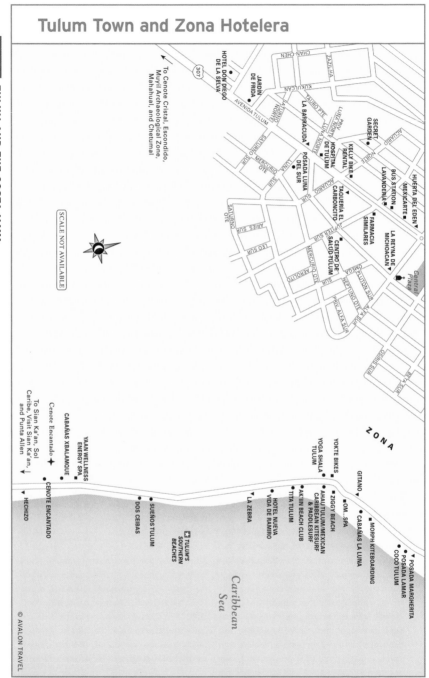

307

To Cenote Cristal, Escondido, Muyil Archaeological Zone, Mahahual, and Chetumal

HOTEL DON DIEGO DE LA SELVA

JARDIN DE FRIDA

AVENIDA TULUM

LA BARRACUDA

SATURNO NORTE

PRIV. NORTE
LUNA NORTE

AURO PTE

KUKULCAN

CHAN-CHEN

ZAZILHA

SECRET GARDEN

AZULIKA

NOBEL

HUERTA DEL EDEN

MEXICARTE

HOSPITAL DE TULUM

KELLY BIKE RENTAL

POSADA LUNA DEL SUR

SATURNO SUR

MERCURIO OTE

LUNA SUR

ACUARIO SUR

BUS STATION

LAVANDERIA

LA REYNA DE MICHOACAN

TAQUERIA EL CARBONCITO

CENTRO DE SALUD TULUM

FARMACIA SIMILARES

SCALE NOT AVAILABLE

ARIES SUR

JUPITER SUR

SATURNO OTE

MERCURIO SUR

MERCURIO OTE

OMEGA

Central Plaza

LEO SUR

APOLITO

NEPTUNO OTE

PLUTON SUR

PRIV. ALFA SUR

ALFA SUR

BETA SUR

OSIRIS SUR

Z O N A

To Sian Ka'an, Sol Caribe, Visit Sian Ka'an, and Punta Allen

Cenote Encantado

CABAÑAS XBALAMQUE

YAAN WELLNESS ENERGY SPA

YOKTE BIKES

YOGA SHALA TULUM

OM... SPA

ZIGGY BEACH

AHAU TULUM/MEXICAN CARIBBEAN KITESURF & PADDLESURF

AK'IIN BEACH CLUB

TITA TULUM

HOTEL NUEVA VIDA DE RAMIRO

LA ZEBRA

GITANO

CABAÑAS LA LUNA

MORPH KITEBOARDING

POSADA MARGHERITA

POSADA LAMAR

COCO TULUM

CENOTE ENCANTADO

HECHIZO

DOS CEIBAS

SUEÑOS TULUM

TULUM'S SOUTHERN BEACHES

Caribbean Sea

© AVALON TRAVEL

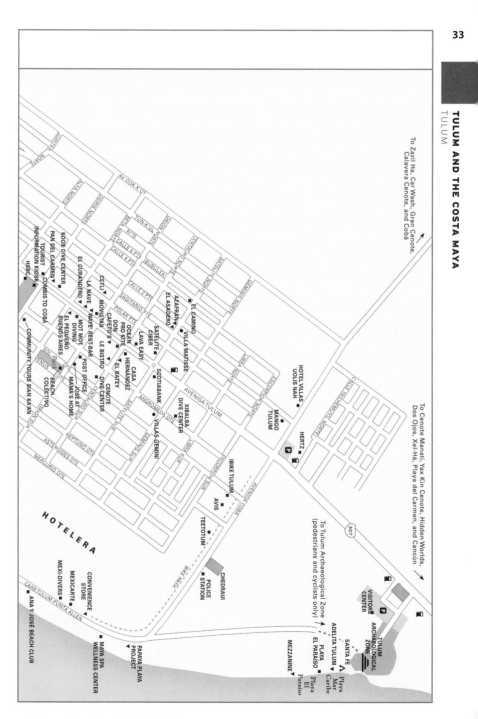

shared bathrooms are actually quite nice, with modern basin sinks, rainshower heads, hot water, and thrice-daily cleaning. And if sharing a bathroom really is beyond the pale, they've got a tower with three deluxe rooms, each with private bathroom, fan, and stellar views. Wind- and solar-powered electricity is available 24 hours. There's also a new Italian restaurant on-site and an area where spa treatments are given.

Tita Tulum (Carr. Tulum-Punta Allen Km. 8, tel. 984/877-8513, www.titatulum. com, US$185-205 s/d) has a lovely beachfront and low-key atmosphere—a great option for families and travelers who prefer modest comforts and a lower rate (especially off-season) over boutique eco-chic embellishments. Ten guest rooms form a semicircle around a sandy, palm-fringed lot; they're a bit worn around the edges but have polished cement floors, clean bathrooms, and indoor and outdoor sitting areas, plus fans, Wi-Fi, and 24-hour electricity. Tita is a charming and attentive proprietor, and prepares authentic Mexican dishes in the hotel's small restaurant.

Posada Lamar (Carr. Tulum-Punta Allen Km. 6, cell tel. 984/106-3682, www. posadalamar.com, US$160-220 s/d) has

eight comfortable and artful bungalows, with salvaged-wood detailing and rich colors and fabrics. There are no fans or air-conditioning, and electricity (solar powered) is available only at night; fortunately, the sea breezes keep the units cool (and the bugs at bay) most nights. The bungalows are a bit too close together, diminishing privacy, especially since you often need the windows and doors open, but the beach here is clean and beautiful, with plenty of chairs, beds, and *palapas*. Continental breakfast is included, served every morning on your private terrace.

Dos Ceibas (Carr. Tulum-Punta Allen Km. 10, tel. 984/877-6024, www.dosceibas. com, US$100-190 s/d) has eight comfortable, if a bit garish, bungalows on a beautiful stretch of beach. Bungalows range from a top-floor honeymoon unit to a "bargain" bungalow with a detached bathroom (and near enough the road to hear passing cars). Most have polished cement floors, brightly painted walls, and firm beds with mosquito nets hanging from the *palapa* roof; all but the two breezy oceanfront rooms and budget rear unit have ceiling fans (electricity available at night only).

Tulum offers idyllic beachfront hotels.

OVER US$200

Nestled in a jungly plot facing a glorious stretch of beach, **Hotel Nueva Vida de Ramiro** (Carr. Tulum-Punta Allen Km. 8.5, tel. 984/877-8512, www.tulumnv.com, US$115-413 s/d) has a large number (and variety) of accommodations, from spacious suites with pillow-top mattresses and gorgeous ocean views to simple thatch-roof bungalows, including some with kitchenette, and even an adults-only area. (The oldest rooms can be dark, however, and aren't a great value, despite being cheaper.) There's 24-hour clean power, but no air-conditioning, just fans and sea breezes. Complimentary continental breakfast (including a bottomless cup of joe) is served at the hotel's restaurant, Casa Banana Steakhouse, located across the street.

Artful, spirit-minded decor is nothing new in Tulum, but ★ **Sueños Tulum** (Carr. Tulum-Punta Allen Km. 8.5, cell tel. 984/115-4338, www.suenostulum.com, US$220-285 s/d, US$485 s/d with hot tub) takes the theme further than most. Each of the hotel's 12 suites is decorated according to an essential force—Earth, Rain, Moon, etc.—and there's Maya imagery inside and out. All have ceiling fans, most rooms have ocean views, and two are reserved for families. A small clean pool is an added bonus, even with beaches as gorgeous as these. Located at the far southern end of the hotel zone, Sueños is quiet and isolated, even by Tulum's standards. Continental breakfast is included.

Accommodations at the lovely and well-liked **Cabañas La Luna** (Carr. Tulum-Punta Allen Km. 6.5, U.S. tel. 818/631-9824, Mex. cell tel. 984/146-7737 [urgent matters only], www.cabanaslaluna.com, US$125-250 s/d, US$290-530 2- and 4-bdrm villas) range from cozy beachfront bungalows to spacious split-level villas, but share essential details like comfortable mattresses, high ceilings, fans and 24-hour electricity, and bright artful decor. The beach is stunning, of course, and the property is big enough for a sense of isolation, yet within walking distance of shops and restaurants in Punta Piedra. Service is excellent.

In Town

UNDER US$50

Known for its elaborate daily breakfasts, **José at Mama's Home** (Calle Orion Sur btwn Calles Venus and Sol Ote., tel. 984/871-2272, US$10 pp dorm, US$12 pp dorm with a/c, US$50 s/d with a/c) is a popular spot for budget travelers. Two mixed dorms and eight private rooms—all with thick mattresses—open onto a colorful courtyard with Maya-inspired murals, hammocks, and long tables. There's a small communal kitchen plus a living room with a couple of computers for Internet access (there's also Wi-Fi). Weekly themed events like "Margarita Night," "Flamenco & Sangria," and "Hollywood Movie Night" make it easy to meet other travelers.

Mango Tulum (Calle Polar Pte. near Av. Cobá, tel. 984/169-9097, www.mangotulum.com, US$20 pp dorm with a/c, US$70-75 s/d with a/c) is a pleasantly sparse hotel with whitewashed walls, polished cement floors, and a spacious garden with mature trees and a refreshing pool. Dorms are limited to two bunk beds with en suite bathroom; sheets, towels, and lockers are included. The private rooms are bright and airy; some have king-size beds. Continental breakfast is provided, but there's no communal kitchen, unfortunately. Look for the hotel behind the OXXO convenient store on Avenida Cobá.

Villa Matisse (Av. Satélite at Calle Sagitario, tel. 984/871-2636, villamatisse@hotmail.com, US$50 s/d) has six simple, comfortable rooms, a pleasant garden and reading area (with book exchange), and a community kitchen. The rooms are spotless, and the grounds and common areas are equally well maintained; the multilingual owner sets out coffee and small snacks in the morning and often supplies rooms with fresh flowers. There's no air-conditioning, but rooms have fans and good cross ventilation. Use of the hotel's bikes is included in the rate.

US$50-100

Tucked into a quiet residential street, ★ **Secret Garden** (Calle Sagitario near

Calle Acuario, tel. 984/157-8001, www.secretgardentulum.com, US$55-65 s/d with a/c, US$75 s/d with a/c and kitchenette, US$65-75 palapa bungalow with fan and kitchenette) offers stylish, comfortable rooms at affordable rates (guests over age 16 only). Units vary in size and layout (some with kitchenettes, some with lofts), but all have fashionable colors, artful stencils, and high-end linens. Rooms open onto a long, leafy central garden with hammocks and low couches, perfect for relaxing day or night. Service is outstanding; purified water, fruit, and baked goods are offered daily.

Located on the southern end of town, **Jardín de Frida** (Av. Tulum near Calle Kukulcán, tel. 984/871-2816, www.fridastulum.com, US$16 pp dorm, US$62 s/d, US$81 s/d with kitchenette, US$92 s/d with kitchenette and a/c) is an artsy hotel with a jungly garden replete with mango and palm trees, a lounge that feels like a global traveler's living room (think tapestries, eclectic furnishings, artworks, and an intriguing library), a spacious common kitchen, and lots of outdoor spaces for hanging out. All the units have spectacular murals—from jungle scenes to modern art. Dorms have twin beds (no bunks here) and en suite bathrooms. Private rooms are different in style and size but are comfortable and homey. Continental breakfast and Wi-Fi are included in the rate.

Hotel Don Diego de la Selva (Av. Tulum s/n, cell tel. 984/114-9744, www.dondiegodelaselva.com, US$85-110 s/d with a/c) offers spacious rooms and bungalows with classy understated decor, comfortable beds, and large glass doors looking onto a shady rear garden. There's a large pool, and the hotel restaurant serves good French-Mexican cuisine; half-board options are available. The only catch is the location, about a kilometer (0.6 mile) south of the plaza. The hotel rents bikes, but most guests find a rental car indispensable. It's very popular with French travelers; wireless Internet and continental breakfast are included.

Set in a leafy garden on the road to Cobá, **Hotel Villas Uolis Nah** (Carr. Tulum-Cobá Km. 0.2, tel. 984/876-4965, www.uolisnah.com, US$63 s/d with kitchen, US$80 s/d with kitchen and a/c) has six simple studios with little touches like mosquito-net canopies, mosaic-tile bathrooms, and palapa-shaded terraces with hammocks. All units have fully equipped kitchens (even ovens), and one of Tulum's main supermarkets is just down the street. There's also a well-kept pool near the front of the property—perfect for cooling off. Continental breakfast, bike rentals, and wireless Internet are included in the rate.

US$100-200

Rooms at **Posada Luna del Sur** (Calle Luna Sur near Av. Tulum, tel. 984/871-2984, www.posadalunadelsur.com, US$120 s/d with a/c) are compact but tidy and pleasant, with whitewashed walls, comfortable beds (king or two twins), and small terraces overlooking a leafy garden. Each has a kitchenette for light food prep—there aren't microwaves or hot plates—though you may not use it much considering the full à la carte breakfast and the many restaurant recommendations of the food-savvy owner who lives on-site. The rooftop lounge is a great evening hangout, with plenty of tables, chairs, and Wi-Fi. Service is friendly and accommodating. The hotel is for ages 16 and over only.

A short distance from town on the road to the beach, **Teetotum** (Av. Cobá Sur s/n, cell tel. 984/143-8956, www.hotelteetotum.com, US$130 s/d with a/c) has four sleek minimalist rooms—ceramic basin sinks, low bed stands—and artful decor throughout, including playful oversized murals in the dining room. All rooms have air-conditioning, Wi-Fi, and iPod docks, but no TV or telephone. Guests enjoy free continental breakfast and bike rentals, and a lovely plunge pool and rooftop sun beds, too. Various massages and other spa treatments are available on request. The restaurant serves a little of everything, from vegetable dumplings to bacon cheeseburgers, with an equally varied (and enticing) drink menu.

★ **Villas Geminis** (Calle Andrómeda at

Calle Gemini, tel. 984/871-3556, www.villas-geminis.com, US$145 s/d with a/c, US$170 penthouse studio with a/c, US$155/205 one/two bdrm with a/c) has spacious penthouse studios and one- and two-bedroom condos with modern kitchens and private terraces (there's also one hotel room); all are simple but elegant in decor. There's 24-hour security and daily maid service, and the owners and staff are attentive and capable. The interior courtyard has a nice swimming pool surrounded by a leafy garden. There's a large supermarket nearby, plus restaurants, bars, and dive shops. The property has cable TV and Wi-Fi, and bikes for rent. All in all, this is an amazing deal, especially considering most units sleep four people.

FOOD

Many Zona Hotelera restaurants are cash only; be sure to bring enough pesos to cover your meal so you're not stuck washing dishes. In Tulum town, most sit-down restaurants accept credit cards, but the taco stands and mom-and-pop eateries do not.

Zona Hotelera

Adelita Tulum (Carr. Tulum-Punta Allen, 2.2 kilometers/1.3 miles north of junction, tel. 984/116-7645, 10am-midnight, US$10-19) is a hip-without-the-attitude beachfront restaurant/bar with a strong menu of gourmet seafood dishes and beach munchies. Tables and hammocks are set up under slatted wood structures, *palapas,* or on the beach. There's also a great bar with swings for seats and dreamy cocktails.

Located well down the coastal road, ★ **Hechizo** (Carr. Tulum-Punta Allen Km. 10.2, tel. 984/879-5020, 6:30pm-11pm Mon.-Sat., US$19-30) is considered by many to be Tulum's finest restaurant. Specializing in gourmet Mexican fare, it features innovative creations like lobster and green tomato *pozole* and seared ahi tuna on jicama-green apple salad. Prix fixe five-course dinners (US$50-60) also are offered nightly. Seating is at long handmade tables in a softly lit dining room

or outside, under the stars with a view of the surf. The chefs and owners, who also happen to be married, are Ritz-Carlton transplants.

Thai is the specialty at **Mezzanine** (Carr. Tulum-Punta Allen, 1.3 kilometers/0.8 mile north of junction, cell tel. 984/131-1596, www.mezzaninetulum.com, 8am-10pm daily, US$10-23), one of Tulum's chicest hotels on the beach. Curries—red, green, sweet potato, pineapple—and house specialties like crispy-style whole fish and lemongrass soup are among the dishes served in a fashionable dining area or on a shaded outdoor patio, both with fine sea views. A full bar and cool music make this a place to linger.

La Zebra (Carr. Tulum-Punta Allen, 4.8 kilometers/3 miles south of junction, cell tel. 984/800-1943, www.lazebratulum.com, 8am-10pm Mon.-Sat., 8am-midnight Sun., US$10-23) serves up classic Mexican dishes like tortilla soup, chicken in mole sauce, and chiles rellenos (stuffed peppers). For lighter fare, check out the ceviche bar, with everything from fish and shrimp to octopus and tuna (there's even a vegan option!). Tables are set up on a lovely beachfront patio and in a *palapa*-roofed dining area; at night, the long entry path is lit by lanterns. On Sunday there's a popular barbecue and salsa party starting at 8pm (free dance classes at 6pm).

Posada Margherita (Carr. Tulum-Punta Allen, 2.4 kilometers/1.5 miles south of junction, tel. 984/801-8493, www.posadamargherita.com, 7am-9:30pm daily, US$10-30) specializes in homemade pastas and breads. Service is personalized to the point of having no menus—instead, the waiter pulls up a chair to discuss the dishes being prepared that night (ask for prices before ordering—many customers are shocked when the bill arrives). It's busy most nights, so expect a wait—fortunately, the cocktails and the view are killer.

In Town

One of the best breakfast places in town, ★ **Azafrán** (Av. Satélite near Calle Polar, cell tel. 984/129-6130, www.azafrantulum.com, 8am-3pm daily, US$5-11) serves up superb morning meals made with gourmet products: homemade bagels with prosciutto and Brie, crepes stuffed with an assortment of fresh fruits, *chaya* omelets, and pâté platters with freshly baked bread. Organic coffee is a must, as is the fresh-squeezed orange juice. The only bummer about this place is that it gets crowded fast—come early to beat the morning rush.

★ **El Asadero** (Av. Satélite near Calle Sagitario, tel. 984/157-8998, 4:30pm-11:30pm Mon.-Sat., US$6-19) is the go-to steak house for locals and expats looking for a spectacular meal without breaking the bank. Meat, chicken, and yes, even veggies, are grilled in the open kitchen, the flavorful smells wafting throughout the dining room and out to the streetside tables. Try the hearty taco plate with your choice of fillings, cooked to order. All meals come with crispy tortilla chips and a trio of homemade salsas.

Taquería El Carboncito (Av. Tulum btwn Calles Acuario and Jupiter; 6pm-2am Wed.-Mon., US$1-5) serves up hot tacos at plastic tables in the driveway of an auto shop that's closed for the night. That is, it's a great place for a cheap tasty meal, and popular with local families.

For seafood, don't miss **La Barracuda** (Av. Tulum near Calle Luna Norte, tel. 984/160-0325, noon-8pm Tues.-Sun., US$6-13), a popular Mexican eatery with plastic tables and chairs located on the main drag. Ceviche and fish soup are the specialty, but the shrimp cocktail and made-to-order fish dishes are mouthwatering. All to say, the seafood here is super fresh, super tasty, and served in generous portions.

Cetli (Calle Polar Norte at Calle Orion Norte, cell tel. 984/108-0681, 5pm-10pm Thurs.-Tues., US$10-20) serves up modern Mexican creations by Chef Claudia Pérez, a Mexico City transplant and a graduate of one of Mexico's top culinary schools. The menu is full of the unique and unexpected, from chicken and *chaya* roll in peanut mole to *agua de pepino con yerba buena* (mint cucumber water). Chef Pérez herself is a delight and often comes out to chat with diners. Reservations are required and can be made via Facebook.

Le Bistro (Calle Centauro near Av. Tulum, cell tel. 984/134-4507, 8:30am-11:30pm daily, US$4-15) is a bustling café offering a full range of French delicacies—from freshly baked croissants to duck confit. Tables are set up outdoors, either on the front porch or under umbrellas in the back courtyard; neither is particularly charming, but the food is so good, it's easy to overlook.

Don't let the nautical theme fool you: **La Nave** (Av. Tulum between Calles Beta and Osiris, tel. 984/871-2592, 7am-11pm Mon.-Sat., US$7-14) is more about thin crispy pizza than fish fry. Whether you go all out with a Brie and prosciutto pizza or stick with a classic margherita, you'll leave satisfied. Pasta dishes and hefty appetizers are excellent alternatives.

El Pequeño Buenos Aires (Av. Tulum btwn Calles Orion and Beta, tel. 984/871-2708, 11am-11pm daily, US$7-30) serves excellent cuts of beef, including a *parrillada Argentina,* which comes piled with various cuts, plus chicken and sausage. The menu also includes crepes, a few vegetarian dishes, and lunch specials.

For home-style Mexican cooking, head to **Don Cafeto's** (Av. Tulum btwn Calles Centauro and Orion, tel. 984/871-2207, 7am-11pm daily, US$5-18), serving Mexican staples like mole and enchiladas, plus ceviche plates that are meals unto themselves. On a hot day, try a tall cold *chayagra,* an uplifting blend of pineapple juice, lime juice, cucumber, and *chaya* (similar to spinach).

Sweets and Groceries

A classic Mexican bakery, **Pan del Carmen** (Av. Tulum near Calle Osiris, 6am-11pm daily, US$0.50-1.50) is a bustling shop offering everything from fresh rolls to chocolate-filled *cuernos* (croissants). Be sure to grab a metal tray and tongs to make your selections.

La Reyna de Michoacan (Calle Alfa Sur at Calle Sol Ote, no phone, 7:30am-11:30pm, US$1.50-3) specializes in *paletas* (frozen ice pop), *helado* (ice cream), *aguas* (juices), and *licuados* (smoothies), all made with fresh fruits. There's a huge variety of flavors—from coconut and strawberry to guava and pineapple with chile. It's a perfect stop while strolling about town.

The Zona Hotelera's largest market is a convenience store (Punta Piedra, 9am-9pm daily), which is filled with snack food, canned goods, water, liquor, and sunscreen.

For a supermarket with the basics and then some, head to the Chedraui (Av. Cobá s/n, 7am-10pm daily), located between Tulum town and the Zona Hotelera; beyond fresh, dry, and canned food, you'll find a bakery, a beachwear and shoe section, even home appliances.

Tulum Pueblo has a great local fruit and vegetable shop, Huerta del Eden (Av. Tulum at Calle Alfa Norte, no phone, 7am-9pm daily). On Sunday, check out the Tianguis Orgánico y Natural (central plaza, 10am-3pm), a farmers market featuring organic produce, artisanal products, and homeopathic medicines.

INFORMATION AND SERVICES
Tourist Information
A tourist information kiosk (no phone, 9am-5pm daily) is located on the central plaza, across from the HSBC bank. The chief attendant is quite knowledgeable, her teenage disciples less so. You often can glean useful information from the stacks of brochures there. The website www.todotulum.com also offers good information on current goings-on and offerings in Tulum.

Emergency Services
Hospital de Tulum (Av. Tulum btwn Calles Luna and Acuario Norte, tel. 984/871-2271, www.hospitaldetulum.com, 24 hours daily) is a small private hospital offering emergency and preventative services with a bilingual staff. For minor medical issues, Tulum's local clinic, Centro de Salud Tulum (Calle Andrómeda btwn Calles Jupiter and Alfa, tel.

984/871-2050, 24 hours) is a decent option. For serious health problems, head to Playa del Carmen or Cancún.

Farmacia Similares (Av. Tulum at Calle Jupiter Sur, tel. 984/871-2736) is open 8am-10pm Monday-Saturday and 8am-9pm Sunday; it also has a doctor on staff for simple consultations 9am-9pm Monday-Saturday and 9am-3pm Sunday.

The police (toll-free tel. 066, 24 hours) share a large station with the fire department, about two kilometers (1.2 miles) from Tulum Pueblo on the road to the Zona Hotelera.

Money
HSBC (Av. Tulum at Calle Alfa next to city hall, 9am-5pm Mon.-Fri.) has reliable ATM machines and will change foreign cash and AmEx travelers checks. If there's a line, ScotiaBank (Av. Tulum at Calle Satélite, 8:30am-4pm Mon.-Fri.) is a good option, too. There are also several bank ATMs at the Chedraui supermarket on Avenida Cobá.

Media and Communications
Tulum's post office (Calle Orion Sur at Calle Andrómeda Sur) is open 8am-4:30pm Monday-Friday and 8am-noon Saturday.

In the Zona Hotelera, most hotels offer free Wi-Fi in the reception or restaurant area for guests. In town, Satélite Ciber (Av. Satélite near Av. Tulum, 8:30am-10:30pm daily, US$1/hour) has flat-screen computers and killer air-conditioning. Another good option is Movistar (Av. Tulum at Calle Orion, 9am-10pm daily, US$1/hour), which has Skype-enabled computers plus direct-dial international calls (US$0.25-0.40/minute).

Laundry and Storage
Lava Easy (Av. Tulum btwn Av. Satélite and Calle Centauro, 8am-8pm Mon.-Sat.) charges US$1.15 per kilo (2.2 pounds), with a three-kilo (6.6-pound) minimum.

Near the bus station, a no name *lavandería* (Av. Tulum near Calle Jupiter Norte, 7am-7pm Mon.-Sat.) charges US$1.50

Tulum Bus Schedule

Departures from the **bus terminal** (Av. Tulum btwn Calles Alfa and Jupiter, tel. 984/871-2122) include:

Destination	Price	Duration	Schedule
Cancún	US$7.15-9.25	2-2.5 hrs	every 15-60 mins midnight-11:15pm
Carrillo Puerto	US$4.75-7.15	1.5 hrs	every 15-90 mins 12:30am-11:30pm
Chetumal	US$13.50-24	3.5-4 hrs	every 30-90 mins 12:30am-11pm
Chichén Itzá	US$7.50-14.75	3-3.5 hrs	8:30am and 9am
Cobá	US$3.25-5.25	45-60 mins	every 30-60 mins 7:15am-11am and 3:30pm-8pm
Mahahual	US$18.50	2.5 hrs	1 departure 9am
Mérida	US$23	4 hrs	5 departures 2:30am-8:30pm
Playa del Carmen	US$3-5.50	1 hr	every 30-60 mins 12:15am-11:15pm
Valladolid	US$6.50-8.50	1.5-2hrs	every 30-90 mins 2:30am-8:30pm

per kilo for two-hour service with a three-kilo (6.6 pound) minimum.

The **bus terminal** (Av. Tulum btwn Calles Alfa and Jupiter, tel. 984/871-2122, 24 hours) has luggage storage for US$1.50 per hour or US$7.75 per 8-24 hours.

Language and Instruction
El Camino (Av. Satélite Norte at Calle 4 Pte., tel. 984/135-8118, www.elcaminotulum.com, 8am-8pm daily) is a new language school offering all levels of Spanish language instruction. Classes are offered one-on-one (US$15/hour) or in small groups (US$215-375 for 15-45 hours). Homestays with local families as well as accommodations at local hotels or condos can be arranged by the school.

GETTING THERE
Bus
Tulum's **bus terminal** (Av. Tulum btwn Calles Alfa and Jupiter, tel. 984/871-2122) is

at the south end of town, a block from the main plaza.

Combi
Combis are white collective vans that zip between Tulum and Playa del Carmen all day, every day (US$3.25, 1 hour, every 10 minutes 5am-10pm). They leave more frequently than buses and are handier for intermediate stops, like Dos Ojos, Akumal, and Xpu-Há. Flag them down anywhere on Avenida Tulum or Highway 307.

Combis also go to Cobá (US$4.75, 1 hour), stopping at cenotes along the way. They leave hourly 8am-5pm from a stop on Avenida Tulum at Calle Osiris Norte. You can also catch them at the intersection of Highway 307 and the Cobá/Zona Hotelera road.

Tukan Kin (tel. 984/871-3538, www.fromcancunairport.com) operates an **airport shuttle** from Tulum to Cancún airport (US$45 adult, US$22.50 child), with six designated pickup stops around Tulum town and door-to-door service from the Zona Hotelera. Service from the airport to Tulum also is available for the same one-way rate. The trip takes just under two hours; advance reservations are required.

Car

Highway 307 passes right through the middle of Tulum Pueblo, where it is referred to as Avenida Tulum. Coming south from Cancún or Playa del Carmen, you'll first pass the entrance to Tulum archaeological site, on your left. A kilometer and a half later (1 mile) you'll reach a large intersection, where you can turn left (east) toward the beach and Zona Hotelera, or right (west) toward Cobá. Continuing straight ahead takes you into Tulum Pueblo, then onward to the Costa Maya.

GETTING AROUND
Bicycle

A bike can be very handy, especially for getting to or from the beach, or anywhere along the now-paved road through the Zona Hotelera.

In the Zona Hotelera, check out **Yokte Bikes** (Carr. Tulum-Punta Allen Km. 7.5, cell tel. 984/145-4061, 9am-6pm daily), which rents beach cruisers for US$9.25 per 24 hours, including helmet, lock, and safety vest. Drop-off and pick-up at your hotel is included.

In town, **iBike Tulum** (Av. Cobá Sur at Calle Venus, tel. 984/802-5518, www.ibiketulum.com, 9am-5:30pm Mon.-Sat.) rents a variety of bikes, including beach cruisers and mountain bikes (US$10-19 per 24 hours), most in top condition. All come with helmet, lock, lights, and roadside assistance. Child seats and bikes are also available. The shop also offers enjoyable tours, including to cenotes and dry caves.

Another option in town is **Kelly Bike Rental** (Av. Tulum at Calle Acuario, cell tel.

984/114-4657, 8:30am-8pm daily), which has decent bikes for US$5 per 12 hours; helmet, lock, and safety vest are included.

Beach Shuttle

There is a local *colectivo* (US$1.15) labeled "Cabañas" that goes from Tulum town to the arch at the southern end of the Zona Hotelera and back again, every 20-30 minutes 6am-8pm. Another *colectivo* (US$0.75) labeled "Ruínas," goes from town to the northern end of the Zona Hotelera at 8am, 8:30am, 5:30pm, and 6pm. Both routes start at the corner of Calle Sol Ote and Orion Sur. You also can catch both *colectivos* along Avenida Tulum and on the road to and along the beach. Schedules often change, so be sure to confirm the current departures (and return times!).

Car

A car can be very useful in Tulum, especially in the Zona Hotelera, even if you don't plan on using it every day. Renting a car from the airport in Cancún is the easiest and most affordable option for most travelers, especially if you book online and in advance. In Tulum, agencies include **Avis** (Av. Cobá Sur at Calle Sol Ote, cell tel. 984/120-3972, toll-free Mex. tel. 800/288-8888, www.avis.com, 8am-8pm daily) and **Hertz** (Hwy. 307 at Carr. Tulum-Cobá, toll-free Mex. tel. 800/709-5000, www.hertz.com, 7am-10pm daily), located next to Super San Francisco supermarket.

Taxi

Taxis are plentiful, and fares run about US$3 in town and US$8-12 to get to the Zona Hotelera (depending on where exactly you're going). In the Zona Hotelera, there is a taxi stand in Punta Piedra; rates are roughly the same within the Zona Hotelera or back into Tulum Pueblo. From either area, a ride to Tulum ruins costs about US$5.

Cobá

The Maya ruins of Cobá make an excellent complement—or even alternative—to the memorable but vastly overcrowded ruins at Tulum. Cobá doesn't have Tulum's stunning Caribbean view and beach, but its structures are much larger and more ornate—in fact, Cobá's main pyramid is the second tallest in the Yucatán Peninsula, and it's one of few you are still allowed to climb. The ruins are also surrounded by lakes and thick forest, making it a great place to see birds, butterflies, and tropical flora.

★ COBÁ ARCHAEOLOGICAL ZONE

Cobá (8am-5pm daily, US$4.50) is especially notable for the complex system of *sacbeob*, or raised stone causeways, that connected it to other cities, near and far. (The term *sacbeob*—whose singular form is *sacbé*—means white roads.) Dozens of such roads crisscross the Yucatán Peninsula, but Cobá has more than any other city, underscoring its status as a commercial, political, and military hub. One road extends in an almost perfectly straight line from the base of Cobá's principal pyramid to the town of Yaxuna, more than 100 kilometers (62 miles) away—no small feat considering a typical *sacbé* was 1-2 meters (3.3-6.6 feet) high and about 4.5 meters (15 feet) wide, and covered in white mortar. In Cobá, some roads were even bigger—10 meters (32.8 feet) across. In fact, archaeologists have uncovered a massive stone cylinder believed to have been used to flatten the broad roadbeds.

History

Cobá was settled as early as 100 BC around a collection of small lagoons; it's a logical and privileged location, as the Yucatán Peninsula is virtually devoid of rivers, lakes, or any other aboveground water. Cobá developed into an important trading hub, and in its early existence had a particularly close connection with the Petén region of present-day Guatemala. That relationship would later fade as Cobá grew more intertwined with coastal cities like Tulum, but Petén influence is obvious in Cobá's high steep structures, which are reminiscent of those in Tikal. At its peak, around AD 600-800, Cobá was the largest urban center in the northern lowlands, with some 40,000 residents and over 6,000 structures spread over 50 square kilometers (31 square miles). The city controlled most of the northeastern portion of the Yucatán Peninsula during the same period before being toppled by the Itzás of Chichén Itzá following a protracted war in the mid-800s. Following a widespread Maya collapse—of which the fall of Cobá was not the cause, though perhaps an early warning sign—the great city was all but abandoned, save as a pilgrimage and ceremonial site for the ascendant Itzás. It was briefly reinhabited in the 12th century, when a few new structures were added, but had been abandoned again, and covered in a blanket of vegetation, by the time of the Spanish conquest.

Cobá Group

Passing through the entry gate, the first group of ruins you encounter is the Cobá Group, a collection of over 50 structures and the oldest part of the ancient city. Many of Cobá's *sacbeob* initiate here. Its primary structure, La Iglesia (The Church), rises 22.5 meters (74 feet) from a low platform, making it Cobá's second-highest pyramid. The structure consists of nine platforms stacked atop one another and notable for their round corners. Built in numerous phases beginning in the Early Classic era, La Iglesia is far more reminiscent of Tikal and other Petén-area structures than it is of the long palaces and elaborate facades typical of Puuc and Chenes sites. Visitors are no longer allowed to climb

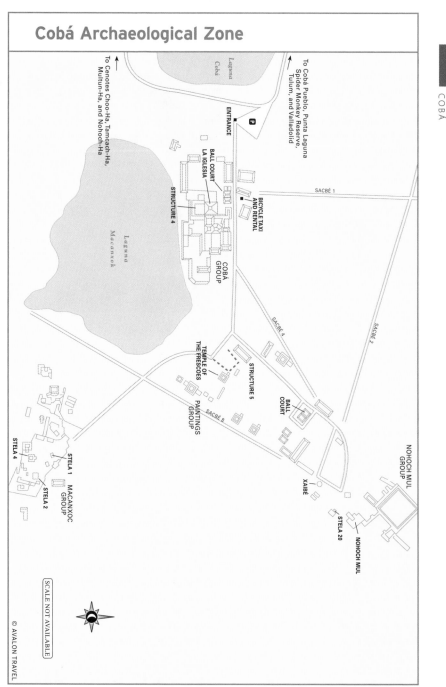

Cobá Archaeological Zone

Laguna
Cobá

To Cobá Pueblo, Punta Laguna
Spider Monkey Reserve,
Tulum, and Valladolid

ENTRANCE

P

BALL COURT
LA IGLESIA

STRUCTURE 4

BICYCLE TAXI
AND RENTAL

SACBÉ 1

COBÁ
GROUP

To Cenotes Choo-Ha, Tamcach-Ha,
Multun-Ha, and Nohoch-Ha

Laguna
Macanxok

SACBÉ 4

SACBÉ 2

TEMPLE OF
THE FRESCOES

STRUCTURE 5

PAINTINGS
GROUP

BALL
COURT

SACBÉ 8

XAIBÉ

STELA 4

STELA 1

MACANXOC
GROUP

STELA 2

STELA 20

NOHOCH MUL
GROUP

NOHOCH MUL

SCALE NOT AVAILABLE

© AVALON TRAVEL

the Iglesia pyramid due to the poor state of its stairs, but it is crowned with a small temple where archaeologists discovered a cache of jade figurines, ceramic vases, pearls, and conch shells.

The Cobá Group also includes one of the city's two **ball courts,** and a large acropolis-like complex with wide stairs leading to raised patios. At one time these patios were connected, forming a long gallery of rooms that likely served as an administrative center. The best-preserved structure in this complex, **Structure 4,** has a long vaulted passageway beneath its main staircase; the precise purpose of this passageway is unclear, but it's a common feature in Cobá and affords a close look at how a so-called Maya Arch is constructed.

The Cobá Group is directly opposite the stand where you can rent bicycles or hire bike taxis. Many travelers leave it for the end of their visit, after they've turned in their bikes.

Nohoch Mul Group

From the Cobá Group, the path winds nearly two kilometers (1.2 miles) through dense forest to Cobá's other main group, Nohoch Mul. The name **Nohoch Mul** is Yucatec Maya for Big Mound—the group's namesake pyramid rises an impressive 42 meters (138 feet) above the forest floor, the equivalent of 12 stories. (It was long believed to be the Yucatán Peninsula's tallest structure until the main pyramid at Calakmul in Campeche was determined to be some 10 meters higher.) Like La Iglesia in the Cobá Group, Nohoch Mul is composed of several platforms with rounded corners. A long central staircase climbs steeply from the forest floor to the pyramid's lofty peak. A small temple at the top bears a fairly well-preserved carving of the Descending God, an upside-down figure that figures prominently at Tulum but whose identity and significance is still unclear. (Theories vary widely, from Venus to the god of bees.)

Nohoch Mul is one of few Maya pyramids that visitors are still allowed to climb, and

The view from atop Cobá's highest pyramid, Nohoch Mul, is spectacular, but watch your step!

the view from the top is impressive—a flat green forest spreading almost uninterrupted in every direction. A rope running down the stairs makes going up and down easier.

Where the path hits Nohoch Mul is **Stela 20,** positioned on the steps of a minor structure, beneath a protective *palapa* roof. It is one of Cobá's best-preserved stelae, depicting a figure in an elaborate costume and headdress, holding a large ornate scepter in his arms—both signifying that he is an *ahau,* or high lord or ruler. The figure, as yet unidentified, is standing on the backs of two slaves or captives, with another two bound and kneeling at his feet. Stela 20 is also notable for the date inscribed on it—November 30, 780—the latest Long Count date yet found in Cobá.

Xaibé and the Ball Court

Between the Cobá and Nohoch Mul Groups are several smaller but still significant structures. Closest to Nohoch Mul is a curiously conical structure that archaeologists have dubbed **Xaibé,** a Yucatec Maya word for crossroads. The name owes to the fact that it's near the intersection of four major *sacbeob,* and for the same reason, archaeologists believe it may have served as a watchtower. That said, its unique design and imposing size suggest a grander purpose. Round structures are fairly rare in Maya architecture, and most are thought to be astronomical observatories; there's no evidence Xaibé served that function, however, particularly since it lacks any sort of upper platform or temple. Be aware that the walking path does not pass Xaibé—you have to take the longer bike path to reach it.

A short distance from Xaibé is the second of Cobá's **ball courts.** Both courts have imagery of death and sacrifice, though they are more pronounced here: a skull inscribed on a stone in the center of the court, a decapitated jaguar on a disc at the end, and symbols of Venus (which represented death and war) inscribed on the two scoring rings. This ball court also had a huge plaque implanted on one of its slopes, with over 70 glyphs and dated AD 465; the plaque in place today is a replica, but the original is under a *palapa* covering at one end of the court, allowing visitors to examine it more closely.

Paintings Group

The Paintings Group is a collection of five platforms encircling a large plaza. The temples here were among the last to be constructed in Cobá and pertain to the latest period of occupation, roughly AD 1100-1450. The group's name comes from paintings that once lined the walls, though very little color is visible now, unfortunately. Traces of blue and red can be seen in the upper room of the **Temple of the Frescoes,** the group's largest structure, but you aren't allowed to climb up to get a closer look.

Although centrally located, the Paintings Group is easy to miss on your way between the more outlying pyramids and groups. Look for a sign for **Structure 5,** where you can leave your bike (if you have one) and walk into the group's main area.

Macanxoc Group

From the Paintings Group, the path continues southeasterly for about a kilometer (0.6 mile) to the Macanxoc Group. Numerous stelae have been found here, indicating it was a place of great ceremonial significance. The most famous of these monuments is **Stela 1,** aka the Macanxoc Stela. It depicts a scene from the Maya creation myth—"the hearth stone appears"—along with a Long Count date referring to a cycle ending the equivalent of 41.9 billion, billion, billion years in the future. It is the most distant Long Count date known to have been conceived and recorded by the ancient Maya. Stela 1 also has reference to December 21, 2012, when the Maya Long Count completed its first Great Cycle, equivalent to 5,125 years. Despite widespread reports to the contrary, there is no known evidence, at Cobá or anywhere, that the Maya believed (much less predicted) that the world would end on that date.

Flora and Fauna

The name Cobá (Water Stirred by the Wind in Maya) is surely a reference to the group of shallow lagoons here (Cobá, Macanxoc, Xkanha, and Sacakal). The archaeological site and the surrounding wetlands and forest are rich with birdlife—herons, egrets, motmot, parrots, and the occasional toucan are not uncommon. Arrive early to see the most birds—at the very least you'll get an earful of their varied songs and cries. Later, as the temperature climbs, you'll start to see myriad colorful butterflies, including the large, deep-blue morphidae and the bright yellow-orange barred sulphur.

If you look on the ground, you'll almost certainly see long lines of leaf-cutter ants. One column carries freshly cut leaves to the burrow, and the other marches in the opposite direction, empty-jawed, returning for more. The vegetation decays in their nests, and the fungus that grows on the compost is an important staple of the ants' diet—a few scientists even claim that this makes leaf-cutter ants the world's second species of agriculturists. Only

Deciphering the Glyphs

For years, scholars could not agree whether the fantastic inscriptions found on Maya stelae, codices, and temple walls were anything more than complex records of numbers and dates. Many thought the text was not "real writing," as it did not appear to reproduce spoken language. Even those who believed the writing to be more meaningful despaired at ever reading it.

Mayanist and scholar Michael D. Coe's *Breaking the Maya Code* (Thames and Hudson, 2012) is a fascinating account of the decipherment of Maya hieroglyphics. Coe describes how, in 1952, reclusive Russian scholar Yuri Valentinovich Knorosov made a crucial breakthrough by showing that Maya writing did in fact convey spoken words. Using a rough alphabet recorded by Fray Diego de Landa (the 16th-century bishop who, ironically, is best known for having destroyed numerous Maya texts), Knorosov showed that ancient texts contain common Yucatec Maya words such as *cutz* (turkey) and *tzul* (dog). Interestingly, Knorosov conducted his research from reproductions only, having never held a Maya artifact or visited an ancient temple. (When he did finally visit Tikal in 1990, Coe says Knorosov wasn't very impressed.)

The decoding of glyphs led to major breakthroughs in understanding ancient Maya history and culture.

But Knorosov's findings were met with staunch resistance by some of the field's most influential scholars, which delayed progress for decades. By the mid-1980s, however, decipherment picked up speed; one of many standouts from that era is David Stuart, the son of Maya experts, who went to Cobá with his parents at age eight and passed the time copying glyphs and learning Yucatec Maya words from local playmates. As a high school student he served as chief epigrapher on a groundbreaking exploration in Belize, and at age 18 he received a US$128,000 MacArthur Fellowship (aka "Genius Award") to, as he told Michael Coe, "play around with the glyphs" full-time.

Researchers now know that Maya writing is like most other hieroglyphic systems. What appears at first to be a single glyph can have up to four parts, and the same word can be expressed in pictorial, phonetic, or hybrid form. Depending on context, one symbol can have either a pictorial or phonetic role; likewise, a particular sound can be represented in more than one way. The word *cacao* is spelled phonetically as "ca-ca-u" but is written with a picture of a fish (*ca*) and a comb-like symbol (also *ca,* according to Landa) and followed by -u. One of David Stuart's great insights was that for all its complexity, much of Maya glyphic writing is "just repetitive."

But how do scholars know what the symbols are meant to sound like in the first place? Some come from the Landa alphabet, others are suggested by the pictures that accompany many texts, still others from patterns derived by linguistic analyses of contemporary Maya languages. In some cases, it is simply a hunch that, after applying it to a number of texts, turns out to be right. If this seems like somewhat shaky scientific ground, it is—but not without a means of being proved. The cacao decipherment was confirmed when the same glyph was found on a jar with cacao residue still inside.

Hundreds of glyphs have been deciphered, and most of the known Maya texts can be reliably translated. The effort has lent invaluable insight into Maya civilization, especially dynastic successions and religious beliefs. Some archaeologists lament, not unreasonably, that high-profile glyphic studies divert attention from research into the lives of everyday ancient Maya, who after all far outnumbered the nobility but are not at all represented in the inscriptions. That said, it's impossible not to marvel at how one of the world's great ancient civilizations is revealed in the whorls and creases of fading stone pictures.

particular types of leaves will do, and the columns can be up to a kilometer (0.6 mile) long.

Practicalities

Cobá's main groups are quite spread apart, and visiting all of them adds up to several kilometers. Fortunately, you can rent a bicycle (US$3) or hire a *triciclo* (US$9.50 for 80 minutes, US$15 for 2 hours) at a large stand a short distance past the entryway, opposite the Cobá Group. Whether you walk or ride, don't forget a water bottle, comfortable shoes, bug repellent, sunscreen, and a hat. Watch for signs and stay on the designated trails. Guide service is available—prices are not fixed but average US$52 per group (1.5 hours, up to 6 people). Parking at Cobá is US$3.

Cobá is not nearly as crowded as Tulum (and is much larger), but it's still a good idea to arrive as early as possible to beat the ever-growing crowds.

COBÁ PUEBLO

It's fair to say that the town of Cobá, a rather desultory little roadside community, has never regained the population or stature that it had as a Maya capital more than 1,000 years ago. Most travelers visit Cobá as a day trip from Tulum or Valladolid, or on a package tour from resorts on the coast. There are two decent hotels in town, used mostly by those who want to appreciate Cobá's rich birdlife, which means being at the gate right when the site opens at 8am; if you're lucky, the gatekeeper may even let you in early.

Sights

Cobá Pueblo itself doesn't have much in the way of sights—besides the ruins, of course—but a number of small eco-attractions have cropped up, all a short distance from town.

RESERVA DE MONOS ARAÑAS PUNTA LAGUNA

The **Punta Laguna Spider Monkey Reserve** (cell tel. 985/107-9182, puntalagunamexico@gmail.com, 7:30am-5:30pm daily, US$5) is a nationally protected forest

that's home to various families of boisterous spider monkeys, as well as smaller groups of howler monkeys—it's estimated that there are up to 800 individual monkeys living in the reserve. There are also numerous bird species as well as coati, white-tailed deer, and even pumas. A short path winds through the reserve, passing a small unexcavated Maya ruin and a large lagoon where you can rent canoes (US$8.50). There's also a zipline and a place to rappel into a cenote, but it's typically reserved for large groups. Your best chance of spotting monkeys is by going in late afternoon, and by hiring one of the guides near the entrance (US$10 pp, minimum 2 people). The reserve (whose official name is Otoch Ma'ax Yetel Kooh, Yucatec Maya for House of the Spider Monkey and Puma) is operated by a local cooperative, whose members live in the nearby village and serve as guides; most speak at least some English. Be sure to wear good walking shoes and bring plenty of bug repellent. The reserve is located 18 kilometers (11 miles) north of Cobá, on the road toward Nuevo X'can.

★ CENOTES

If you've got a car, a cluster of three well-maintained and well-run cenotes (no phone, 8am-5pm daily) are a great addition to a day spent at Cobá. **Choo-Ha, Tamcach-Ha,** and **Multun-Ha** are southwest of Cobá and are operated jointly (US$5/7/10 for 1/2/3 cenotes); a fourth cenote called **Nohoch-Ha** is a bit farther and requires a separate entrance fee (US$4). Each is slightly different—one has a high roof and platform for jumping, another is wide and low—but all are impressive enclosed chambers bristling with stalactites, filled with cool crystalline water that's heaven on a hot day. Cement or wooden stairways lead down to pools; showers and changing areas are available at Choo-Ha. To get there, continue past the Cobá ruins on the road to Tepich and follow the signs.

Accommodations

The low-key **Hotel Sac Be** (Calle Principal,

tel. 984/206-7140, US$34 s/d, US$42 s/d with a/c) has friendly service and spotless rooms with one or two beds, televisions, Wi-Fi, and a small desk. All have private bathrooms and open onto a long outdoor corridor. Guests get 10 percent off at the hotel restaurant (which is the small one right above the mini-mart reception area; the much larger attached restaurant has a different owner). If it's booked, consider heading to Tulum or Valladolid, each about 45 minutes away by car or bus—the other options in town are pretty grim.

Food

With a large raised patio overlooking the lagoon, **La Pirámide** (Calle Principal at Laguna Cobá, no phone, 7:30am-9pm daily, US$6-15) is a nice place for lunch après-ruins or beer and snacks in the evening. The restaurant receives a number of tour groups, and it often has a buffet set up (US$12.50); otherwise the menu has grilled fish, chicken, and meat dishes as well as typical Mexican fare.

A few doors down, **Nicte Ha** (facing Laguna Cobá, tel. 984/206-7025, 8am-7pm daily, US$3-8) is a small place serving tacos, enchiladas, and various pork dishes.

Across the street from the church, **Abarrotes Neftali** (Calle Principal s/n, 7am-11pm daily) is a mini-mart that sells canned goods, bread, and some fresh produce.

Information and Services

Cobá has neither an official tourist office nor a health clinic. There also are no banks or ATMs—the nearest banking and medical services are in Tulum and Valladolid.

Facing the lagoon, **Farmacia El Porvenir** (Calle Principal s/n, no phone, 9am-1pm and 2pm-9pm Mon.-Sat.) is a small shop selling basic medicines and toiletries.

The **police station** (toll-free tel. 066) is halfway down the main drag, before you hit the lagoon.

Getting There and Around

You can easily walk to any of the listed businesses in town; the archaeological site is a five-minute walk down the main road, alongside the lagoon.

BUS

A tiny bus station operates out of El Bocadito restaurant (Calle Principal). For the coast, the lone first-class bus departs Cobá at 3:10pm, with stops in Tulum (US$5.15, 1 hour), Playa del Carmen (US$9.25, 2.5 hours), and Cancún

Hotel Sac Be

(US$14.50, 3.5 hours). Second-class buses to the same destinations cost a bit less but take longer; departures are at 9:30am, 10:30am, 1:30pm, 3:30pm, 4pm, and 6pm.

CAR

Getting to Cobá is easiest by car. No matter what direction you're coming from, the roads are smooth and scenic, cutting through pretty farmland and small towns. Keep your speed down, however, as there are innumerable *topes* (speed bumps) and occasional people and animals along the shoulder. Buses ply the same routes, but somewhat infrequently.

Three different roads lead to Cobá; none are named or marked, so they are known by the towns on either end. There are no formal services along any of the roads, save a gas station in the town of Chemax.

The Cobá-Tulum road (45 kilometers/28 miles) is the busiest, cutting southeast to Tulum and the coastal highway (Hwy. 307). The other two roads connect to Highway 180, the main highway between Cancún and Chichén Itzá. The Cobá-Nuevo X'Can road (47 kilometers/29 miles) angles northeast, connecting with Highway 180 about 80 kilometers (50 miles) outside Cancún and passing places like the Punta Laguna monkey reserve along the way. The Cobá-Chemax road (30 kilometers/19 miles) angles northwest to the town of Chemax; from there it's another 20 kilometers (12.4 miles) to Valladolid and Highway 180, connecting to the highway about 40 kilometers (25 miles) from Chichén Itzá.

All three roads, plus the short access road to Cobá, intersect at a large roundabout just north of Cobá village. Pay close attention to which road you want to avoid a long detour.

Sian Ka'an Biosphere Reserve

Sian Ka'an is Yucatec Maya for "where the sky is born," and it's not hard to see how the original inhabitants arrived at such a poetic name. The unkempt beaches, blue-green sea, bird-filled wetlands and islets, and humble accommodations are manna for bird-watchers, artists, snorkelers, and kayakers. But most visitors come here for the fishing. Sian Ka'an is one of the best fly-fishing spots in the world, with all three Grand Slam catches: bonefish, tarpon, and permit.

The reserve was created in 1986, designated a UNESCO World Heritage Site in 1987, and expanded in 1994. It now encompasses around 1.3 million acres of coastal and mangrove forests and wetlands, and some 113 kilometers (70 miles) of pristine coral reefs just offshore. A huge variety of flora and fauna thrive in the reserve, including four species of mangrove, many medicinal plants, and about 300 species of birds, including toucans, parrots, frigate birds, herons, and egrets. Monkeys, foxes, crocodiles, and boa constrictors also populate the reserve and are spotted by locals and visitors with some regularity. Manatees and jaguars are the reserve's largest animals but also the most reclusive: You need sharp eyes and a great deal of luck to spot either one. More than 20 Maya ruins have been found in the reserve, though most are unexcavated.

Spending a few days in Sian Ka'an is the best way to really appreciate its beauty and pace. Hotels and tour operators there can arrange fishing, bird-watching, and other tours, all with experienced local guides. But if time is short, a number of tour operators in Tulum offer day trips into the reserve as well.

SIGHTS
Muyil Archaeological Zone

The most accessible Maya site within the Sian Ka'an reserve is **Muyil** (Hwy. 307, 25 kilometers/15.5 miles south of Tulum, 8am-5pm daily, US$4), on the western edge of the park. Also known as Chunyaxché, it is one of the oldest archaeological sites in the Maya world,

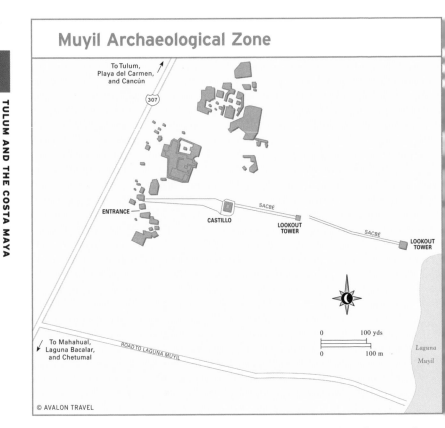

Muyil Archaeological Zone

To Tulum,
Playa del Carmen,
and Cancún

307

SACBE

ENTRANCE

CASTILLO

LOOKOUT
TOWER

SACBE

LOOKOUT
TOWER

0   100 yds
0   100 m

To Mahahual,
Laguna Bacalar,
and Chetumal

ROAD TO LAGUNA MUYIL

Laguna
Muyil

© AVALON TRAVEL

dating back to 300 BC and occupied continuously through the conquest. It's believed to have been primarily a seaport, perched on a limestone shelf near the edge of Laguna Muyil; it is connected to the Caribbean via a canal system that was constructed by ancient Maya traders and still exists today.

Only a small portion of the city has been excavated, so it makes for a relatively quick visit. There are six main structures ranging from two-meter-high (6.6-foot) platforms to the impressive **Castillo.** At 17 meters (56 feet), it is one of the tallest structures on the peninsula's Caribbean coast. The Castillo is topped with a unique solid round masonry turret from which the waters of the Caribbean Sea can be seen. Unfortunately, climbing to the top is prohibited.

A *sacbé* (raised stone road) runs about a half kilometer (0.3 mile) from the center of the site to the edge of the **Laguna Muyil.** Part of this *sacbé* is on private property, however, so if you want to access the lagoon from the ruins—you also can get to it by car—there is an additional charge of US$4 per person. Along the way, there is a lookout tower with views over Sian Ka'an to the Caribbean.

Once you arrive at the water's edge, it's possible to take a **boat tour** (US$46 pp) that crosses both Muyil and Chunyaxché Lagoons, which are connected by a canal that was carved by the ancient Maya in order to reach the ocean. It's a pleasant way to enjoy the water, and you'll also get a view of several otherwise inaccessible ruins along the lagoons' edges and through the mangroves, with the final stop being **Xlapak ruins,** a small site thought to have been a trading post. If arriving by car, look for signs to Muyil Lagoon on Highway 307, just south of the similarly named archaeological site. More thorough tours of this part of Sian Ka'an can be booked in Tulum.

★ Bahía de la Ascensión

Ascension Bay covers about 20 square kilometers (12.4 square miles), and its shallow flats and tangled mangrove islands teem with bonefish, tarpon, and huge permit—some of the biggest ever caught, in fact. It is a fly fisher's dream come true, and it has been attracting anglers from around the world since the mid-1980s. Don't fly-fish? No worries: The spin fishing is also fantastic, while the offshore reef yields plenty of grouper, barracuda, dorado, tuna, sailfish, and marlin.

SPORTS AND RECREATION
Sportfishing

Sportfishing is world-class in and around Sian Ka'an—it's hard to go wrong in the flats and mangrove islands, or with the Caribbean lapping at its shores. All the hotels listed in this section arrange fishing tours, and most specialize in it, using their own boats and guides.

If you prefer to go with an independent operator, recommended outfits include **Pesca Maya** (7 kilometers/4.3 miles north of Punta Allen, tel. 998/848-2496, toll-free U.S. tel. 888/894-5642, www.pescamaya.com, 8am-7pm daily); the **Palometa Club** (Punta Allen, north of the central plaza, toll-free U.S. tel. 888/824-5420, www.palometaclub.com, 8am-6pm daily); and **Club Grand Slam** (near the entrance to Punta Allen, cell tel. 984/139-2930, www.grandslamfishinglodge.com).

Weeklong fly-fishing trips range US$3,400-4,000 per person, in shared room and shared boat, depending largely on the style and comforts afforded by the lodge. Most packages include airport transfer, daily guided fishing, meals, and admission to the reserve, but it's always a good idea to confirm this before booking. For private room or private boat, expect to pay an additional US$100-200 per day; shorter trips are available, but may incur extra transportation costs to and from the airport. Fishing day trips can be arranged through most hotels; rates start at around US$360 for a private full-day tour, including lunch and admission and license fees. Variations like renting gear, adding people, and half-day options can also be arranged.

dolphin spotting in the Sian Ka'an Biosphere Reserve

Sport- and Game Fishing

The Riviera Maya is well known for trolling and deep-sea fishing, while Ascension Bay and the Costa Maya have terrific fly-fishing. Although you can hook into just about any fish at any time of the year, below is information on the peak and extended seasons for a number of top target species. Those fish not listed—tuna, barracuda, yellowtail, snapper, grouper, and bonefish—are prevalent year-round.

SPORTFISHING

Fish	Peak Season	Extended Season	Description
Sailfish	Mar.-June	Jan.-Sept.	Top target species, with a dramatic dorsal fin and a high-flying fighting style.
Blue Marlin	Apr.-Aug.	Mar.-Sept.	Largest Atlantic billfish, up to 500 pounds locally, but much larger elsewhere.
White Marlin	May-July	Mar.-Aug.	Smaller than the blue marlin, but still challenging.
Wahoo	Nov.-Jan.	June-Feb.	Lightning fast, with torpedo-like shape and distinctive blue stripes.
Dorado	May-July	Feb.-Aug.	Hard fighter with shimmery green, gold, and blue coloration; aka dolphin or mahimahi.

FLAT-WATER FISHING

Fish	Peak Season	Extended Season	Description
Tarpon	Mar.-Aug.	Feb.-Oct.	Big hungry tarpon migrate along the coast in summer months.
Snook	July-Aug.	June-Dec.	Popular trophy fish, grows locally up to 30 pounds.
Permit	Mar.-Sept.	year-round	March and April see schools of permit, with some 20-pound individuals.

Bird-Watching

Sian Ka'an is also an excellent place for bird-watching. Trips to Bird Island and other spots afford a look at various species of water birds, including male frigates showing off their big red balloon-like chests in the winter. Tours often combine bird-watching with snorkeling and walking around one or more bay islands. Hotels in Punta Allen and along the coastal road can arrange tours, as can outfits in Tulum. Prices are typically per boat, so don't be shy to approach other travelers in town about forming a group.

In Punta Allen, **Punta Allen Coop** (no phone, 6:30am-2pm daily) is a local cooperative that offers bird-watching tours

(US$120-145, 2-3 hours, up to 6 pax); look for their two-story wooden shack along the main road near the entrance to town. Other operators to consider include **Community Tours Sian Ka'an** (Calle Osiris Sur near Calle Sol Ote, tel. 984/871-2202, www.siankaantours.org, 7am-7pm daily); and, if your budget permits, **Visit Sian Ka'an** (Sian Ka'an Biosphere Reserve, Carr. Tulum-Punta Allen Km. 15.8, cell tel. 984/141-4245, www.visitsiankaan.com), which offers customized private tours.

Kayaking

The tangled mangrove forests, interconnected lagoons, and scenic bays make Sian Ka'an ideal for kayaking. **Community Tours Sian Ka'an** (Calle Osiris Sur near Calle Sol Ote, tel. 984/871-2202, www.siankaantours.org, 7am-7pm daily) offers several kayak excursions, with tours starting at US$75 per person.

ACCOMMODATIONS

Punta Allen is the only town on the peninsula and has the most options for lodging, food, tours, and other services. Along the long unpaved road leading there is a smattering of lodges and private homes, amid miles and miles of deserted coastline. **Note:** The town of Punta Allen often switches off the electricity grid at midnight—and hotels outside of town are entirely off the grid—so air-conditioning and TV are not functional unless the establishment has a generator. (Fans work as long as the hotel has solar or wind power.) If you're staying in a room with kitchen facilities, keep the fridge shut as much as possible to conserve the cold.

Toward Punta Allen

Eight kilometers (5 miles) north of Punta Allen, ★ **Sol Caribe** (cell tel. 984/139-3839, www.solcaribe-mexico.com, US$185 s/d, US$175-250 *cabaña,* US$100/40 extra per adult/child all-inclusive) offers modern rooms and *cabañas* set on a breezy, palm-tree-laden beach. All feature tropical wood furnishings, terraces with hammocks, 24-hour electricity (fan only), and gorgeous views of the ocean— a true hidden getaway of the Riviera Maya. There's a full-service restaurant on-site, too.

For more luxury than you'd rightly expect in a remote natural reserve, **Grand Slam Fishing Lodge** (cell tel. 984/139-2930, www.grandslamfishinglodge.com, US$370 s/d with a/c) has gigantic guest rooms in two-story villas, each with one or two king-size beds, fully-stocked minibars, marble bathrooms, and

A handful of beachfront hotels dot the road between Tulum and Punta Allen.

satellite service on large flat-screen TVs, plus 24-hour electricity for air-conditioning and Wi-Fi. The grounds include a tidy beach and aboveground pool, both with drink service, and a spacious restaurant-lounge. Guides and boats are first-rate.

Punta Allen

Facing the central plaza, ★ Posada Sirena (cell tel. 984/139-1241, www.casasirena. com, US$38-75 s/d) offers simple Robinson Crusoe-style rooms. Most are quite spacious, sleeping 6-8 people, and all have private bathrooms, fully equipped kitchens, and plenty of screened windows to let in the ocean breeze. Area excursions, including fly-fishing, snorkeling, and bird-watching, can be arranged on-site.

The accommodations at Serenidad Shardon (road to the lighthouse, cell tel. 984/107-4155, www.shardon.com, US$150 s/d, US$200 s/d with kitchen, US$375 2-bdrm apartment for up to 4 guests, US$500 beach house for up to 8 guests) vary from oceanfront *cabañas* to a large beach house; all have basic furnishings but are clean and well equipped. You also can camp using your own gear, or rent deluxe tents with real beds, electric lighting, and fans; access to hot showers and a full kitchen is included, too.

A dedicated fishing lodge, The Palometa Club (north of the central plaza, toll-free U.S. tel. 888/824-5420, www.palometaclub. com) has just six rooms in a two-story structure facing the beach. Each has two double beds, air-conditioning, and a private bathroom. Meals are served family-style, with cocktails and snacks (including freshly made ceviche) available at the club's outdoor bar, après fishing. The Palometa is designed for serious anglers, with a fly-tying study, one-to-one guiding, and an emphasis on landing permits (*palometa* in Spanish, hence the name). The all-inclusive seven-night/six-day rate is US$3,650 per person (non-anglers US$2,000/person). Rates are for shared room and boat. Private add-ons and shorter packages are also available.

FOOD

Punta Allen isn't a foodie's village, but it does have a handful of eateries, all specializing in fresh seafood. A few mini-marts and a tortilleria round things out a bit, especially if you're planning on staying more than a couple of days.

With a gorgeous view of the Caribbean, Muelle Viejo (just south of the central plaza, no phone, 11am-10pm Mon.-Sat., US$6-14) serves up fresh seafood dishes and cold beers—perfect for a long lazy lunch.

Casa de Ascensión (tel. 984/801-0034, 8am-10pm daily, US$4-17) offers a wide variety of Mexican dishes, pizza and pasta, and (of course) seafood. Seating is outdoors, under a large *palapa*. It's located two blocks from the beach, near the entrance to town.

There are three mini-marts in town: on the north end (near the road to the lagoonside dock), south end (two blocks west of Cuzan Guesthouse), and near the central plaza (one block west). Each sells basic foodstuffs and snacks, though you may have to visit all three to find what you're looking for. If you plan to cook a lot, stock up on supplies in Tulum.

INFORMATION AND SERVICES

Don't expect much in the way of services in Sian Ka'an—if there is something you can't do without, definitely bring it with you. There are no banking services, and few of the hotels or tour operators accept credit cards. There is one Internet café (9am-9pm Mon.-Fri., 9am-2pm Sat., US$1/hour), located inside a mini-mart near the southwest corner of the central plaza; many hotels have Wi-Fi. Cell phones typically don't work in Sian Ka'an, but there are public telephones in town. Punta Allen also has a modest medical clinic—look for it on the main road as you enter town. There is no laundry, but most hotels will provide the service.

Volunteer Work

Global Vision International (www.gvi.

co.uk) operates a popular volunteer-for-pay program in Sian Ka'an in partnership with Amigos de Sian Ka'an, a local nonprofit. GVI "expedition" fees are reasonable considering how much diving is involved (including open-water scuba certification, if needed): US$2,767-8,932 for 4-24 weeks, including room, board, and equipment, but not airfare. Advance registration is required.

GETTING THERE

Many of the hotels include airport pickup/drop-off, which is convenient and helps you avoid paying for a week's car rental when you plan on fishing all day. That said, a car is useful if you'd like to do some exploring on your own.

Bus

Public transport to and from Punta Allen is unpredictable at best—build some flexibility into your plans in case of missed (or missing) connections.

A privately run **Tulum-Punta Allen shuttle** (cell tel. 984/115-5580, US$22, 4 hours) leaves Tulum at 2pm most days. You can catch it at the taxi station on Avenida Tulum between Calles Centauro and Orion, or anywhere along the Zona Hotelera road; advance reservations are required. To return, the same shuttle leaves Punta Allen for Tulum at 5am.

You also can get to Punta Allen from Carrillo Puerto, a slightly cheaper but much longer and more taxing trip. State-run *combis* leave from the market in Carrillo Puerto (a block from the main traffic circle) for a bone-jarring four-hour trip down a private road to the small settlement of Playón (US$10, 10am and 3pm daily), where water taxis wait to ferry passengers across the lagoon to Punta Allen (US$2.50 pp, 15 minutes). The *combi* back to Carrillo Puerto leaves Playón at 6am.

Car

To get to Punta Allen by car, head south along the coast through (and past) Tulum's Zona Hotelera. About eight kilometers (5 miles) from the Tulum/Zona Hotelera junction is *el arco* (the arch), marking the reserve boundary where you register and pay a US$2.85 per person per day park fee. From there it's 56 kilometers (35 miles) by dirt road to Punta Allen. The road is much improved from years past, and an ordinary car can make it in 2-3 hours. It can be much more difficult after a heavy rain, however. Be sure to fill the tank in Tulum—there is no gas station along the way or in Punta Allen, though some locals sell gas from their homes.

The Costa Maya

The coastline south of Tulum loops and weaves like the tangled branches of the mangrove trees that blanket much of it. It is a mosaic of savannas, marshes, lagoons, scattered islands, and three huge bays: Bahía de la Ascensión, Bahía del Espíritu Santo, and Bahía de Chetumal. Where it's not covered by mangroves, the shore has sandy beaches and dunes, and just below the turquoise sea is one of the least-impacted sections of the great Mesoamerican Coral Reef. Dozens of Maya archaeological sites have been discovered here, but few excavated, and much remains unknown about pre-Hispanic life here. During the conquest, the snarled coastal forest proved an effective sanctuary for indigenous rebels and refugees fleeing Spanish control, not to mention a haven for pirates, British logwood cutters, and Belizean anglers.

In the 1990s, Quintana Roo officials launched an effort to develop the state's southern coast, which was still extremely isolated despite the breakneck development taking place in and around Cancún. (It has always been a famous fly-fishing area, however.) The first order of business was to construct a huge

The Caste War

On July 18, 1847, a military commander in Valladolid learned of an armed plot to overthrow the government that was being planned by two indigenous men—Miguel Antonio Ay and Cecilio Chí. Ay was arrested and executed. Chí managed to escape punishment and on July 30, 1847, led a small band of armed men into the town of Tepich. Several officials and Euro-Mexican families were killed. The military responded with overwhelming force, burning villages, poisoning wells, and killing scores of people, including many women, children, and elderly. The massacre—and the longstanding oppression of indigenous people at its root—sparked spontaneous uprisings across the peninsula, which quickly developed into a massive, coordinated indigenous rebellion known as the Caste War.

Indigenous troops tore through colonial cities, killing and capturing scores of non-Maya. In some cases, the Maya turned the tables on their former masters, forcing them into slave labor, including building the church in present-day Carrillo Puerto's central plaza. Valladolid was evacuated in 1848 and left abandoned for nearly a year, and by 1849, the peninsula's indigenous people were close to expelling the colonial elite. However, as they were preparing their final assaults on Mérida and Campeche City, the rainy season came early, presenting the Maya soldiers with a bitter choice between victory and (were they to miss the planting season) likely famine. The men turned their backs on a hard-fought and near-certain victory to return to their fields to plant corn.

Mexican troops immediately took advantage of the lull, and the Maya never regained the upper hand. For the next 13 years, captured indigenous soldiers (and increasingly *any* indigenous person) were sold to slave brokers and shipped to Cuba. Many Maya eventually fled into the forests and jungles of southern Quintana Roo. The fighting was rekindled when a wooden cross in the town of Chan Santa Cruz (today, Carrillo Puerto) was said to be channeling the voice of God, urging the Maya to keep fighting. The war ended, however, when troops took control of Chan Santa Cruz in 1901. An official surrender was signed in 1936.

cruise ship port, which they did in the tiny fishing village of Mahahual. They also needed a catchy name, and came up with the "Costa Maya." The moniker generally applies to the coastal areas south of Tulum, particularly the Sian Ka'an Biosphere Reserve; the towns of Mahahual and Xcalak; Laguna Bacalar; and Chetumal, the state capital and by far the largest city in the area.

It's hard not to be a little cynical about cruise liners coming to such a remote area, whose entire population could fit comfortably on a single ship. The town of Mahahual, nearest the port, is utterly transformed when cruise ships arrive, their passengers moseying about Mahahual, beer bottles in hand, the beaches packed with sun worshippers serenaded by the sound of Jet Skis. Then again, it's doubtful the area would have paved roads, power lines, or telephone service if not for the income and demand generated by cruise ships. Driving down the

old rutted coastal road to Xcalak (an even smaller town south of Mahahual) used to take a half day or more; today, a two-lane paved road has cut the trip to under an hour. The state government has vowed to control development by limiting hotel size and density, monitoring construction methods, and protecting the mangroves and coral reef. Small, ecofriendly bed-and-breakfasts have thrived, not surprisingly, and more and more independent travelers are drawn to the Costa Maya for its quiet isolation and pristine natural beauty.

CARRILLO PUERTO

Highway 307 from Tulum to Chetumal passes through Carrillo Puerto, the gateway to the Costa Maya. It's a small city that holds little of interest to most travelers except an opportunity to fill up on gas. Historically, however, it played a central role in the formation of Quintana Roo and the entire peninsula.

History

Founded in 1850, the town of Chan Santa Cruz (present-day Carrillo Puerto) was the center of a pivotal movement during the Caste War. As the Maya lost ground in the war, two indigenous leaders enlisted a ventriloquist to introduce the *Cruz Parlante* (Talking Cross) in Chan Santa Cruz. The cross "spoke" to the battle-weary population, urging them to continue fighting, even issuing tactical orders and predicting victory in the long, bitter conflict. Thousands joined the sect of the cross, calling themselves Cruzob (a Spanish-Maya conflation meaning People of the Holy Cross). Some accounts portray the talking cross as little more than political theater for a simpleminded audience, while others say most Cruzob understood it as a ruse to instill motivation. Some people, of course, believe in the cross's divinity. Whatever the case, it reinvigorated the Maya soldiers, and Chan Santa Cruz remained the last redoubt of organized indigenous resistance, finally submitting to federal troops in 1901. Once residing in Carrillo Puerto's Santuario de la Cruz Parlante, the Talking Cross is today housed in a small sanctuary in the town of Tixcal.

The town's name was changed in 1934 in honor of a former governor of Quintana Roo, much revered by indigenous and working-class people for his progressive reforms, for which he was ultimately assassinated.

Sights

The **Santuario de la Cruz Parlante** (Calle 69 at Calle 60, no phone, irregular hours, free) is a sacred place where the Talking Cross and two smaller ones were originally housed (they now reside in the nearby town of Tixcal). Today, there are several crosses in their place, all dressed in *huipiles,* which is customary in the Yucatán. Shoes and hats must be removed before entering. Be sure to ask permission before snapping any photographs.

Carrillo Puerto's main church, the **Iglesia de Balam Nah** (facing the central plaza, no phone), was reportedly built by white slaves—mostly Spaniards and light-skinned Mexicans—who were captured during the Caste War. It was constructed in 1858 to house the Talking Cross and its two companion crosses because the original sanctuary had become too small to accommodate its worshippers. Unfortunately, at the end of the Caste War, federal troops used the church as an army storeroom, desecrating it in the eyes of many Maya; this led to the transfer of the Talking Cross to the town of Tixcal.

Museo Maya Santa Cruz (central plaza, no phone, 9am-8:30pm Mon.-Fri., 10am-2pm and 5pm-9pm Sat.-Sun., free) is a small museum located in an exterior wing of the main church. Inside you'll find a mishmash of folk art, modern paintings, and modern Maya woodwork. It's not worth making a special stop but is a nice diversion if you're spending the night in Carrillo Puerto.

Despite outward appearances, Maya nationalism is still very much alive, and its adherents are not blind of the sometimes invasive effects of mass tourism. Don't miss the beautifully painted **Central Plaza Mural**, next to the Casa de Cultura, that reads: *La zona Maya no es un museo etnográfico, es un pueblo en marcha* (The Maya region is not an ethnographic museum, it is a people on the move).

Accommodations

Owned by one of the founding families of the city, **Hotel Esquivel** (Calle 63 btwn Calles 66 and 68, tel. 983/834-0344, US$44 s/d with a/c, US$52 suite with a/c and kitchenette) offers 37 rooms in four buildings, each with private bathroom, cable TV, and Wi-Fi. The main building has by far the best rooms—gleaming tile floors, simple furnishings, decent beds, and even some with balconies overlooking a pleasant park. The suites are in a large building across the street—recently remodeled, they are spacious and sparse with kitchenettes for basic cooking (microwave only). They open onto a large garden with swing sets and even a wading pool—perfect if you're traveling with small children (or are desperate to cool off).

Carrillo Puerto Bus Schedule

Departures from the bus terminal (Calle 65 near central plaza, tel. 983/834-0815) include:

Destination	Price	Duration	Schedule
Bacalar	US$5	1.5-2 hrs	17 departures 2am-11pm
Cancún	US$11.50	3.5-4 hrs	23 departures 1am-11:30pm
Chetumal	US$6.75	2-2.5 hrs	17 departures 2am-11pm
Limones	US$3.50	45-60 min	17 departures 2am-11pm
Mérida	US$15.25	6 hrs	13 departures midnight-9pm
Tulum	US$4.50	1-1.5 hrs	23 departures 1am-11:30pm
Valladolid	US$7	2.5 hrs	3 departures 9:30am-10:30pm

Food

El Faisán y el Venado (Av. Benito Juárez at Calle 67, tel. 983/834-0043, 6am-10pm daily, US$5-8) is Carrillo Puerto's best-known restaurant, as much for its location and longevity than for any particular noteworthiness of its food. The menu is filled with reliable Yucatecan standards, including 8-10 variations of fish, chicken, and beef, plus soup and other sides.

Located just off the central plaza, Café Luna Violeta (Calle 63 at Calle 68, tel. 983/700-3847, 7am-noon and 7pm-midnight Mon.-Sat., US$3-8) is a cozy little place serving light fare like sandwiches and pastries plus a variety of coffee drinks and teas.

Information and Services

The tourist office (Av. Benito Juárez at Av. Santiago Pacheco Cruz, tel. 983/267-1452) is open 8am-2pm and 6pm-9pm Monday-Friday.

The Hospital General (Calle 51 btwn Av. Benito Juárez and Calle 68, tel. 983/834-0092) is open 24 hours daily. Try Farmacia Similares (Av. Benito Juárez at Av. Lázaro Cárdenas, tel. 983/834-1407, 8am-10:30pm Mon.-Sat., 9am-10:30pm Sun.) for meds.

The police department (central plaza, tel. 983/834-0369, 24 hours) is located in the Palacio Municipal (city hall).

Next to the PEMEX station, HSBC (Av. Benito Juárez at Calle 69, 9am-5pm Mon.-Fri., 9am-3pm Sat.) has one 24-hour ATM. There also are two ATMs—HSBC and Santander—inside the bus terminal (Calle 65 near the central plaza).

The post office (Calle 69 btwn Calles 64 and 66) is open 9am-4pm Monday-Friday. Facing the central plaza, Balam Nah Internet (8am-midnight daily) charges US$0.75 per hour.

Getting There

Carrillo Puerto's bus terminal (Calle 65 near the central plaza, tel. 983/834-0815) has second-class service to Mahahual, Chetumal, Cancún, Mérida, and elsewhere.

If traveling by car, fill your gas tank in Carrillo Puerto, especially if you're headed to Mahahual or Xcalak. There are other roadside gas stations ahead (and in Chetumal),

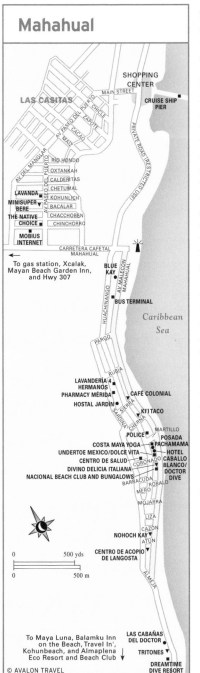

Mahahual

SHOPPING CENTER
MAIN STREET
LAS CASITAS
CRUISE SHIP PIER
AV PASEO DEL PUERTO
CHICLE
ZAPOTE
CACAO
MAIZ
PRIVATE ROAD (RESTRICTED USE)
AV DEL MANGLAR
RÍO HONDO
OXTANKAH
PASEO DEL PUERTO
CALDERITAS
CHETUMAL
LAVANDA
KOHUNLICH
MINISUPER BERE
BACALAR
THE NATIVE CHOICE
CHACCHOBEN
CHINCHORRO
MOBIUS INTERNET
CARRETERA CAFETAL MAHAHUAL
← To gas station, Xcalak, Mayan Beach Garden Inn, and Hwy 307
BLUE KAY
AV MALECÓN MAHAHUAL
HUACHINANGO
BUS TERMINAL
Caribbean Sea
PARGO
RUBIA
LAVANDERÍA 4 HERMANOS
PHARMACY MÉRIDA
CAFÉ COLONIAL
HOSTAL JARDÍN
KI'I TACO
SARDINA
SIERRA
CHERNA
MARTILLO
POLICE
POSADA PACHAMAMA
COSTA MAYA YOGA
UNDERTOE MEXICO/DOLCE VITA
HOTEL
CENTRO DE SALUD
CABALLO BLANCO
DIVINO DELICIA ITALIANA
CORONADO
DOCTOR DIVE
NACIONAL BEACH CLUB AND BUNGALOWS
BARRACUDA
ROBALO
MERO
MOJARRA
LIZA
CAZON
NOHOCH KAY
ATÚN
CENTRO DE ACOPIO DE LANGOSTA
AL MEJÍA
0   500 yds
0   500 m
To Maya Luna, Balamku Inn on the Beach, Travel In', Kohunbeach, and Almaplena Eco Resort and Beach Club ↓
LAS CABAÑAS DEL DOCTOR
TRITONES
DREAMTIME DIVE RESORT
© AVALON TRAVEL

but they get less and less reliable—having either no gas or no electricity to pump it—as the stretches of empty highway grow longer and longer.

MAHAHUAL

Mahahual is a place of two faces: cruise ship days, when the town's one road is packed with day-trippers looking to buy T-shirts and throw back a few beers; and non-cruise-ship days, when Mahahual is sleepy and laid-back, and the narrow white-sand beaches are free to walk for miles. Whether you stay here a night or a week, you're likely to see both, which is a good thing. You can be in a major party zone one day, and the next be the only snorkeler in town—all without changing hotels. If you seek long quiet days every day, though, definitely stay outside of town.

Whether or not there is a cruise ship in town, Mahahual is pretty easy to manage. Most of its hotels and services are located on, or just off, Avenida Mahahual (aka El Malecón), the three-kilometer (1.9-mile) pedestrian walkway that runs through town until it meets up with the coastal road heading south, the Carretera Antigua (literally, Old Highway). Just northwest of town, the tiny residential community of Las Casitas has additional services like an Internet café and a laundry.

Sights
★ BANCO CHINCHORRO

Chinchorro Bank is by some measurements the largest coral atoll in the Northern Hemisphere and a paradise for divers and snorkelers alike. About 44 kilometers (27 miles) east of Mahahual and 65.4 kilometers (40 miles) northeast of Xcalak, Chinchorro is a marine reserve and is known for its spectacular coral formations, massive sponges, and abundant sealife. Scores of ships have foundered on the shallow reefs through the years, but (contrary to innumerable misreports) the wrecks cannot be dived. Not only are they protected as historical sites, but most are on the eastern side of the atoll, where the surf and currents are too strong for recreational diving. The famous **40 Cannons wreck,** in about three meters (10 feet) of water on the atoll's northwest side, is good for snorkeling but not diving, and thanks to looters there are far fewer than 40 cannons there. There are small government and fishermen's huts on Cayo Centro, one of the three cays; as of 2010, tourists are permitted to stay overnight, which means spectacular multiday diving and snorkeling opportunities. To get to Chinchorro, it's a 1.5- to 2-hour boat ride, which can be pretty punishing depending on conditions. Groups typically set out around 7am and return to port around 5pm. Dive shops usually require at least five divers or six snorkelers (or a combination of the two) and may not go for days at a time if the weather is bad (summer months are best).

Sports and Recreation
SCUBA DIVING
Mahahual has terrific diving on the coral reef just offshore, with dozens of sites a short boat ride away. It's also one of two jumping-off points for trips to Chinchorro Bank, the largest coral atoll in the Northern Hemisphere. The other departure point is Xcalak, south of Mahahual.

Tritones (Av. Mahahual Km. 2.4, cell tel. 983/123-7639, www.tritonesdemahahual.com, 8am-6pm daily) is a friendly shop offering a wide array of dives to local sites (US$100 one tank, US$190 two tanks). It also offers fantastic overnight trips to Banco Chinchorro (US$500 pp, 1 night) that include six dives, meals (including a lobster dinner), drinks, and basic lodging in a stilt house on the water's edge. Snorkelers are welcome, too (US$200 pp). Longer trips to Chinchorro also can be arranged.

Doctor Dive (Malécon at Calle Coronado, cell tel. 983/125-2140, www.doctordive.com, 8am-6pm daily) is a small shop offering personalized service for independent travelers; fun dives are US$55 for one tank, US$85 for two; gear is an extra US$15

per day. Specialty trips, including lionfish hunting and diving unexplored locations, also can be arranged.

Don't be deterred by the slew of cruise shippers who crowd into **Dreamtime Dive Resort** (Av. Mahahual Km. 2.5, cell tel. 983/124-0235, U.S. tel. 904/730-4337, www.dreamtimediving.com, 9am-7pm daily)—the shop is an indie operation at heart and sends its students and "regular" guests on separate boats in groups of six divers or fewer. Fun dives cost US$55 for one tank, US$85 for two, and US$110 for three; rental equipment is an additional US$20 per day. The shop also offers Chinchorro Bank trips, all-day exploration trips, night dives, and a full menu of diving instruction and courses.

SNORKELING
You can rent snorkel gear for around US$8-10 a day from the dive shops or from the kiosks that pop up on cruise ship days. Swim or kayak out to the reef for a do-it-yourself experience, or join a guided tour, where you'll likely see more sealife, plus have extra safety and convenience. Mahahual's dive shops all offer guided snorkel trips for US$30-40 per person, including gear and about 90 minutes in the water.

STAND-UP PADDLING
UnderToe Mexico (Calle Coronado near Malécon, cell tel. 983/117-8995,www.undertoemexico.com, hours vary) offers introductory paddleboarding lessons (US$40 for 90 minutes) from certified bilingual instructors. If you already know the basics, rentals are available (US$35/hour) as are a number of SUPing excursions to nearby rivers and lagoons (prices vary).

YOGA
Located in a breezy studio overlooking the Caribbean, **Costa Maya Yoga** (Calle Martillo near Malécon, cell tel. 983/105-8040, www.costa-maya-yoga.com, hours vary) offers vinyasa, hatha, and restorative yoga classes from a handful of talented instructors. Classes

Lionfish

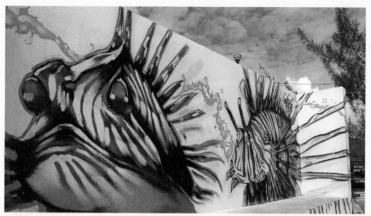

lionfish mural in Puerto Morelos

The lionfish is a spectacular striped fish with a "mane" of fins and poisonous spines that is changing the underwater landscape of the entire Caribbean. Historically found only in the warm regions of the Pacific and Indian Oceans, lionfish were first sighted in Atlantic waters in 1992 in Biscayne Bay, Florida; it's believed they were released into the wild after a private aquarium was swept into the ocean by Hurricane Andrew. Since then, lionfish have been documented in the Florida Keys, the Bahamas, Cuba, and elsewhere; the first lionfish sighting in the region was in Cozumel in January 2009. Voracious hunters with no natural predators, lionfish can grow to 20 inches long and devour everything from small reef fish to commercial fish like snapper and juvenile grouper. They thrive at depths of just a few feet to over 500 feet, and their coloring makes them especially well-suited for coral environments. Government agencies have taken proactive efforts to help curb the growth of this invasive fish, garnering widespread community support. There now are fishing tournaments targeting lionfish, and spear-fishing training for local sport divers; experts are even trying, with some success, to "train" wild sharks and mature grouper to prey on lionfish by introducing them into known hunting grounds. Restaurants are doing their part by creating innovative and tasty dishes from lionfish meat.

run US$20 per person; check the website for the current schedule.

TOURS

The Native Choice (Las Casitas, Av. Paseo del Puerto at Calle Chinchorro, tel. 998/869-3346, www.thenativechoice.com) offers a range of area tours, all led by guides who are extremely knowledgeable about Maya history, culture, and belief systems. Tours include visiting the archaeological sites of Chacchoben, Kohunlich, or Dzibanché (US$55-100 adult, US$45-85 child), a "Mayan Experience Tour,"

which includes touring Chacchoben ruins and a visit to a home in Chacchoben village (US$75 adult, US$65 child), plus a kayaking and hiking trip on and around Laguna Bacalar (US$55 adult, US$40 child). The tours are geared toward the cruise ship crowd, but hotel owners warmly recommend the outfit to independent travelers as well.

Accommodations

Many of Mahahual's lodgings, especially the ones with beachfront, are outside of the village itself, along the Carretera Antigua that hugs the coast south of town. The rest are in town, either on the Malecón or a stone's throw away.

IN TOWN

Under US$50: ★ **Hostal Jardín** (Calle Sardina near Calle Sierra, tel. 983/834-5722, hostal.jardin.mahahual@gmail.com, US$10 pp dorm, US$27 s/d, US$35 s/d with a/c) is an appealing hostel with a small interior garden and a friendly staff. The eight-bed dorm has overhead fans, thick mattresses, and spotless single-sex bathrooms. Four private rooms are located on the other side of the garden, with whitewashed walls, polished cement floors, and artsy touches. The only bummer—there's no communal kitchen.

Near the entrance to town, **Blue Kay** (Malecón btwn Carretera Cafetal and Calle Pargo, tel. 983/834-5868, www.bluekaymahahual.com, US$7.50 pp camping, US$11.50 pp dorm, US$32-39 s/d cabin with shared bathroom) has 27 tiny wood-plank cabins, lined up in three tidy rows in front of a long, gorgeous beach. Except for the waterbeds (yes, waterbeds), the cabins are basic—wood floor, a bed, a light—with a private porch for relaxing in the evenings; campers can set up in a garden just steps from the beach (BYO gear). Shared bathrooms are located in a *palapa*-roofed

building—they're huge and clean enough. All guests enjoy use of the hotel's beach club and its amenities, though on cruise ship days, it can get pretty busy.

Set on a grassy lot facing the ocean, **Las Cabañas del Doctor** (Av. Mahahual Km. 2, tel. 983/832-2102, www.lascabanasdeldoctor.com, US$7 pp camping, US$37-50 s/d *cabaña,* US$50 s/d, US$69 s/d with a/c) has a good range of accommodations: camping on the beach with access to cold-water bathrooms (BYO gear); simple *palapa*-roofed *cabañas* with tile floors and fans; and hotel rooms with recently remodeled bathrooms, modern decor, and private porches. All units—and camping spots—have Wi-Fi, too.

US$50-100: Posada Pachamama (Calle Huachinango btwn Calles Martillo and Coronado, tel. 983/834-5762, www.posadapachamama.net, US$68-76 s/d with a/c) is a small hotel a block from the beach. Rooms are small but appealingly decorated with modern furnishings and stone-inlaid floors; they are starting to show a bit of wear and tear, but nothing that impedes a comfortable stay. All have air-conditioning, wireless Internet, and satellite TV. The higher-priced rooms have small balconies, some with partial beach views. Guests also

Even the waves take it easy in Mahahual.

enjoy complimentary use of the beach club at Barba Roja, just in front.

With direct access to the beach and a rooftop bar with a spectacular view, **Hotel Caballo Blanco** (Malecón btwn Calles Martillo and Coronado, tel. 983/834-5830, www.hotelelcaballoblanco.com, US$77-115 s/d suite with a/c) is a great place to land. Rooms are modern and comfortable with air-conditioning, flat-screen TVs, mini-fridges, and Wi-Fi. All have private balconies, the more expensive ones overlooking the Caribbean. The only quirk about the place? Dramatic murals of old-world villages.

Over US$100: ★ **Nacional Beach Club and Bungalows** (Malécon near Calle Coronado, tel. 983/834-5719, www.nacionalbeachclub.com, US$62-112 s/d bungalows, US$112-127 s/d with a/c) is a tasteful beachfront hotel with spectacular ocean views and excellent service. Units vary from thatched-roof bungalows with private terraces to spacious hotel rooms with high ceilings and Mexican tile bathrooms. There's a small pool right on the Malécon and a good restaurant on-site. Guests are welcome to use the hotel beach club and its amenities, too.

OUTSIDE OF TOWN
US$50-100: Kohunbeach (Carr. Antigua Km. 7, cell tel. 983/700-2820, www.kohunbeach.com, US$54-77 s/d) offers three simple and spacious *cabañas* on the beach. Each has a queen bed, a foldout futon sofa, picture windows, and a mosaic-tile bathroom. All are solar powered. Kayaks and plenty of hammocks are available to guests, too.

Owned and operated by friendly Canadian expats, ★ **Balamku Inn on the Beach** (Carr. Antigua Km. 5.7, tel. 983/732-1004, www.balamku.com, US$85 s, US$95 d) offers artfully decorated rooms in a handful of *palapa*-roofed buildings. All run on solar power, wind turbines, and a nonpolluting wastewater system. Full breakfast is included, as is use of the hotel's kayaks, board games, and library. Wi-Fi is available in all the rooms, too.

Maya Luna (Carr. Antigua Km. 5.6, tel. 983/836-0905, www.hotelmayaluna.com, US$89 s/d) has four modern bungalows with 24-hour solar/wind power, rainwater showers, and *palapa*-shaded porches. Each has a private rooftop terrace with views of the Caribbean in front and the jungle in back; all have Maya- or ocean-themed murals, too. A hearty and healthy breakfast is included in the rate. Pets are welcome (and will join a cadre of friendly cats and a dog who live on-site).

Over US$100: About 20 minutes south of town, **Almaplena Eco Resort and Beach Club** (Carr. Antigua Km. 12.5, cell tel. 983/137-5070, www.almaplenabeachresort.com, US$135-145 s/d) is a small boutique resort with just eight rooms facing a gorgeous isolated stretch of beach. All have king-size beds, ceiling fans (no air-conditioning), cool stone floors, and tasteful decor. Suites are on the top floor and have private terraces, while standards share a wooden patio with direct access to the beach. All have Wi-Fi, too. Continental breakfast is included, and the on-site restaurant serves fine Mediterranean and Mexican meals.

About 21 kilometers (13 miles) north of Mahahual, **Mayan Beach Garden Inn** (cell tel. 983/130-8658, www.mayanbeachgarden.com, US$96-125 s/d, US$125 s/d with kitchenette, US$25 extra for a/c at night) is a quiet hotel (children over age 12 only) with several rooms and one *cabaña,* all with white-washed walls and Mexican-style decor, most with ocean views. A hearty breakfast is included in the rate, as are Wi-Fi and the use of kayaks. All-inclusive meal packages are also available. In the high season, there's a three-night minimum.

Food
IN TOWN
An open-air eatery and beach club, ★ **Nohoch Kay** (Big Fish in English, Malecón btwn Calles Liza and Cazón, no phone, 8am-7pm Mon.-Tues., 8am-10pm Wed.-Sun., US$5-14) serves up some of the best fish tacos in town. Thick pieces of fish—fried or grilled—are served with small

tortillas, onion, cilantro, and plenty of lime. On cruise ship days, it gets overrun with clients, but otherwise it's a laid-back place to get a beachfront meal.

Ki'i Taco (Calle Huachinango at Calle Cherna, no phone, 11am-10pm Mon.-Sat., US$2-6) offers equally good fish tacos without the cruise ship scene. For a treat, order the garlic shrimp tacos.

A breezy restaurant with hanging shell lamps and a *palapa* roof, ★ **Divino Delicia Italiana** (Calle Huachinango at Calle Coronado, no phone, 5pm-11pm Tues.-Sun., US$7-14) serves up freshly made pastas, seafood salads, and wooden tablets loaded with gourmet cheeses and meats. Thin crust pizzas also are baked in the wood-burning stove, visible from the dining room. An extensive wine list combined with friendly service round out a meal nicely.

Café Colonial (Calle Sierra near Malécon, no phone, 7am-5pm daily, US$3-6) is a good place to grab breakfast. Package deals include a hearty plate of eggs with bread, coffee, and juice for US$6. À la carte items like fruit plates and breakfast sandwiches also are offered. Tables are in a small wood house or on the pedestrian walkway in front.

Dolce Vita (Malécon at Calle Coronado, no phone, 8am-10pm daily, US$3-7) is a small shop specializing in homemade gelato, pastries, crepes, and milkshakes. And if you're looking for a mean cappuccino, look no further.

If you're cooking for yourself, consider buying fresh lobster from the local lobster fisherman's co-op, **Centro de Acopio de Langosta** (Calle Huachinango near Calle Almeja, no phone, 7am-7pm daily). At this roadside shack, you can take your pick of lobsters; they generally sell for US$30 per kilo (2.2 pounds). Fresh conch also is sold here for about US$16 per kilo.

OUTSIDE OF TOWN

A longtime favorite, **Travel In'** (Carr. Antigua Km. 5.8, cell tel. 983/110-9496, www.travel-in.com.mx, 5:30pm-9pm Tues.-Sat., US$5-20)

is a great little restaurant a few kilometers down the coastal road. Homemade pita bread is baked fresh every day—order it as an appetizer with an assortment of homemade dips. Daily seafood specials vary according to the day's catch. Open on Monday Christmas-Easter.

For basic groceries, try **Minisuper Bere** (Las Casitas, Av. Paseo del Puerto near Calle Kohunlich, 8am-11pm daily).

Information and Services

Cruise ships have brought considerable modernization to this once-isolated fishing village, but services are still somewhat limited.

EMERGENCY SERVICES

The **Centro de Salud** (Calle Coronado btwn Calles Huachinango and Sardina, no phone, 8am-2:30pm daily, after 5pm emergencies only) offers basic health services. For serious health matters, head to Chetumal.

For meds, try **Pharmacy Mérida** (Calle Sardina btwn Calles Rubia and Sierra, cell tel. 983/132-1845, 7am-11pm Mon.-Fri., 9am-11pm Sat.-Sun.), the best-stocked pharmacy in town.

The **police department** (Calle Huachinango near Calle Martillo, toll-free Mex. tel. 066) is open 24 hours.

MONEY

There is no bank in town, but there are a handful of **ATMs,** all along El Malécon. At the time of research, however, none were affiliated with local banks, so withdrawal charges were hefty. Another option is to go to the gas station outside of town, where there's an **HSBC ATM** (though it often runs out of cash); alternatively, consider bringing enough money to get you through your stay.

MEDIA AND COMMUNICATIONS

The only Internet café is in Las Casitas, where **Mobius Internet** (Calle Chinchorro near Av. Paseo del Puerto, 9am-10pm Mon.-Fri., 9am-2pm and 5pm-10pm Sat.) charges US$1.50 per hour and offers international telephone service, too (US$0.35-0.45/minute calls to the United States and Europe). Most hotels and some restaurants offer wireless Internet as well.

LAUNDRY

Lavandería 4 Hermanos (Calle Huachinango near Calle Rubia, 7am-8pm daily) offers same-day laundry service for US$1.50 per kilo (2.2 pounds).

In Las Casitas, try Lavanda (Av. Paseo del Puerto at Calle Chetumal, 9am-6pm daily), which charges US$1.25 per kilo (2.2 pounds).

Getting There and Around

Just south of the grubby roadside town of Limones, a good paved road with signs to Mahahual breaks off Highway 307 and cuts through 58 kilometers (36 miles) of coastal forest and wetlands tangled with mangroves. It's a scenic stretch, whether in a car or on a bus, along which you can occasionally see egrets, herons, and other water birds.

Mahahual proper is very walkable—in fact, the main road that runs through town, El Malecón, is a three-kilometer (1.9-mile) pedestrian walkway. If you're staying outside of town, a car certainly comes in handy, but plenty of people manage without; dive shops and tour operators typically offer hotel pickup, and there are cabs and a local bus.

BUS

Mahahual's bus terminal is a modest affair near the entrance to town—basically, a parking lot in front of Koox Quinto Sole Hotel. Buses to Cancún (US$28.50, 4.5 hours) leave at 5pm daily, stopping at Carrillo Puerto (US$10.25, 2 hours), Tulum (US$18.50, 3 hours), Playa del Carmen (US$24, 3.5 hours), and Puerto Morelos (US$23, 4 hours) along the way. To Chetumal (US$6.25, 2.5 hours) and Laguna Bacalar (US$5.75, 1.5 hours), buses depart at 7:40am and 5:40pm daily. All buses stop in Limones (US$3.50, 1 hour).

Note: Buses entering Mahahual stop in Las Casitas before arriving at the bus terminal; be

sure you get off at the latter if you're headed to the beach or any of the hotels.

CAR AND TAXI

There is a PEMEX gas station (24 hours) on the main road to Mahahual, just east of the turnoff to Xcalak. It occasionally runs out of gas, so definitely fill your tank in Carrillo Puerto or Chetumal on your way here.

Note: There's often a military checkpoint set up just west of the turnoff to Xcalak, where officials conduct searches for illicit drugs and other contraband. As long as you or your passengers don't have anything illegal in the car, the longest you should be delayed is a couple of minutes.

Cabs abound in this town, especially on cruise ship days. Rates are set by zone; in general, rates run around US$1 per kilometer (0.6 mile). If in doubt, ask to see the *tarifario* (official rate chart).

AIRPORT

Mahahual has a small airport just outside of town. Well, it's more like a well-maintained airstrip with a nice shelter. At the time of research, it was only used by private or chartered planes.

XCALAK

The tiny fishing village of Xcalak lies just a short distance from the channel that marks the Mexico-Belize border, and a blessed long way from anything else. The town started out as a military outpost and didn't get its first real hotel until 1988. Villagers had to wait another decade to get a paved road; before that, the only way in or out of town was by boat or via 55 kilometers (34 miles) of rutted beach tracks. Electrical lines were installed in 2004 but only in the village proper, so many outlying areas (including most of the better hotels) still rely on solar and wind power, as well as generators. The town has no bank, no public phones, and no gas station. That is to say: perfect!

The area doesn't have much beach but makes up for it with world-class fly-fishing, great snorkeling and diving, and a healthy coral reef and lagoon. A growing contingent of expats, mostly American and Canadian, have built homes here, some for personal use, others for rent, others as small hotels. Large-scale tourism may be inevitable but still seems a long way off, and Xcalak remains a small and wonderfully laid-back place, perfect for those looking for some honest-to-goodness isolation.

Sights

PARQUE NACIONAL ARRECIFES DE XCALAK

Xcalak Reef National Park was established at the end of 2003, affording protection to the coastal ecosystem as well as Xcalak's nascent tourist economy. The park spans nearly 18,000 hectares (44,479 acres), from the Belize border to well north of town, and includes the reef—and everything else down to 100 meters (328 feet)—as well as the shoreline and numerous inland lagoons.

The main coral reef lies just 90-180 meters (100-200 yards) from shore, and the water is less than 1.5 meters (5 feet) deep almost the whole way out. Many snorkelers prefer the coral heads even closer to shore, which have plenty to see and less swell than the main reef. The shallow waters keep boat traffic to a minimum, and anglers are good about steering clear of snorkelers (you should still stay alert at all times, however).

Divers and snorkelers also can explore the reef at 20 or so official sites and many more unofficial ones. Most are a short distance from town, and shops typically return to port between tanks. La Poza is one of the more distinctive dives, drifting through a trench where hundreds, sometimes thousands, of tarpon congregate, varying in size from one-meter (3-foot) "juveniles" to two-meter (7-foot) behemoths.

A fee of US$4 per day technically applies to all divers and snorkelers (and kayakers and anglers) in the Parque Nacional Arrecifes de Xcalak; dive shops typically add it to their rates, while most hotels have a stack of wristband permits to sell to guests who want to snorkel right from shore.

Sports and Recreation

SCUBA DIVING AND SNORKELING

XTC Dive Center (north end of town, across bridge, no phone, www.xtcdivecenter.com, 8am-6pm daily) is a highly recommended full-service dive shop offering dives to dozens of sites within Xcalak Reef National Marine Park (US$70 for one tank, US$110 for two tanks). It also specializes in trips to Chinchorro Bank (US$239 for two tanks or US$179 per person for snorkelers, including lunch, drinks, and a hike on Cayo Centro, the main cay; overnight trips are also offered). A variety of dive classes also are available; a nice three-meter-deep (9-foot) pool on-site is used for the open-water certification course. Snorkeling tours run US$40-75 per person depending on how long and far you go; five-hour trips include jaunts into Chetumal Bay and Bird Island, which can be fascinating, especially in January and February when the birds are most plentiful.

STAND-UP PADDLING

XTC Dive Center (north end of town, across bridge, no phone, www.xtcdivecenter.com, 8am-6pm daily) was on the brink of launching its SUPing class offerings when we passed through town. At the time, though, it offered paddleboard rentals with half- and full-day options (US$35-55).

SPORTFISHING

Xcalak boasts world-class sportfishing, with huge saltwater and brackish flats where hooking into the grand slam of fly-fishing—tarpon, bonefish, and permit—is by no means impossible. Add a snook, and you've got a super slam. Oceanside, tarpon and barracuda abound, in addition to grouper, snapper, and others.

Costa de Cocos (3 kilometers/1.9 miles north of town, no phone, www.costadecocos.com) is the area's oldest fishing resort, with highly experienced guides and numerous magazine write-ups. Three- to seven-night packages include transfer to and from the airport, lodging, meals, open bar, fishing license, marine park wristband, and, of course, nonstop fly-fishing (US$2,030-4,305 s, US$1,620-3,295 d). The resort also offers half- and full-day fishing trips (US$175-350), in case you want to fish while in Xcalak without making it a full-on fishing vacation.

Hotel Tierra Maya (2.1 kilometers/1.3 miles north of town, tel. 983/839-8012, www.tierramaya.net) also offers fly-fishing packages for 6-7 nights (US$3,040-3,684 s, US$1,950-2,400 d), though they don't include all the perks—like airport transportation, open bar, and fishing license fees—that the Costa de Cocos packages do.

XTC Dive Center (north end of town, across bridge, no phone, www.xtcdivecenter. com, 8am-6pm daily) offers half-day and full-day fly-fishing excursions (US$249-349) that include drinks, snacks, and a guide. BYO gear.

Accommodations

Xcalak's most appealing accommodations are on the beach road heading north out of town. Few places accept credit cards on-site, but many have payment systems on their websites.

UNDER US$50

Next to Restaurant Toby, Hotel Caracol Caribe (center of town, across from volleyball court, tel. 983/839-8381, US$27-31 s/d) is a simple, if aging, hotel offering the basics: a decent bed, a clean bathroom, a bare bulb, and a fan. There are two extras though: 24-hour electricity (huge in this part of the world) and a full breakfast (huge anywhere). Service is friendly, too.

US$50-100

Part of the XTC Dive Center, Flying Cloud Hotel (north end of town, across bridge, no phone, www.xtcdivecenter.com, US$45-55 s/d, US$65 s/d with kitchenette) is a three-room hotel with whitewashed walls, polished cement floors, and spectacular ocean views. Mattresses are thick and bathrooms are spotless. While each room is different—a collection of dive magazines, a private solarium, a king-size bed—each is comfortable. Guests enjoy use of the dive shop's pool and sea kayaks, too. When we passed through, plans were in the works to build a larger hotel just next door.

★ Hotel Tierra Maya (2.1 kilometers/1.3 miles north of town, tel. 983/839-8012, www.tierramaya.net, US$90-100 s/d,

The Costa Maya is home to some of the world's best fishing.

US$150 apartment) is a pleasant hotel with ample rooms decorated with simple furnishings and colorful Mexican rugs. All have private terraces or balconies with views of the Caribbean. Continental breakfast is included in the rate and served in the hotel's excellent beachfront restaurant. Fly-fishing and dive packages are also available.

US$100-150

It's hard not to feel at home at ★ **Sin Duda** (8 kilometers/5 miles north of town, Can. tel. 306/500-3240, www.sindudavillas.com, US$84 s/d, US$110 studio, US$120 apartment), a gem of a hotel with beautifully decorated rooms and apartments featuring Mexican folk art and breathtaking views. Evening often brings cocktail hour, when guests can join the friendly Canadian hosts for margaritas in the cozy lounge that doubles as a common kitchen and library. Kayaks and bicycles are available for guests, as are a rooftop solarium and hammocks on the beach. A healthy continental breakfast is included in the rate.

Four cheerful units with fully equipped kitchenettes make **Casa Carolina** (2.5 kilometers/1.6 miles north of town, U.S. tel. 678/446-9817, www.casacarolina.net, US$120 s/d) a great choice for indie travelers. Add ocean views from private balconies and a wide beach with palm trees, and it's a classic beach vacation. Full breakfast is included in the rate and is served in a pleasant *palapa*-roofed dining area. Kayaks, snorkel gear, and bicycles are available to guests free of charge, too. Snorkeling and fishing trips also can be arranged, with pickup at the hotel's private dock.

OVER US$150

Playa Sonrisa (6.9 kilometers/4.3 miles north of town, no phone, www.playasonrisa. com, US$150-175 s/d, US$175-250 suite) is a clothing-optional resort on a palm-tree-laden stretch of beach. Units are clean and comfortable, though they lack the charm that you'd expect for the rate. What you mostly pay for is the freedom to enjoy the Caribbean in the buff. A continental breakfast is included in the rate, as is Wi-Fi. Geared at naturist couples, the hotel welcomes naturist families during the low season only.

Food

Locally run **Restaurant Toby** (center of town, across from volleyball court, cell tel. 983/107-5426, 11am-9pm Mon.-Sat., US$7-14) is a popular seafood restaurant serving up, among other tasty dishes, heaping plates of ceviche, coconut shrimp, and fish soup. It's a friendly, low-key place perfect for a beer and a good meal after a day of diving or relaxing on the beach. Wi-Fi is available, too.

The Maya Grill (Hotel Tierra Maya, 2.1 kilometers/1.3 miles north of town, tel. 983/839-8012, www.tierramaya.net, 6:30am-9pm daily, US$6-14) is a hotel beachfront restaurant with spectacular floor-to-ceiling windows with views of the Caribbean. The menu is solidly Mexican—tacos, quesadillas, enchiladas—with a fair share of seafood, too. Ingredients are fresh and portions are hearty.

The restaurant at Costa de Cocos, **The Reel Inn** (3 kilometers/1.9 miles north of town, no phone, www.costadecocos.com, 7am-8:30pm daily, US$6-28) serves up breakfast classics, burgers, steak, pizza, and all manner of tall tales—though with fishing as good as it is, many just happen to be true. The service is seriously lacking, but the schedule, reservations policy (none required), and full bar make it a reliable option.

If you are cooking for yourself, a **grocery truck** passes through town and down the coastal road several times per week—ask at your hotel for the current schedule. It comes stocked with eggs, yogurt, grains, basic produce, fresh meats, and canned food. You also can buy a broom or two. In town, there are a handful of small **mini-marts** selling basic canned and dried foods. Most are open 9am-9pm daily.

Information and Services

Xcalak has **no bank, ATM, or currency-**

exchange office, and only a few places take credit cards—plan accordingly!

There's a basic **health clinic** (no phone, 8am-noon and 2pm-6pm Mon.-Fri.) two blocks from the soccer field, near the entrance of town.

The **police station** (toll-free Mex. tel. 066) is located behind the lighthouse.

Most hotels have Wi-Fi; in a pinch many hotel owners will let you use their computers to send a quick email. For more time on the net, **San Jordy** (center of town, hours vary, US$2/hour) is a reliable Internet café. To make an international or domestic call, head to **Telecomm/Telégrafos** (2 blocks north of the lighthouse, 9am-3pm Mon.-Fri.).

Getting There and Around

Bus service is somewhat erratic in Xcalak. Theoretically, buses bound for Chetumal (US$7.75, 4-5 hours) with stops in Mahahual (US$3, 1 hour) and Limones (US$5.50, 2.5 hours) leave twice daily, typically around 5am and 2pm, but it's not unusual for one or both departures to be delayed or canceled. Upon arrival, your hotel may send a car to pick you up; otherwise a taxi from town is about US$10. A cab from Mahahual runs around US$40.

Most travelers come in a rental car, which certainly simplifies life here. The closest gas station is on the main road to Mahahual, near the turnoff for Xcalak. However, it occasionally runs out of gas, so you should fill up on Highway 307 as well—Carrillo Puerto is a good spot. In a pinch, a few Xcalak families sell gas from barrels in their front yards; ask your hotel owner for help locating them.

If your budget permits, there also is a well-maintained airstrip approximately 2 kilometers (1.2 miles) west of town. Despite rumors that commercial flights will begin using it regularly, at the time of research, it was only used sporadically by private or chartered planes.

CHACCHOBEN ARCHAEOLOGICAL ZONE

Chacchoben (8am-5pm daily, US$4) got its name from archaeologists who, after uncovering no inscription indicating what the city's original residents called it, named it after the Maya village to which the land pertained. The meaning of that name is also lost, even to local villagers, though the accepted translation is Place of Red Corn. The area may have been settled as early as 1000 BC, and most of the building activity probably took place between AD 200-700, the Classic period.

Chaccoben's Temple 24 has unusual rounded corners.

Chacchoben Archaeological Zone

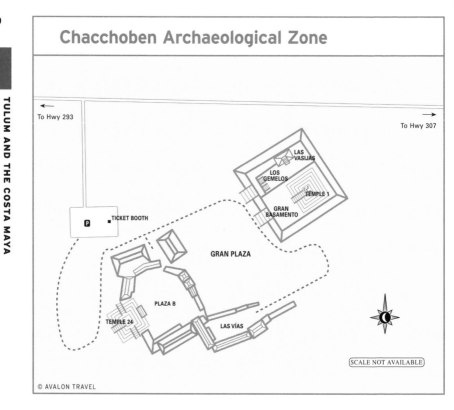

← To Hwy 293

To Hwy 307 →

LAS VASIJAS

LOS GEMELOS

TEMPLE 1

GRAN BASAMENTO

P   ■ TICKET BOOTH

GRAN PLAZA

PLAZA B

TEMPLE 24

LAS VÍAS

SCALE NOT AVAILABLE

© AVALON TRAVEL

Visiting the Ruins

Entering the site, a short path leads first to **Temple 24,** a squat pyramid that is the primary structure of a small enclosed area called **Plaza B.** Across that plaza—and the larger Gran Plaza beyond it—is a massive raised platform, the **Gran Basamento,** with the site's largest pyramid, **Temple 1,** atop it; this pyramid is believed to have served astronomical and religious purposes. Also on the platform, two smaller structures, dubbed **Las Vasijas** and **Los Gemelos,** were likely used for ceremonial functions. The site has some well-preserved stucco and paint, and for that reason none of the pyramids can be climbed.

Though it can get crowded when there's a cruise ship at Mahahual, Chacchoben has an appealingly remote feel, nestled in the forest with towering mahogany and banyan trees, and paths dotted with bromeliads.

Practicalities

Chacchoben is located about 70 kilometers (43 miles) north of Mahahual and 4 kilometers (2.5 miles) west of Limones. By **car,** take Highway 307 and turn west at the sign to Chacchoben ruins and like-named town, about 3 kilometers (1.9 miles) down a well-paved road. Alternatively, take a **bus** to Limones and then a **cab** (US$5) to the ruins.

Laguna Bacalar

Almost 50 kilometers (31 miles) long, Laguna Bacalar is the second-largest lake in Mexico and certainly among the most beautiful. Well, it's not technically a lake: A series of waterways do eventually lead to the ocean, making Bacalar a lagoon, but it is fed by natural springs, making the water on the western shore, where the hotels and town are, 100 percent *agua dulce* (fresh water).

The Maya name for the lagoon translates as Lake of Seven Colors. It is an apt description, as you will see on any sunny day. The lagoon's sandy bottom and crystalline water turn shallow areas a brilliant turquoise, which fades to deep blue in the center. If you didn't know better, you'd think it was the Caribbean.

The hub of the Laguna Bacalar region is the town of Bacalar. Located on the west side of the lake, it won't win any prizes for charm, but it does have a terrific museum, one of the best hotels around, a handful of decent restaurants, and, of course, gorgeous views of the lagoon.

SIGHTS AND EVENTS
★ Fuerte San Felipe Bacalar

The mid-18th-century **Fuerte San Felipe Bacalar** (central plaza, no phone, Av. 3 at Calle 20, 9am-7pm Tues.-Sun., US$2.50 adult, US$1.25 child) was built by the Spanish for protection against English pirates and Maya that regularly raided the area. In fact, attacks proved so frequent—and successful—that the fort was captured in 1858 by Maya during the Caste War. It was not returned to Mexican officials until 1901. Today, the star-shaped stone edifice has been restored to its former glory: drawbridge, cannons, moat, and all. The fort also houses the excellent **Museo del Fuerte de San Felipe Bacalar,** a modern museum with exhibits on the history of the area, including details on the pirates who regularly attacked these shores.

Cenote Azul

As good or better than Laguna Bacalar for swimming, **Cenote Azul** (Hwy. 307 Km. 15) is two kilometers (1.2 miles) south of town. It's the widest cenote in Mexico, some 300 meters

Fuerte San Felipe Bacalar is a restored fort with an excellent museum inside.

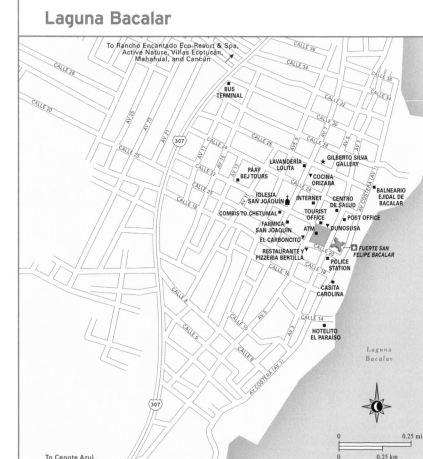

Laguna Bacalar

To Rancho Encantado Eco-Resort & Spa,
Active Nature, Villas Ecotucán,
Mahahual, and Cancún

BUS TERMINAL

CALLE 36
CALLE 34
CALLE 32
CALLE 30
CALLE 28
CALLE 26
CALLE 24
CALLE 20
CALLE 18
CALLE 16
CALLE 14
CALLE 8
CALLE 6
CALLE 10

GILBERTO SILVA GALLERY
LAVANDERÍA LOLITA
PÁAY BEJ TOURS
COCINA ORIZABA
IGLESIA SAN JOAQUÍN
INTERNET
CENTRO DE SALUD
BALNEARIO EJIDAL DE BACALAR
COMBIS TO CHETUMAL
TOURIST OFFICE
POST OFFICE
FÁRMICA SAN JOAQUÍN
ATM
DUNOSUSA
EL-CARBONCITO
RESTAURANTE Y PIZZERIA BERTILLA
FUERTE SAN FELIPE BACALAR
POLICE STATION
CASITA CAROLINA
HOTELITO EL PARAÍSO

Laguna Bacalar

307

To Cenote Azul,
Centro Holístico
Akal Ki, and Chetumal

To Hotel
Laguna Bacalar

0   0.25 mi
0   0.25 km

© AVALON TRAVEL

(984 feet) across at its widest, and 150 meters (492 feet) deep, with crystalline blue water. A rope stretches clear across, so even less-conditioned swimmers can make it to the far side. A large, breezy **restaurant** (tel. 983/834-2038, 7:30am-8pm daily, US$6-16) has the only entrance to the cenote, and charges a small admission fee (US$0.75) only if you don't order something.

Gilberto Silva Gallery

Gilberto Silva, an accomplished sculptor of Maya art, has a small **gallery and workshop** (Calle 26 btwn Calles 5 and 7, tel. 983/834-2657, hours vary) where some of his works are displayed and sold. Most are intricately carved limestone pieces, which are then cast in clay. Notably, his works have been displayed at the Museum of Natural History in New York City.

Festival Mágico Bacalar

Held in early June, the Festival Mágico Bacalar (www.festivalmagicobacalar.com) is a five-day event showcasing Bacalar's water sports and culture. The festival features a two-day, 74-kilometer (44.5-mile) **Paddle Marathon** for adult sea kayakers and paddleboarders; for youths, there's a 2-kilometer (1.2-mile) **regatta.** Other popular events include a two-day **kayaking film festival** (who knew there were so many movies about kayaking?) as well as several live music and dance performances and art exhibits. There's also an expo of the latest paddle-sport gear, with top vendors and professionals on-site—a go-to stop if you're an aficionado or just curious about developments in the industry.

Fiesta de San Joaquín

Every July, the town of Bacalar celebrates San Joaquín, its patron saint. For nine consecutive days, different neighborhoods host festive celebrations, each trying to outdo the other for the year's best party. Visitors are welcome and should definitely join the fun—expect plenty of food, music, dancing, and performances of all sorts. Cockfights also are popular, and a three-day **hydroplane race** usually follows the festivities in early August.

SPORTS AND RECREATION
Ecotours

A friendly German couple founded **Active Nature** (Hotel Villas Ecotucán, Hwy. 307 Km. 27.3, cell tel. 983/120-5742, www.activenaturebacalar.com) after fate and car trouble cut short their planned tour of the Americas and left them in lovely Laguna Bacalar. Tour options include kayaking through mangrove channels, outrigger canoe tours, sunrise birding walks, and more. Day trips cost US$12.50-60 per person, including gear and often lunch and water; children under 10 are free, under 14 half off. Tours begin at Villas Ecotucán, whose guests get a 10 percent discount. Overnight tours can also be arranged.

Páay bej Tours (Posada Casa Madrid, Av. 22 btwn Calles 11 and 13, tel. 983/154-7580, www.bacalar-tours-paaybej.com) offers mellow hiking and kayaking trips in the lagoon (US$38.50 pp) and guided tours of Maya ruins like Kohunlich, Dzibanché, and Chacchoben (US$42-69 pp, including transport and entrance fees), led by a friendly multi-lingual guide. You can also rent bikes here (US$0.75/hour, US$7.75/day).

Swimming

Though you'll have to walk through a bit of mud to get to the entrance, the **Balneario Ejidal de Bacalar** (Av. Costera near Calle 26, no phone, 7am-7pm, US$0.25) is a public swimming area complete with *palapas* for rent (US$3/day), bathrooms, and a restaurant (9am-7pm, US$3-10). Located just 250 meters (0.2 mile) from the central plaza, it's a convenient and inexpensive place to enjoy the water.

Other good swimming spots on Laguna Bacalar include **Rancho Encantado** (2 kilometers/1.2 miles north of town, tel. 998/884-2071, www.encantado.com) and **Hotel Laguna Bacalar** (Blvd. Costero 479, tel. 983/834-2205, www.hotellagunabacalar.com); plan on ordering something from the hotel restaurant to be able to use the waterfront.

ACCOMMODATIONS
In Town

One of the area's most charming and convenient accommodations, ★ **Casita Carolina** (Av. Costera btwn Calles 16 and 18, tel. 983/834-2334, www.casitacarolina.com, US$37.50-54 s/d, some with shared kitchen) offers lagoon-front units that open onto a large grassy garden. Units are either stand-alone or occupy a converted home, but all have a private bathroom, a fan, and a homey feel. The friendly American owner lives on-site and is a wealth of information on area sights.

Hotelito el Paraíso (Av. Costera at Calle 14, tel. 983/834-2787, www.hotelitoelparaiso. com.mx, US$61/73 d/t with a/c) has 14 stark hotel rooms, with minifridges, cable TV, and Wi-Fi. All open onto a large grassy area that runs to the lakeshore; there's a *palapa* shade, plenty of chairs, and even a grill.

Outside of Town

Villas Ecotucán (Hwy. 307 Km. 27.3, cell

tel. 983/120-5743, www.villasecotucan. info, US$73 s/d) has ten solar-powered, *palapa*-roofed *cabañas,* each spacious and artfully decorated, with a veranda to enjoy the view of the lake and surrounding tropical forest. The verdant grounds included a bird-watching tower, shady hammocks throughout, a dock, and complimentary kayaks. The hotel specializes in guided nature excursions, by bike, kayak, outrigger boat, and on foot.

Built on a bluff just south of town, **Hotel Laguna Bacalar** (Blvd. Costero 479, tel. 983/834-2205, www.hotellagunabacalar. com, US$80-92 d/t with fan, US$100-119 d/t with a/c) has spacious rooms with tolerable nautical-themed decor; pay a bit more for a room with a balcony and dramatic views of the lagoon. Stairs zigzag down to the water, where a pier, a ladder, and a diving board make swimming in the lagoon easy. There's a moderately sized pool and simple restaurant; breakfast can be included for an extra US$5.50 per person.

Rancho Encantado Eco-Resort & Spa (Hwy. 307 Km. 24, tel. 998/884-2071, www. encantado.com, US$140-250, breakfast included) has spacious *palapa*-roofed casitas and modern suites, both featuring Mexican tile floors, good beds, and views of either the lush garden or the lagoon; all but one have air-conditioning. The prettiest spot here, however, is a pier that leads to a shady dock strung with hammocks—it's perfect for swimming and relaxing. Guests can receive massages and body treatments in a small kiosk built over the lake; a hot tub is nearby. The only downer here is the persistent hum of traffic from nearby Highway 307.

Set on the dramatic waters of Laguna Bacalar, ★ **Centro Holístico Akal Ki** (Hwy 307, Km. 12.5, tel. 983/106-1751, www.akalki. com, US$207-330 s/d) is a whole body experience—from the yoga classes and holistic body treatments to the organic foods and breathtaking views. Eleven *cabañas* and suites are simple and elegant, with whitewashed walls, tropical wood floors, thick mattresses, and luxurious linens (and no outlets in any of them, to help guests fully disconnect). Best of all, most units are built over the water—fall asleep to the gentle lapping of the lagoon (or jump in, from your private sundeck, first thing in the morning). Complimentary use of kayaks and bicycles is included. Service is gracious and accommodating.

Find utter peace and tranquility at little-visited Laguna Bacalar.

75

TULUM AND THE COSTA MAYA
LAGUNA BACALAR

Bacalar Bus Schedule

Departures from the bus terminal (Hwy. 307 near Calle 30, no phone) are almost all *de paso* (mid-route service), which means there's often a limited availability of seats. Destinations include:

Destination	Price	Duration	Schedule
Cancún	US$17.75-26.75	5-6 hours	every 30-60 minutes 12:45am-11:50pm
Carrillo Puerto	US$5.25-9.25	1.5-2 hours	take Cancún bus
Chetumal	US$2.50-2.75	50 minutes	every 30-60 minutes 12:30am-11:30pm
Mahahual	US$5.75	1.5-2 hours	6:30am and 5pm
Playa del Carmen	US$14.25-21.75	4-4.5 hours	take Cancún bus
Tulum	US$11.50-15	3 hours	take Cancún bus

FOOD

For good cheap eats, Cocina Orizaba (Av. 7 btwn Calles 24 and 26, tel. 983/834-2069, 8am-6pm daily, US$4.50-12) serves a variety of classic Mexican dishes. The daily *comida corrida* (lunch special) includes an entrée, main dish, and drink.

On the main plaza, the Italian-owned and operated Restaurante y Pizzeria Bertilla (Av. 5 at Calle 20, cell tel. 983/123-4567, 4pm-11pm Tues.-Sun., US$6-15) specializes in authentic homemade pasta and pizza. Service can be a bit grumpy, but think of it as part of the experience. Some traditional Mexican dishes are available, too.

El Carboncito (central plaza, Av. 5 near Calle 20, tel. 983/117-7167, 5pm-11pm daily, US$2.50-8) is a popular *puesto* (food stand) that serves up grilled favorites like hot dogs, hamburgers, and tacos. If you want your meal to go, let the cook know it's "*para llevar.*"

Dunosusa (Calle 22 btwn Avs. 3 and 5, 7:30am-9pm Mon.-Sat., 8:30am-8pm Sun.) is a well-stocked supermarket on the central plaza.

INFORMATION AND SERVICES

Tourist Information

Bacalar's municipal tourist office (Calle 22 between Avs. 3 and 5, 8am-5pm Mon-Fri, 9am-noon Sat., tel. 983/834-2886) is located on the central square. Also, www. bacalarmosaico.com is a bilingual website with useful information on the area's sights, activities, and businesses.

Emergency Services

The Centro de Salud (Av. 3 btwn Calles 22 and 24, tel. 983/834-2756, 24 hours) offers basic medical care; for serious matters, head to Chetumal. For meds, try Farmacia San Joaquín (Av. 7 btwn Calles 20 and 22, no phone, 8am-3pm and 6pm-9pm daily). The police station (Calle 20 near Av. 3, toll-free Mex. tel. 066, 24 hours) is located across from the Fuerte San Felipe Bacalar.

Money

There is no bank in town, but there is a Banorte ATM on the west side of the central plaza. If you need other money services or the ATM has run out of cash, the closest bank is in Chetumal.

Media and Communications

The post office (Av. 3 near Calle 24, 8am-4:30pm Mon.-Fri., 8am-noon Sat.) is just east of the Fuerte San Felipe Bacalar. For email try the no name Internet (Av. 5 near Calle 24,

9am-10pm daily, US$1/hour), operated out of a private home.

Laundry

Lavandería Lolita (Av. 7 btwn Calles 24 and 26, tel. 983/834-2069, 9am-8pm daily) offers same-day service for US$1.25 per kilo (2.2 pounds). Pickup and delivery are available.

GETTING THERE AND AROUND

You can easily walk to all the sites of interest in Bacalar, with the exception of Cenote Azul. A taxi there from town costs around US$3; cabs typically wait for passengers around the central plaza and on Avenida 7 in front of Iglesia San Joaquín.

Bus

Bacalar's modest **bus terminal** (Hwy. 307 near Calle 30) is on the highway, about a 20-minute walk from the central plaza. The buses are almost exclusively *de paso* (midroute) service, which means there's often limited availability (i.e., as soon as you know your schedule, buy your ticket).

Combi

Combis and *taxi colectivos* (US$2-3, every 30 minutes) run between Bacalar and Chetumal daily. You can catch either in front of Iglesia San Joaquín (Calle 22 near Av. 7), one block up from the central plaza.

Chetumal

Chetumal is the capital of Quintana Roo and the gateway to Central America. It's not the prettiest of towns, and most travelers just pass through on their way to or from Belize or southern Campeche. However, Chetumal's modern Maya museum is one of the best you'll find in the region (albeit with few original pieces) and is well worth a visit. And if you're dying to see the Guatemalan ruins of Tikal, a shuttle from Chetumal can get you there in eight hours (cutting through Belize) and back again just as fast; a 90-minute boat ride also will take you to San Pedro, Belize, for a quick overnighter. The area around Chetumal is worth exploring, too, whether the bayside town of Calderitas or the intriguing and little-visited Maya ruins of Kohunlich, Dzibanché, Kinichná, and Oxtankah. North of town is Laguna Bacalar, a beautiful multicolored lake with great swimming and kayaking.

SIGHTS
Museo de la Cultura Maya

One of the best museums in the region, the **Maya Culture Museum** (Av. de los Héroes at Calle Cristóbal Colón, tel. 983/832-6838, 9am-7pm Tues.-Thurs., 9am-8pm Fri.-Sun., US$5 adult, US$2 child) extends over three levels—the upper represents the world of gods, the middle the world of humans, and the lower Xibalba, the underworld. Each floor has impressive, well-designed exhibits describing Maya spiritual beliefs, agricultural practices, astronomy, and more, all in English and Spanish. In fact, the only thing lacking is original artifacts. (The replicas, however, are quite good.) The exhibition area past the ticket booth usually has good temporary art shows, plus a cinema that hosts free screenings of independent films.

Monumento al Mestizo

Across from the Museo de la Cultura Maya is the **Monumento al Mestizo** (Av. de los Héroes s/n), a striking sculpture symbolizing the creation of a new race—the mestizo—through the union of the shipwrecked Spanish sailor Gonzalo Guerrero and Zazil Há, a Maya woman. Hernán Cortés offered to take Guerrero back to Spain, but Guerrero chose to stay in the Americas, wedding Zazil

Há in a Maya marriage ritual. Note that the Maya symbol for the number zero as well as the cycle of life, the snail shell, provides the framework for the entire work of art.

Museo de la Ciudad

The **city museum** (Calle Héroes de Chapultepec btwn Avs. Juárez and de los Héroes, tel. 983/832-1350, 9am-7pm Tues.-Sun., US$1) is small and well organized, and describes the political, economic, and cultural history of Chetumal, spanning the period from its founding in 1898 to the present day. Signage is in Spanish only.

El Malecón

Running six kilometers (3.7 miles) on the Boulevard Bahía, this breezy promenade makes for a fine bayfront stroll. Along it you'll find cafés, monuments, a lighthouse, government buildings, and, hopefully, a cooling breeze. Of particular note are two impressive **murals** found within the **Palacio Legislativo** (end of Av. Reforma, 9am-10pm Mon.-Fri.), a shell-shaped building that houses the State Congress. Created by local artist Elio Carmichael, one mural outlines the state's history—from the creation of man to the devastating effects of Hurricane Janet in 1955—while the other depicts the law of the cosmos. Both are located in the reception area and are open to the public.

Maqueta Payo Obispo

The **Maqueta Payo Obispo** (Calle 22 de Enero near Av. Reforma, 9am-7pm Tues.-Sun., free) is a scale model of Chetumal as it looked in the 1930s, with brightly colored clapboard houses, grassy lots, and plenty of palm trees. It's a reproduction of a model made by long-time resident Luis Reinhardt McLiberty. Look for it in a glass-enclosed building across the street from the Palacio Legislativo, though glare on sunny days can make it hard to see the exhibit. A small history museum of the city also is on-site; signage is in Spanish only.

Trolley Tours

For a breezy overview of Chetumal's attractions, consider taking **Bule Buzz** (cell tel. 983/120-5223, US$7.75 adult, US$4 child), a guided trolley tour of the city. Sites visited include the murals in the Palacio Legislativo, the sculptures along Boulevard Bahía, the Maqueta Payo Obispo, and the Museo de la Cultura Maya. The trolley leaves from the Monumento al Mestizo at noon and 3pm Tuesday-Saturday and 11am Sunday;

The Museo de la Cultura Maya in Chetumal has fascinating displays on Maya sculpture, writing, mathematics, astronomy, and more.

Chetumal

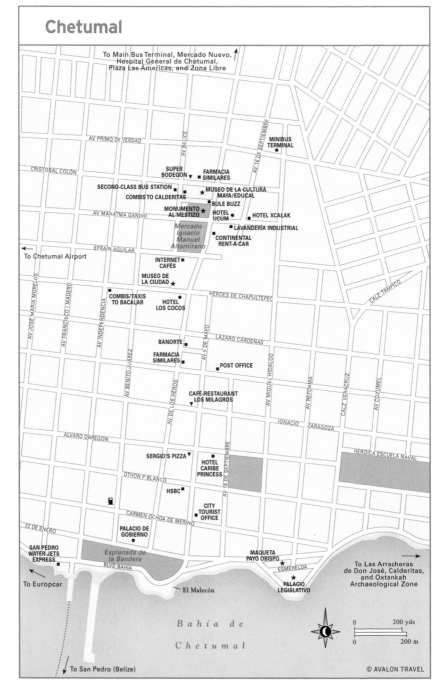

To Main Bus Terminal, Mercado Nuevo,
Hospital General de Chetumal,
Plaza Las Américas, and Zona Libre

AV PRIMO DE VERDAD

CRISTOBAL COLON

AV BELICE

AV 16 DE SEPTIEMBRE

MINIBUS
TERMINAL

SUPER
BODEGÓN

FARMACIA
SIMILARES

SECOND-CLASS BUS STATION

MUSEO DE LA CULTURA
MAYA/EDUCAL

COMBIS TO CALDERITAS

BULE BUZZ

AV MAHATMA GANDHI

MONUMENTO
AL MESTIZO

HOTEL
UCUM

HOTEL XCALAK

Mercado
Ignacio
Manuel
Altamirano

LAVANDERÍA INDUSTRIAL

CONTINENTAL
RENT-A-CAR

EFRAIN AGUILAR

To Chetumal Airport

INTERNET
CAFÉS

MUSEO DE
LA CIUDAD

AV JOSE MARIA MORELOS

AV FRANCISCO I MADERO

AV INDEPENDENCIA

COMBIS/TAXIS
TO BACALAR

HOTEL
LOS COCOS

HEROES DE CHAPULTEPEC

CALZ TAMPICO

AV BENITO JUAREZ

BANORTE

AV 5 DE MAYO

LAZARO CARDENAS

FARMACIA
SIMILARES

POST OFFICE

AV DE LOS HEROS

CAFÉ-RESTAURANT
LOS MILAGROS

AV MIGUEL HIDALGO

AV REFORMA

CALZ VERACRUZ

AV COZUMEL

IGNACIO ZARAGOZA

ALVARO OBREGON

HEROICA ESCUELA NAVAL

SERGIO'S PIZZA

HOTEL
CARIBE
PRINCESS

AV 16 DE SEPTIEMBRE

OTHON P BLANCO

HSBC

CITY
TOURIST
OFFICE

CARMEN OCHOA DE MERINO

22 DE ENERO

PALACIO DE
GOBIERNO

SAN PEDRO
WATER JETS
EXPRESS

Esplanada de
la Bandera

BLVD BAHIA

MAQUETA
PAYO OBISPO

ESMERELDA

To Las Arracheras
de Don José, Calderitas,
and Oxtankah
Archaeological Zone

To Europcar

El Malecón

PALACIO
LEGISLATIVO

B a h í a   d e

C h e t u m a l

0   200 yds
0   200 m

To San Pedro (Belize)

© AVALON TRAVEL

admission to the Museo de la Cultura Maya also is included.

ENTERTAINMENT AND SHOPPING

Sunday on El Malecón

Every Sunday at 6pm, locals gather at the Esplanada de la Bandera (southern end of Av. de los Héroes) to enjoy city-sponsored events, typically performances by the municipal band or local musicians and singers. The events are free and family friendly, with vendors selling drinks and munchies.

Cinema

If you're hankering to watch the latest Hollywood film, head to Cinépolis (Plaza Las Américas, Av. Insurgentes s/n, tel. 983/837-6044, www.cinepolis.com, US$5-8), an 11-screen theater where most films are in English with Spanish subtitles.

Shopping

Educal (Av. de los Héroes at Calle Cristóbal Colón, cell tel. 983/129-2832, www.educal. com.mx, 9am-7pm Tues.-Sat., 9am-2pm Sun.) is a good bookstore located inside the Museo de la Cultura Maya.

Mercado Ignacio Manuel Altamirano (Efraín Aguilar btwn Avs. Belice and de los Héroes, 8am-4pm daily) is a two-story building mostly selling everyday items, from clothing to kitchenware. For travelers, it's a good place to buy a pair of flip-flops, a travel clock, or kitschy souvenirs.

Plaza Las Américas (Av. Insurgentes s/n, 9am-10pm daily) is a classic shopping mall with clothing and shoe boutiques, a Chedraui supermarket, a megaplex movie theater, and all the typical amenities, like ATMs, food court, and public bathrooms.

The Zona Libre (Corozal Duty Free Zone, 9am-7pm daily) is an area just across the Belize border that's jam-packed with stores selling products from around the world, including shoes, clothing, alcohol, and household items. Bring your passport along, but guard it carefully.

ACCOMMODATIONS

Chetumal's status as the state capital and its location on the Belize border make it a busy town, and reservations are recommended.

Under US$50

★ Hotel Xcalak (Av. 16 de Septiembre at Av. Mahatma Gandhi, cell tel. 983/129-1708, www.hotelxcalak.com.mx, US$33 s/d with a/c) is one of the best deals in town: modern rooms with tasteful decor, strong but quiet air-conditioning, SKY TV, and wireless Internet. The hotel restaurant also provides room service (though you've got to order in person). The hotel is located one block from the Museo de la Cultura Maya.

Next door, the moss-colored Hotel Ucúm (Av. Mahatma Gandhi btwn Avs. 5 de Mayo and 16 de Septiembre, tel. 983/832-0711, US$19 s/d with fan, US$23 s/d with fan and cable TV, US$32 s/d with a/c and cable TV) has aging but clean rooms. Beds are hit or miss, unfortunately, and some rooms can be downright stuffy (ask for one on the top floor for the best breeze). There's a decent pool on-site with a separate wading area for kids. There's also a secure parking lot.

Over US$50

Hotel Caribe Princess (Av. Alvaro Obregón btwn Avs. 5 de Mayo and 16 de Septiembre, tel. 983/832-0900, toll-free Mex. tel. 866/337-7342, US$39 s with a/c, US$54 d with a/c) has comfortable nondescript rooms with decent beds, cable TV, and powerful air-conditioning. There's Wi-Fi in the lobby and a self-serve breakfast (i.e., toast, cereal, fruits) every day. Ask for a room facing the interior of the building; the karaoke bar in front blasts music— and keeps the windows rattling—until late.

Hotel Los Cocos (Av. de los Héroes at Calle Héroes de Chapultepec, tel. 983/835-0430, toll-free Mex. tel. 800/719-5840, www. hotelloscocos.com.mx, US$50-65 s/d with a/c) has three categories of rooms, all pleasant with updated furnishings and modern amenities. The more expensive ones have flat-screen TVs, quiet air-conditioning, and more stylish decor. They all open onto a lush garden, which has a small, inviting pool area. The on-site restaurant is great for breakfast.

Outside of Chetumal

On the road to the like-named ruins, ★ **Explorean Kohunlich** (toll-free Mex. tel. 800/504-5000, www.theexplorean.com, US$225-352 s/d bungalow) is a luxurious resort with 40 deluxe bungalows set on 30 hectares (74 acres) of tropical forest. Each has gleaming stone floors, high *palapa* ceilings, elegant furnishings, and privacy walls for sunbathing. Two suites also have plunge pools. The main building houses a fine restaurant, a full-service spa, and a lap pool that overlooks the jungle (you can see the ruins at Kohunlich from here). Excursions like rappelling in the jungle, kayaking through a crocodile reserve, or mountain biking through forgotten forests and ruins are included.

FOOD

A buzzing little place, ★ **Café-Restaurant Los Milagros** (Calle Ignacio Zaragoza near Av. 5 de Mayo, tel. 983/832-4433, 7:30am-9pm Mon.-Sat., 7:30am-1pm Sun., US$3-7) serves up strong coffee drinks and especially good breakfasts. The best seating is outdoors—snag a table where you can, as it can get crowded fast.

Located on the Malecón, ★ **Las Arracheras de Don José** (Blvd. Bahía at Calle Josefa Ortiz de Dominguez, tel. 983/837-6103, 11am-10pm daily, US$4-10) serves some of the best tacos in town. Try the *tacos de arrachera* (broiled skirt steak marinated in lemon and spices), which are only improved when followed with a cold beer.

Sergio's Pizza (Av. 5 de Mayo at Av. Alvaro Obregón, tel. 983/108-1438, 7am-11:30pm daily, US$5-17) serves much more than pizza in its dimly lit dining room. The extensive menu covers the gamut of Italian and Mexican dishes—from meat lasagna to *molletes rancheros*. Meals are hearty, making it popular with families.

Super Bodegón (Calle Cristóbal Colón btwn Avs. Belice and de los Héroes, 5am-9pm Mon.-Sat., 5am-3pm Sun.) has an impressive selection of fresh fruits and veggies. Canned goods, dry foods, and basic toiletries are also sold.

INFORMATION AND SERVICES
Tourist Information

Near the waterfront, the **city tourist office** (Av. 5 de Mayo at Carmen Ochoa de Merino, tel. 983/835-0860, 8:30am-4:30pm Mon.-Fri.) has a decent selection of brochures and maps. There also is a **tourist information booth** in the main bus terminal (Av. Insurgentes at Av. de los Héroes, 9am-8pm daily).

Emergency Services

About two kilometers (1.2 miles) from the center of town, **Hospital General de Chetumal** (Avs. Andrés Quintana Roo at Juan José Isiordia, tel. 983/832-8194, 24 hours) is the city's main hospital.

For meds, try **Farmacia Similares** (Av. de los Héroes near Calle Plutarco Elias, tel. 983/833-2232, 8am-9pm daily) or its **sister store** (Calle Cristóbal Colón btwn Avs. Belice and de los Héroes, tel. 983/833-2331), which is open 24 hours.

The **police** can be reached by dialing toll-free 066.

Money

HSBC (Av. Othon Blanco btwn Av. 5 de Mayo and Av. de los Héroes, 9am-5pm Mon.-Fri.) and **Banorte** (Av. de los Héroes btwn Lázaro Cárdenas and Plutarco Elias, 9am-4pm Mon.-Fri.) are both conveniently located downtown. There also is an ATM at the **main bus station** (Av. Insurgentes at Av. de los Héroes, 9am-8pm daily).

Media and Communications

The **post office** (Av. Plutarco Elias Calles btwn Avs. 5 de Mayo and 16 de Septiembre, 8am-4pm Mon.-Fri., 9am-1pm Sat.) is just a block from the main drag. For Internet access, there is a string of **Internet cafés** across from

Chetumal Bus Schedule

Departures from Chetumal's **main bus terminal** (Av. Insurgentes at Av. de los Héroes, tel. 983/832-5110) are for first-class service, though some second-class buses stop here as well; tickets for either service can be purchased downtown, in the **second-class bus terminal** (Av. Belice at Av. Cristóbal Colón). Destinations from the main bus terminal include:

Destination	Price	Duration	Schedule
Bacalar	US$2.50-2.75	50 minutes	every 30-60 minutes 1:15am-11:45pm
Cancún	US$18.25-30	5.5-6.5 hours	every 30-90 minutes 12:15am-11:45pm
Mahahual	US$6.25	2.5 hours	5:40am and 4:10pm or take Xcalak bus (Mercado Nuevo terminal only)
Mérida	US$34.25	5.5-6 hours	7:30am, 1:30pm, 5pm, and 11:30pm
Playa del Carmen	US$13-29.50	4.5-5.5 hours	take any Cancún bus
Tulum	US$13.50-20.50	3.5-4 hours	take any Cancún bus

Buses for **Belize City** (US$11.50, 3 hours), **Corozal** (US$3, 1 hour), and **Orangewalk** (US$4, 2 hours) leave the **Mercado Nuevo** (Av. de los Héroes at Circuito Segundo, no phone) 18 times daily 4:30am-6:30pm. Some pass the main ADO terminal en route. Buses bound for **Xcalak** (US$7.75, 4-5 hours) also leave from here at 5:40am and 4:10pm.

Buses to the **Zona Libre** (US$2, 30 minutes) leave the **Minibus terminal** (Av. Primo de Verdad at Av. Miguel Hidalgo, no phone) every 15 minutes 6:30am-8pm.

the Mercado Ignacio Manuel Altamirano (Efraín Aguilar btwn Avs. Belice and de los Héroes); most charge US$1 per hour and are open 7am-midnight daily.

Immigration

The **immigration office** (Av. México s/n, tel. 983/834-5046, 9am-1pm Mon.-Fri.) is located half a block from the border with Belize. Heading south on Avenida México, it's on your left-hand side.

Laundry and Storage

Though catering primarily to hotels and restaurants, **Lavandería Industrial** (Av. Mahatma Ghandi near Av. 16 de Septiembre, tel. 983/129-2458, 8am-8pm daily) also takes small loads at US$1.35 per kilo (2.2 pounds). There is no signage, so listen for the huge dryers and look for huge piles of tablecloths.

Conveniently located in the main bus station, **Lockers, Revistas y Novedades Laudy** (Av. Insurgentes at Av. de los Héroes, 8am-8pm daily) stores bags for US$0.65 per hour.

GETTING THERE AND AROUND

Chetumal is a relatively large city, but the parts most travelers are interested in are all within easy walking distance—mostly along Avenida de los Héroes and El Malecón. The exception is the main bus terminal and Mercado Nuevo, both of which are 10-12 grubby blocks from the center. A cab to either terminal, or anywhere around downtown, costs US$2-3.

Air

The **Chetumal International Airport** (CTM, tel. 983/832-6625) receives only a few flights each day. Airlines serving it include **Interjet** (toll-free Mex. tel. 800/011-2345, toll-free U.S. tel. 866/285-9525, www.interjet.com.mx) and the air taxi service **Avioquintana** (tel. 998/734-1975, www.avioquintana.com).

Bus

All first-class buses leave from the **main bus terminal** (Av. Insurgentes at Av. de los Héroes, tel. 983/832-5110), though most second-class buses also stop here on the way in or out of town.

The **second-class bus station** (Avs. Belice and Cristóbal Colón, tel. 983/832-0639) is located just west of the Museo de la Cultura Maya; tickets for first-class buses also can be purchased here if you want to buy your tickets in advance but don't want to make the trek to the main terminal.

Two other terminals—the **Minibus terminal** (Av. Primo de Verdad at Av. Miguel Hidalgo, no phone) and **Mercado Nuevo** (Av. de los Héroes and Circuito Segundo, no phone)—have service to Bacalar, Xcalak, the Zona Libre, and to destinations in Belize.

Combi

Combis and *taxi colectivos* (US$2-3, every 30 minutes) run between Chetumal and Bacalar daily. You can catch either on Avenida Independencia at Calle Héroes de Chapultepec.

Car

The highways in this area are now all paved and well maintained. Car rental agencies in town include **Continental Rent-a-Car** (Av. de los Héroes near Av. Mahatma Gandhi, tel. 983/832-2411, www.continentalcar.com.mx, 8am-8pm daily) and **Europcar** (Chetumal Noor Hotel, Blvd. Bahía at Ave. José Maria, tel. 983/833-9959, www.europcar.com, 8am-8pm daily).

Taxi

Taxis can be flagged down easily in downtown Chetumal. Few are metered, so be sure to agree on a price before you set off toward your destination.

Water Taxi

San Pedro Water Jets Express (Blvd. Bahía near Av. Independencia, tel. 983/833-3201, www.sanpedrowatertaxi.com) offers service to two destinations in Belize: San Pedro (US$60) and Caye Caulker (US$65). The boat leaves Chetumal at 3pm; it returns at 7am from Caye Caulker and 8am from San Pedro. Service varies monthly—be sure to check the website for the most updated information.

Around Chetumal

The area around Chetumal has a number of worthwhile attractions, all the better because so few travelers linger here.

CALDERITAS

Located just seven kilometers (4 miles) north of Chetumal, Calderitas is a bayside town known for its **seafood restaurants** (8am-6pm daily, US$4-10)—most along the waterfront across from the main plaza—and its **public beaches.** During the week it's a mellow scene, but on weekends locals descend upon the town for a day of R&R and some revelry, too.

Boat rides can be arranged at many of the bayside establishments to explore **Chetumal Bay** (US$150, up to 8 people) in search of manatees, which were once abundant in these waters, or to visit **Isla Tamalcab** (US$40, up to 8 people), an uninhabited island with white-sand beaches and good snorkeling, and home to spider monkeys and *tepescuintles* (pacas in English).

If you want to stay overnight, the best place in town is **Yax Há Resort & Explorer** (Av. Yucatán 415, tel. 983/834-4127, www.yaxharesort.com, US$8 pp camping, US$19-27 per RV,

Oxtankah Archaeological Zone

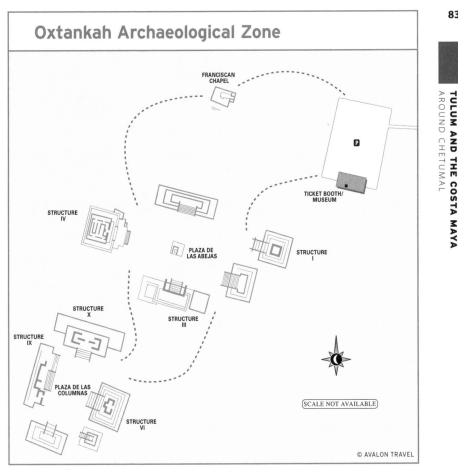

US$38.50 s/d with a/c, US$54-69 s/d with a/c and kitchenette). Located on the waterfront, it offers everything from camp- and RV sites to bungalows. The bungalows themselves range from one-room units with air-conditioning, satellite TV, and minifridges to two-bedroom units with fully equipped kitchens; all have porches with chairs that overlook the bay. There also is a pool and a restaurant on-site.

Getting There

Calderitas is a quick bus ride from downtown Chetumal. *Combis* leave from Avenida Cristóbal Colón, behind the Museo de la Cultura Maya, roughly every half hour 6am-9pm daily (US$0.65, 15 minutes). If you've got a *car,* head east out of Chetumal on Boulevard Bahía, which becomes the main drag in Calderitas. Alternatively (though less scenic), take Avenida Insurgentes east until you get to the turnoff, and follow the signs from there.

OXTANKAH ARCHAEOLOGICAL ZONE

Oxtankah (8am-5pm daily, US$4) is a small archaeological site whose name means Between Branches, so called by early archaeologists after the many trees growing amid, and on top of, the structures. Relatively little is known about Oxtankah—including its true name—but it probably arose during the Classic era, between AD 300 and 600, and was dedicated primarily to trade and salt production. At its height, the city extended to the shores of Chetumal Bay and included the island of Tamalcab.

Oxtankah's principal structures were constructed in this period, suggesting it was a fairly robust city, but it was apparently abandoned around AD 600, for unknown reasons. The city was reoccupied by Maya settlers almost a thousand years later, in the 14th or 15th century, during which time a number of structures were expanded or enhanced. It was still occupied, mostly by modest earthen homes, when the first Spanish explorers arrived.

Some researchers have suggested the infamous Spaniard castaway Gonzalo Guerrero lived here; Guerrero was shipwrecked in this area in 1511 and adopted Maya ways, even marrying a chieftain's daughter. Their children are considered the New World's first mestizos, or mixed-race people.

In 1531, conquistador Alonso de Avila attempted to found a colonial city on the site, but he was driven out after two years of bitter conflict with local residents. He did manage to have a Franciscan chapel built, the skeleton of which remains, including an impressive eight-meter-tall (26-foot) arch.

Today, most of the excavated structures in Oxtankah surround two plazas: **Abejas** (Bees) plaza, the city's main ceremonial and elite residential center, and the somewhat smaller **Columnas** (Columns) plaza, whose large palace probably served an administrative function. Architecturally, the structures are more closely related to those of the Petén region (present-day Guatemala) than to Yucatecan ones, suggesting a close relationship with that area. There's a small **museum** on-site; signage is in Spanish only.

Getting There

Oxtankah is located seven kilometers (4 miles) north of Calderitas, about one kilometer (0.6 mile) off the bayside road. There's no

The famous red-painted masks at Kohunlich are believed to represent the Maya sun god.

public transportation to the site; a **cab** from Calderitas costs US$3 each way; one from Chetumal will run about US$18 round-trip, including wait time.

KOHUNLICH ARCHAEOLOGICAL ZONE

Swallowed by the jungle over the centuries, **Kohunlich** (8am-5pm daily, US$4.50) was first discovered in 1912 by American explorer Raymond Merwin, but it was not until the 1960s that excavation of the site began in earnest. Today, the ruins are in harmony with the surrounding vegetation; wandering through it, you'll be rewarded with more than 200 structures, stelae, and uncovered mounds that have trees growing out of them and moss spreading over their stones—a beautiful sight. Most date to the Late Preclassic (AD 100-200) through the Classic (AD 600-900) periods.

Kohunlich's most famous and compelling structure is the **Temple of the Masks.** Constructed in AD 500, it features six

Kohunlich Archaeological Zone

ACRÓPOLIS

TEMPLE OF THE MASKS

TICKET BOOTH

Plaza de las Estelas

EDIFICIO DE LAS ESTELAS

BALL COURT

PALACE COMPLEX

RESIDENTIAL COMPLEX

PIX'AAN COMPLEX

27 ESCALONES

0   50 yds

0   50 m

© AVALON TRAVEL

two-meter-tall (6.6-foot) stucco masks, be-lieved to be representations of the Maya sun god, with star-incised eyes, mustaches, and nose plugs. Intriguingly, each is slightly dif-ferent, leading some to speculate that they also represent successive members of the rul-ing dynasty; it would not have been unusual for the city's elite to draw an overt connection between themselves and a high god.

Southwest of the Temple of the Masks is **27 Escalones,** the largest and most impressive residential area in Kohunlich. Built on a cliff with a spectacular bird's-eye view of the jun-gle, it is one of the largest palaces in the Maya world, reached by climbing its namesake 27 steps. As you walk through the site, keep an eye out for *aguadas* (cisterns) that once

were part of a complex system of Kohunlich's reservoirs.

Getting There

Kohunlich is located about 60 kilometers (37 miles) west of Chetumal. By **car,** take Highway 186 west and turn south (left) at the sign to Kohunlich. An 8.5-kilometer (5.3-mile) paved road leads straight to the site. There is no public transportation to the site.

DZIBANCHÉ AND KINICHNÁ ARCHAEOLOGICAL ZONES

If the crowds at Chichén Itzá and Tulum get you down, these picturesque twin ruins may be the antidote you need. Dzibanché and its smaller neighbor, Kinichná, see very few visitors—it's not uncommon to have them to yourself, in fact—and feature modest-size temples in varying states of restoration. (A great many structures aren't excavated at all, but even they—abrupt tree-covered mounds—hold a certain mystery and appeal.)

Dzibanché

The larger of the two sites, Dzibanché is Yucatec Maya for Etched in Wood, a name created by archaeologists in reference to a wood lintel inscribed with hieroglyphics that was found in one of the primary temples. A date on the lintel reads AD 618, and the site seems to have flourished between AD 300 and AD 800. Archaeologists believe this area was occupied by a sprawling, widely dispersed city that covered some 40 square kilometers (25 square miles).

The site has three main plazas, each higher than the next. Dzibanché's namesake lintel is still in the temple atop Structure VI, also called the Building of the Lintels, facing one of the plazas. Unfortunately, climbing Structure VI is no longer allowed, but it's just one of several large pyramids here, the rest of which you can clamber up. The largest is Structure II, with an ornate temple at its summit where archaeologists found a tomb of a high-ranking leader (judging from the rich offering found with his remains). The steep stairways and lofty upper temples here are reminiscent of Tikal and other temples in the Petén area of present-day Guatemala, suggesting a strong connection between the two regions.

Kinichná

Kinichná (House of the Sun) has just one structure, but it's a biggie: a massive pyramid whose summit affords a great view of the surrounding countryside. The structure has three distinct levels, each built in a different era over the course of around 400 years. As you climb up, it's fascinating to observe how the craftsmanship and artistry changed—generally for the better—over the centuries. At the top is a stucco image of the sun god, hence the site's name. As in Structure II in Dzibanché, archaeologists uncovered a tomb here, this one containing the remains of two people and a cache of fine jade jewelry and figurines.

Practicalities

Dzibanché and Kinichná are open 8am-5pm daily; admission is US$4 and valid for both archaeological zones. There is no public transportation to or from the area, and precious little local traffic, so a car (or tour van) is essential. To get here, look for the turnoff 50 kilometers (31 miles) west of Chetumal on Highway 186, before reaching the town of Francisco Villa; from there it's 15 kilometers (9 miles) north down a bumpy dirt road. You'll reach Kinichná first, then Dzibanché about 2 kilometers (1.2 miles) later.

Chichén Itzá

Look for ★ to find recommended
sights, activities, dining, and lodging.

Highlights

★ **Chichén Itzá Archaeological Zone:**
Voted one of the New Seven Wonders of the
World, the Yucatán's most famous ruin is all about
hyperbole: the iconic star-aligned pyramid, the
gigantic Maya ball court, even the crush of bikini-
clad day-trippers from Cancún (page 91).

★ **Iglesia y Ex-Convento San
Bernardino de Siena:** Located in a quiet
corner of Valladolid, this elegant church has a
spacious esplanade and beautiful interior, a small
museum, plus a natural cenote inside the convent
walls (page 102).

★ **Ek' Balam Archaeological Zone:** A
stunning stucco frieze with angel-like figures and
a huge "monster mouth" is the highlight of this
small, serene site near Valladolid. A nearby cenote makes for a cool après-ruins swim (page 111).

❙f you can drag yourself away from the beaches, a short trip inland will bring you to two of the Yucatán Peninsula's most intriguing ancient ruins—Chichén Itzá and Ek' Balam. Each is quite different from the other, and together they form

an excellent introduction to Maya archaeology and architecture. Venturing inland also will give you an opportunity to sneak a peek at how ordinary Yucatecans, including modern-day Maya, live today.

Chichén Itzá (200 kilometers/124 miles from Cancún; 150 kilometers/90 miles from Tulum) is one of the most famous ruins in the Maya world, with a massive four-sided pyramid and the largest Maya ball court ever built. About two hours from either Cancún or Tulum, it's inundated with tour groups; get there early to beat the crowds.

Even closer to the coast, but far less visited, is the small ruin of Ek' Balam (175 kilometers/109 miles from Cancún; 125 kilometers/75 miles from Tulum), boasting a beautiful stucco frieze partway up a massive pyramid. The frieze features winged priests and a gaping monster mouth that are so well preserved they look like they could

be modern-day plaster art. A kilometer (0.6 mile) away, a cenote provides a welcome respite from the heat.

PLANNING YOUR TIME

Chichén Itzá and Ek' Balam can each be reached as a day trip from Cancún or Tulum. You can visit both in one or two days, staying overnight at hotels near the sites or in Valladolid, an attractive and centrally located colonial town.

Both sites can be reached by bus or taxi, especially Chichén Itzá. But if you plan on visiting more than one site, a rental car may make your trip easier and more rewarding. You won't be tied to a bus schedule, and you'll be able to beat the crowds by getting to the sites bright and early. There also are numerous organized tours to Chichén Itzá from Cancún (though fewer to Ek' Balam). While certainly convenient, many travelers find the large groups off-putting.

Previous: Valladolid's Calzada de los Frailes; Chichén Itzá's El Castillo. **Above:** Iglesia de San Gervasio in Valladolid.

Chichén Itzá

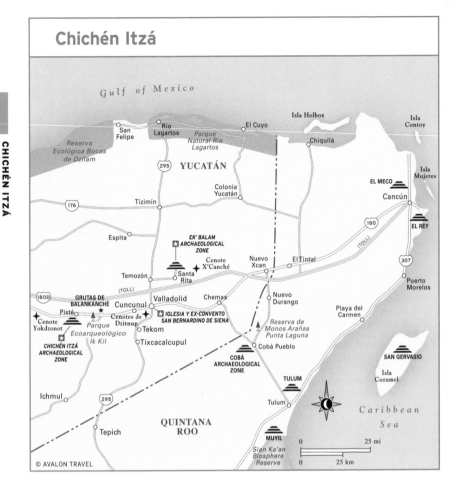

Chichén Itzá

Chichén Itzá is one of the finest archaeological sites in the northern part of the peninsula, and in all of Mesoamerica. It is also one of the most visited. Located just two hours from both Cancún and Mérida, the site is inundated by tour groups, many of them bikini-clad day-trippers on loan from the pool at their all-inclusive. That fact should not dissuade independent travelers from visiting—crowded or not, Chichén Itzá is a truly magnificent ruin and a must-see on any archaeology tour of the Yucatán. That said, you can make the most of your visit by arriving right when the gates open, so you can see the big stuff first and be exploring the outer areas by the time the tour buses start to roll in.

Pisté is a one-road town that is strangely underdeveloped considering it is just two kilometers (1.2 miles) from such an important and heavily visited site. The hotels and restaurants here are unremarkable, and there's not much to do or see in town.

★ CHICHÉN ITZÁ ARCHAEOLOGICAL ZONE

Chichén Itzá (8am-5pm daily, US$16.50 per adult, US$0.50 for children under 12) is a monumental archaeological site, remarkable for both its size and scope. The ruins include impressive palaces, temples, and altars, as well as the largest-known ball court in the Maya world. One of the most widely recognized (and heavily visited) ruins in the world, it was declared a World Heritage Site by UNESCO in 1988 and one of the New Seven Wonders of the World in 2007. In 2012, INAH (Instituto Nacional de Antropología e Historia) partnered with Google to photograph—by bicycle—the site for Google Street View maps.

History

What we call Chichén Itzá surely had another name when it was founded. The name means Mouth of the Well of the Itzá, but the Itzá, an illiterate and semi-nomadic group of uncertain origin, didn't arrive here until the 12th century. Before the Itzá, the area was controlled—or at least greatly influenced—by Toltec migrants who arrived from central Mexico around AD 1000. Most of Chichén's most notable structures, including its famous four-sided pyramid, and images like the reclining *chac-mool,* bear a striking resemblance to structures and images found at Tula, the ancient Toltec capital, in the state of Hidalgo. Before the Toltecs, the area was populated by Maya, evidenced by the Puuc- and Chenes-style design of the earliest structures here, such as the Nunnery and Casa Colorada.

The three major influences—Maya, Toltec, and Itzá—are indisputable, but the exact chronology and circumstances of those groups' interaction (or lack thereof) is one of the most hotly contested issues in Maya archaeology. Part of the difficulty in understanding Chichén Itzá more fully is that its occupants created very few stelae and left few Long Count dates on their monuments. In this way Chichén Itzá is different from virtually every other ancient city in the Yucatán. It's ironic,

actually, that Chichén Itzá is the most widely recognized "Maya" ruin considering it was so deeply influenced by non-Maya cultures, and its history and architecture are so atypical of the region.

Chichén Itzá's influence ebbed and flowed over its many centuries of existence and occupation. It first peaked in the mid-9th century, or Late Classic period, when it eclipsed Cobá as the dominant power in the northern Yucatán region. The effects of a widespread collapse of Maya cities to the south (like Calakmul, Tikal, and Palenque) reached Chichén Itzá in the late 900s, and it too collapsed abruptly. The city rose again under Toltec and later Itzá influence, but went into its final decline after an internal dispute led to the rise of Mayapán, which would come to control much of the Yucatán Peninsula. Chichén Itzá was all but abandoned by the early 1200s, though it remained an important religious pilgrimage site even after the arrival of the Spanish.

El Castillo/Temple of Kukulcán

The most dramatic structure in Chichén Itzá is El Castillo (The Castle), also known as the Temple of Kukulcán. At 24 meters (79 feet), it's the tallest structure on the site, and certainly the most recognizable. Dating to around AD 850, El Castillo was built according to strict astronomical guidelines. There are nine levels, which, divided by the central staircase, make for 18 platforms, the number of months in the Maya calendar. Each of the four sides has 91 steps, which, added together along with the platform on top, total 365— one for each day of the year. And there are 52 inset panels on each face of the structure, equal to the number of years in each cycle of the Calendar Round.

On the spring and autumn equinoxes (March 21 and September 22), the afternoon sun lights up a bright zigzag strip on the outside wall of the north staircase as well as the giant serpent heads at the base, giving the appearance of a serpent slithering down the steps. Chichén Itzá is mobbed during those

Chichén Itzá Archaeological Zone

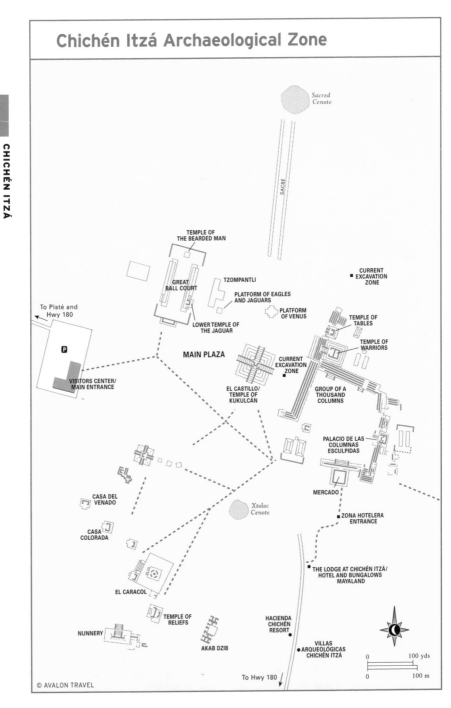

Sacred Cenote

SACBÉ

TEMPLE OF THE BEARDED MAN

TZOMPANTLI

CURRENT EXCAVATION ZONE

GREAT BALL COURT

PLATFORM OF EAGLES AND JAGUARS

PLATFORM OF VENUS

TEMPLE OF TABLES

To Pisté and Hwy 180

LOWER TEMPLE OF THE JAGUAR

TEMPLE OF WARRIORS

MAIN PLAZA

CURRENT EXCAVATION ZONE

P

VISITORS CENTER/ MAIN ENTRANCE

EL CASTILLO/ TEMPLE OF KUKULCÁN

GROUP OF A THOUSAND COLUMNS

PALACIO DE LAS COLUMNAS ESCULPIDAS

CASA DEL VENADO

Xtoloc Cenote

MERCADO

ZONA HOTELERA ENTRANCE

CASA COLORADA

THE LODGE AT CHICHÉN ITZÁ/ HOTEL AND BUNGALOWS MAYALAND

EL CARACOL

TEMPLE OF RELIEFS

HACIENDA CHICHÉN RESORT

NUNNERY

AKAB DZIB

VILLAS ARQUEOLÓGICAS CHICHÉN ITZÁ

0   100 yds

0   100 m

To Hwy 180

© AVALON TRAVEL

periods, especially by spiritual-minded folks seeking communion with the ancient Maya. The effect also occurs in the days just before and after the equinox, and there are significantly fewer people blocking the view.

Climbing El Castillo used to be a given for any visit to Chichén Itzá, and the views from its top level are breathtaking. However, an elderly tourist died in 2005 after tumbling from near the top of the pyramid to the ground. The accident, combined with longtime warnings from archaeologists that the structure was being irreparably eroded by the hundreds of thousands of visitors who climbed it yearly, prompted officials to close it off. Pyramids at other sites have been restricted as well, and it's looking more and more like a standard policy at Maya archaeological zones.

Deep inside El Castillo and accessed by way of a steep, narrow staircase are several chambers; inside one is a red-painted, jade-studded bench in the figure of a jaguar, which may have served as a throne of sorts. You used to be able to climb the stairs to see the chambers and throne—a fascinating, albeit humid and highly claustrophobic affair—but access was closed at the same time climbing the pyramid was prohibited.

Great Ball Court

Chichén Itzá's famous Great Ball Court is the largest ball court in Mesoamerica by a wide margin. The playing field is 135 meters (443 feet) by 65 meters (213 feet), with two parallel walls 8 meters high (26 feet) and scoring rings in impossibly high perches in the center. The players would've had to hit a 12-pound rubber ball through the rings using only their elbows, wrists, and hips (they wore heavy padding). The game likely lasted for hours; at the game's end, the captain of one team—or even the whole team—was apparently sacrificed, possibly by decapitation. There's disagreement about *which* team got the axe, however. Some say it was the losers—otherwise the game's best players would constantly be wiped out. Some argue that it was the winners, and that being sacrificed would have been the ultimate

honor. Of course, it's likely the game varied from city to city and evolved over the many centuries it was played. Along the walls, reliefs depict the ball game and sacrifices.

On the outside of the ball court, the **Lower Temple of the Jaguar** has incredibly fine relief carvings depicting the Maya creation myth. An upper temple is off-limits to visitors, but is decorated with a variety of carvings and remnants of what were likely colorful murals.

The Platforms

As you make your way from the ball court to the Temple of Warriors, you'll pass the gruesome **Tzompantli** (Wall of Skulls). A low T-shaped platform, it is decorated on all sides with row upon row of carved skulls, most with eyes staring out of the large sockets. Among the skulls are images of warriors holding the heads of decapitated victims, skeletons intertwined with snakes, and eagles eating human hearts (a common image in Toltec design, further evidence of their presence here). It is presumed that ceremonies performed on this platform culminated in a sacrificial death for the victim, the head then left on display, perhaps with others already in place. It's estimated that the platform was built AD 1050-1200. Nearby, the **Platform of Venus** and **Platform of Eagles and Jaguars** are smaller square structures, each with low stairways on all four sides, which were likely used for ritualistic music and dancing.

Sacred Cenote

This natural well is 300 meters (984 feet) north of the main structures, along the remains of a *sacbé* (raised stone road) constructed during the Classic period. Almost 60 meters (197 feet) in diameter and 30 meters (98.4 feet) down to the surface of the water, it was a place for sacrifices, mostly to Chaac, the god of rain, who was believed to live in its depths. The cenote has been dredged and scoured by divers numerous times, beginning as early as 1900, and the remains of scores of victims, mostly children and young adults, have been recovered, as well as innumerable

The Maya Collapse

Something went terribly wrong for the Maya between the years AD 800 and 900. Hundreds of Classic Maya cities were abandoned, monarchies disappeared, and the population fell by millions, mainly due to death and plummeting birthrates. The collapse was widespread, but was most dramatic in the Southern Lowlands, a swath of tropical forest stretching from the Gulf of Mexico to Honduras and including once-glorious cities such as Palenque, Tikal, and Copán. (Archaeologists first suspected a collapse after noticing a sudden drop-off in inscriptions; it has been confirmed through excavations of peasant dwellings from before and after that period.)

There are many theories for the collapse, varying from climate change and epidemic diseases to foreign invasion and peasant revolt. In his carefully argued book *The Fall of the Ancient Maya* (Thames and Hudson, 2002), archaeologist and professor of anthropology at Pennsylvania State University David Webster suggests it was a series of conditions, rather than a single event, that led to the collapse.

sculpture at Museo Maya de Cancún

To a certain degree, it was the very success of Maya cities during the Classic era that set the stage for their demise. Webster points to a population boom just before the collapse, which would have left agricultural lands dangerously depleted just as demand spiked. Classic-era farming techniques were ill-suited to meet the challenge; in particular, the lack of draft animals kept productivity low, meaning Maya farmers could not generate large surpluses of corn and other food. (Even if they could, storage was difficult given the hot, humid climate.) The lack of animals also limited how far away farmers could cultivate land and still be able to transport their crops to the city center; as a result, available land was overused. As Webster puts it, "Too many farmers [growing] too many crops on too much of the landscape left the Classic Maya world acutely vulnerable to an environmental catastrophe, such as drought or crop disease."

Certain kingdoms reached their tipping point before others (prompting some to launch 11th-hour military campaigns against weakened rivals), but few escaped the wave of malnutrition, disease, lower birthrates, and outright starvation that seems to have swept across the Maya world in the 9th century. Kings and nobility would have faced increasing unrest and insurrection—after all, their legitimacy was based on their ability to induce the gods to bestow rain, fertility, and prosperity—further destabilizing the social structure and food supply.

The collapse was not universal, of course, and the fall of lowland powers gave other city-states an opportunity to expand and gain influence. But the Maya world was dramatically and permanently changed by it; the grand cities built by the Classic Maya were abandoned to the jungle, most never to be reoccupied, and, as Webster notes, "Cortés and his little army almost starved in 1525 while crossing a wilderness that had supported millions of people seven centuries earlier."

jade and stone artifacts. (Most are now displayed at the Museo Nacional de Antropología in Mexico City.) On the edge of the cenote is a ruined sweat bath, probably used for purification rituals before sacrificial ceremonies. The name Chichén Itzá (Mouth of the Well of the Itzá) is surely derived from this deeply sacred cenote, and it remained an important Maya pilgrimage site well into the Spanish conquest.

Temple of Warriors and Group of a Thousand Columns

The Temple of Warriors is where some of the distinctive reclining *chac-mool* figures are found. However, its name comes from the rectangular monoliths in front, which are carved on all sides with images of warriors. (Some are also prisoners, their hands tied behind their backs.) This temple is also closed to entry, and it can be hard to appreciate the fading images from the rope perimeter. You may be able to get a closer look from the temple's south side, where you can easily make out the figures' expressions and dress (though access is sometimes blocked there as well). The south side is impressive for its facade, too, where a series of well-preserved human and animal figures adorn the lower portion, while above, human faces emerge from serpents' mouths, framed by eagle profiles, with masks of Chaac, the hook-nosed god of rain, on the corners.

The aptly named Group of a Thousand Columns is adjacent to the Temple of Warriors. It's perfectly aligned cylindrical columns likely held up a grand roof structure.

Across the plaza, the **Palacio de las Columnas Esculpidas** (Palace of Sculptured Columns) also has cylindrical columns, but with intricate carvings, suggesting this was the ceremonial center of this portion of the complex. Continuing through the trees, you'll reach the **Mercado** (market). The name is purely speculative, though it's easy to imagine a breezy bustling market here, protected from the sun under a wood and *palapa* roof built atop the structure's remarkably high columns.

Osario, El Caracol, and the Nunnery

From the market, bear left (away from El Castillo, just visible through the trees) until you meet the path leading to the site's southern entrance. You'll pass the **Osario** (ossuary), also known as the Tomb of the High Priest. Like a miniature version of El Castillo, the pyramid at one time had four stairways on each side and a temple at the crest. From the top platform, a vertical passageway leads into a chamber where seven tombs were discovered, along with numerous copper and jade artifacts indicating the deceased were of special importance (and hence the temple's name). Continuing on, you'll pass two more large structures, **Casa del Venado** (House of the Deer) and **Casa Colorada** (Red House).

The highlight of this portion of Chichén Itzá is **El Caracol** (The Snail Shell), also known as the Observatory, and perhaps the most graceful structure at Chichén Itzá. A two-tiered circular structure is set atop a broad rectangular platform, with window slits facing south and west, and another aligned

El Caracol was used by the Maya to track celestial events and patterns.

according to the path of the moon during the spring equinoxes. Ancient astronomers used structures like this one to track celestial events and patterns—the orbits of the Moon and Venus, and the coming of solar and lunar eclipses, for example—with uncanny accuracy.

Beyond El Caracol is the Nunnery, so-named by Spanish explorers who thought it looked like convents back home. Judging from its size, location, and many rooms, the Nunnery was probably an administrative palace. Its exuberant facades show strong Chenes influence, another example of the blending of styles in Chichén Itzá.

Sound and Light Show

Recently revamped, the site puts on a nightly high-tech sound and light show at 7pm in the winter (Oct.-Apr.) and at 8pm in the summer (May-Sept.). Tickets cost US$15.50 and are separate from the general admission to the ruins. The sound and light show is presented in Spanish, but for an additional US$3.50, you can rent headphones with a recorded English-language translation of the program.

Practicalities

The grounds are open 8am-5pm daily. Admission is US$16.50 per adult, US$0.50 for children under 12; it must be paid in two parts—the state fee and the federal fee—at two separate windows. Additionally, there's a US$4 fee to enter with a video camera; parking is US$2.50.

Guides can be hired at the entrance according to fixed and clearly marked prices: US$45 for a two-hour tour in Spanish, US$60 in English, French, Italian, or German. Prices are per group, which can include up to eight people. Tips are customary and not included in the price. The visitors center has restrooms, an ATM, free luggage storage, a café, a bookstore, a gift shop, and an information center.

MAYALAND PLANETARIUM

Mayaland Resort (Zona Hotelera, Carr. Mérida-Valladolid Km. 120, www.mayaland. com, US$10) offers half-hour shows about Maya astronomy and scientific advances at a modern planetarium on the resort's grounds. Built in 2013, the planetarium replicates the shape of Chichén Itzá's famous Caracol structure, itself believed to be an observatory and located just steps from the resort's rear entrance. A planetarium show is part of several pricey all-day Chichén Itzá package tours from Cancún or Mérida, including a "Be Maya" tour that also has Maya cuisine and numerology components. Independent travelers can see the show for US$10; show times vary, and a schedule and tickets available at the resort.

GRUTAS DE BALANKANCHÉ

Six kilometers (3.7 miles) east of Chichén Itzá, the Balankanché Caves (9am-5pm daily, US$8.50, child under 9 free) are a disappointment. The 1959 excavation of the caves by National Geographic archaeologist Dr. E. Wyllys Andrews uncovered numerous artifacts and ceremonial sites, giving researchers a better understanding of ancient Maya cosmology, especially related to the notion of Xibalba (the underworld). Nowadays, the caves are basically a tourist trap—a wide path meandering 500 meters (0.3 mile) down a tunnel with urns and other artifacts supposedly set up in their original locations. Wires and electric lights illuminate the path, but the recorded narration does nothing of the sort—it's so garbled you can hardly understand it, no matter what language it's in.

Entry times are fixed according to language: English at 11am, 1pm, and 3pm; Spanish at 9am, noon, and 2pm; and French at 10am. A minimum of six visitors are needed for the 45-minute tour to depart.

PARQUE ECOARQUEOLÓGICO IK KIL

Three kilometers (1.9 miles) east of Pisté, the centerpiece of the **Ik Kil Eco-Archaeological Park** (Carr. Mérida-Cancún Km. 122, tel. 985/851-0002, 8am-6pm daily Apr.-Oct., 8am-5pm daily Nov.-Mar., US$5.50 adult, US$2.75 child) is the immense, perfectly round **Cenote Sagrado Azul,** with a partial stone roof. Although the cenote is real, the alterations to its natural state—supported walls, a set of stairs leading you in, a waterfall—make it feel pretty artificial. While not representative of the typical cenote experience, this is a good option if you are traveling with small children and need a spot to cool off. Lockers are available for US$2.50. The cenote and on-site restaurant (breakfast US$7, lunch buffet US$13) get packed with tour groups 12:30pm-2:30pm; try visiting outside those times for a mellower experience. Better yet, stay at one of the on-site bungalows (US$100 s/d with a/c).

ACCOMMODATIONS

A handful of upscale hotels make up the small Zona Hotelera on the east side of Chichén Itzá, complete with its own entrance to the ruins. Nearby, in the town of Pisté, there are also a few budget and mid-range options. Be sure to reserve early during the spring and fall equinoxes. All the options below (except Ik Kil) have Wi-Fi available, though often in the reception area only. Book rooms online for the lowest rates.

Under US$50

On the eastern end of Pisté toward the ruins, **Pirámide Inn** (Calle 15 No. 30, tel. 985/851-0115, www.chichen.com, US$42 s/d with a/c) is a low, sprawling hotel with large rooms that are clean though a bit dark. The decor is distinctly 1970s den, with some rooms sporting bubblegum paint jobs and lacquered brick walls. The air conditioners appear to be from the same era, and can be loud. Cement seating frames a pool in a pleasant fruit tree garden. Backpackers can **camp** or **rent a hammock** here (US$4-8 pp), with access to the pool and cleanish shared bathrooms.

Posada Olalde (Calle 6 at Calle 17, tel. 985/851-0086, US$23/27 s/d with fan) is the best budget option in town. Seven simple rooms are brightly painted, with a long shared porch facing a leafy courtyard. The hotel also has four pressed-earth bungalows, which sound nice but have saggy beds, bad light, and a dank feel—better to stick with the rooms.

Many Maya today live in homes not much different than those built by their ancestors, more than a millennium ago.

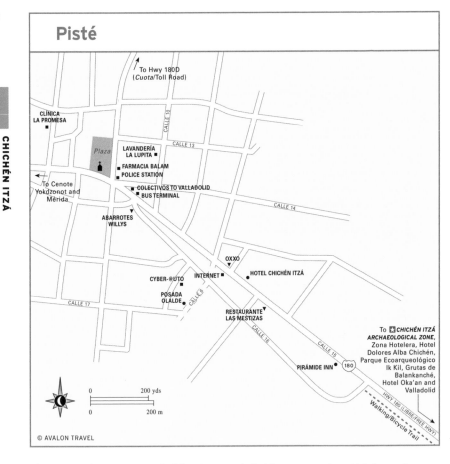

Pisté

The access road is easy to miss—look for it just west of (and across the street from) the OXXO mini-mart. Street parking only.

US$50-100

Hotel Chichén Itzá (Calle 15 s/n, tel. 998/887-2495, toll-free Mex. tel. 800/235-4079, www.mayaland.com, US$68-94 s/d with a/c) is the nicest hotel in Pisté, featuring rooms with a king or two queen beds, comfortable furnishings, large modern bathrooms, and simple Mexican decor. The less-expensive rooms face the street and can be noisy, while the top-floor ones are larger and overlook the hotel's attractive garden and pool area. There's free Wi-Fi plus a cavernous restaurant that's often packed with tour groups, but which frequently has live music and dance performances.

★ **Hotel Dolores Alba Chichén** (Carr. Mérida-Cancún Km. 122, tel. 985/851-0117, www.doloresalba.com, US$50 s with a/c, US$54 d with a/c) has simple and small rooms with good beds, satellite TV, and air-conditioning. There's a pleasant outdoor restaurant and two well-kept swimming pools, including one with a natural stone bottom with swim-throughs and channels reminiscent of an ocean reef. The hotel also provides free shuttle service to the ruins during the day (though not back); it's US$2 per person round-trip for an evening shuttle to the sound and light show. All that plus it's in a choice location: three kilometers (1.9 miles) from the ruins, one kilometer (0.6 mile) from Balankanché Caves, and across the street from the Parque Ecoarqueológico Ik Kil.

Just steps from the ruins, **Villas Arqueológicas Chichén Itzá** (Zona Hotelera, Carr. Mérida-Valladolid Km. 120, tel. 985/851-0187, toll-free Mex. tel. 855/532-2213, www.villasarqueologicas.com.mx, US$65 s/d with a/c, US$109 suite with a/c) is a two-story hotel with a mellow ambience. Boxy, somewhat dated rooms are set around a lush courtyard with an inviting L-shaped pool. In the standard units, alcove walls bracket the ends of the beds, which might make for a cramped night for tall guests. An open-air common room with comfy couches, Wi-Fi, TV, and lots of books also faces the courtyard. A decent restaurant and a tennis court (with nighttime lighting and racquets to borrow) rounds out the hotel nicely.

US$100-150

Set in a lush forest, ★ **Parque Ecoarqueológico Ik Kil** (Carr. Mérida-Cancún Km. 122, tel. 985/858-1525, US$100 s/d with a/c) offers 14 modern and ultra-comfortable bungalows. All are spacious and have whirlpool tubs and comfortable beds, and a handful sport pullout sofas. Silent air-conditioning and a private porch make it all the better. Guests get unlimited use of the on-site cenote, including after hours. It's a fantastic value, especially for those traveling with kids.

A holistic retreat center in a forest setting, **Hotel Oka'an** (Carr. Mérida-Cancún Km. 122, cell tel. 985/105-8402, www.hotelokaan.com, US$130-150 s/d with a/c, US$185 suite with a/c) beckons with a full spa, yoga workshops, and the occasional spiritual ceremony. Ample standard rooms have balconies with hammocks, and corner units have an extra set of picture windows letting in more light. Larger and more luxurious bungalows have decorative stone butterflies and turtles detailing the floors and earthy contemporary architecture, plus private terraces. Continental breakfast is served in a draped open-air restaurant, offering regional, international, and vegetarian options. For post-ruin lounging, an infinity pool cascades into smaller shaded basins, but don't miss the killer view from the *mirador* terrace—Chichén Itzá's El Castillo pops up over the (arduously manicured) treeline. Look for the road marquis just west of the Hotel Dolores Alba and continue 1.5 kilometers (0.9 mile) on an unpaved road; it's a US$8 taxi ride from Pisté.

Over US$150

Once the headquarters for the Carnegie Institute's Chichén Itzá expedition, the **Hacienda Chichén Resort** (Zona Hotelera, Carr. Mérida-Valladolid Km. 120, tel. 999/920-8407, toll-free U.S. tel. 877/631-4005, www.haciendachichen.com, US$179-299 with a/c) is now a tranquil hotel set in a lush tropical garden. Newer units are quite comfortable, with tile floors, exposed beam ceilings, and wood furnishings. Many of the older units occupy the original cottages used by archaeologists who conducted their first excavations of Chichén Itzá—very cool in theory, though the cinder-block walls and pervasive mustiness diminish the charm. Still, the latter are usually booked solid. Be sure to wander the grounds with an eye for the original hacienda (blocks from the ruins are incorporated into the main building) and narrow-gauge railroad tracks that were used to transport artifacts from Chichén Itzá. There's also a gorgeous pool, full-service spa (7:30am-9:30pm daily), and an upscale dining room.

The Lodge at Chichén Itzá (Zona Hotelera, Carr. Mérida-Valladolid Km. 120, tel. 998/887-9162, toll-free Mex. tel. 800/719-5465, toll-free U.S. tel. 800/235-4079, www.mayaland.com, US$374-498 s/d with a/c) is part of the larger Mayaland Resort, which is at the rear entrance to the ruins (visitors must pass through the resort—and two of its gift shops—to get to the ticket booth). The grounds are gorgeous: 100 acres of tamed tropical jungle with walking and horseback riding trails, a full-service spa, three restaurants, and three pools. The *palapa*-roofed bungalows are spacious and pleasant with stained-glass windows, hardwood furniture, and shared terraces. Units are typically reserved for independent travelers, and their location—including a separate access road and parking lot—makes for a relaxed environment. Still, you're bound to encounter flocks of day-trippers, especially in the restaurants, which diminishes the charm for some.

FOOD

Eating options are pretty limited in Pisté but improve somewhat if you have a car and can get to and from the large hotels.

★ **Restaurante Las Mestizas** (Calle 15 s/n, tel. 985/851-0069, 7:30am-10:30pm daily, US$5-8) is the best place to eat in Pisté, with an airy, colonial-style interior and tasty, good-sized portions. The food is classic Yucatecan fare, from *panuchos* to *pollo pibil*. Service is exceptional.

Set in a 16th-century hacienda and its lush gardens, the ★ **Hacienda Chichén Resort's restaurant** (Zona Hotelera, tel. 999/920-8407, 7am-10pm daily, US$14-25) is a soothing place to eat after a long day at the ruins. The menu is varied—Yucatecan specialties, pastas, sandwiches—and on the occasional evening, a trio plays regional music. Much of the produce is grown in its beautiful organic garden, too.

If you can stand the tour groups, the lunch buffet at **Hotel and Bungalows Mayaland** (Zona Hotelera, Carr. Mérida-Valladolid Km. 120, tel. 985/851-0100, noon-4:30pm daily, US$15) offers a variety of hot and cold dishes that will definitely fill you up. Live music, ballet *folklórico* shows, and outdoor seating are nice touches.

For groceries, **Abarrotes Willy's** (Calle 2 s/n, 7am-10pm daily) has the best selection and prices in town. Follow the pulsating music a block southeast of the plaza.

INFORMATION AND SERVICES

There is no tourist office in Pisté; hotel receptionists are sometimes helpful—depends who you get—as are other travelers. Pisté also doesn't have a bank, but there are three local ATMs: inside the OXXO market, across the street from OXXO, and in Chichén Itzá's visitors complex.

Emergency Services

The **police** have an office (tel. 985/851-0365) in the Palacio Municipal, facing the church. An officer is on duty 24 hours a day, and there's usually one waving through traffic near the plaza. **Clínica La Promesa** (Calle 14 btwn Calles 13 and 15, tel. 985/851-0005, 24 hours) is one of two clinics in town. For anything serious, you're better off going to Mérida or Cancún. **Farmacia Balam** (Calle 15 s/n, tel. 985/851-0358, 7am-midnight daily) is just north of the Palacio Municipal.

Media and Communications

In the middle of town, across from the OXXO mini-mart, a **no-name Internet place** (Calle 15 s/n, 10am-10pm daily, US$0.75/hour) has a fast connection plus international telephone service (US$0.30/minute to the United States and Canada, US$0.60/minute to Europe).

Off the road that parallels the main drag, and across from the cemetery, **Ciber-@uto** (Calle 4A, 9am-7pm daily, US$1/hour), is a combination Internet café-and-car-wash run out of a family home.

Laundry

Lavandería La Lupita (Calle 10 near Calle 13, 8am-8pm Mon.-Sat.) charges US$1.85 per kilo (2.2 pounds) to wash and dry clothes; they'll do same-day service if you drop your load off first thing in the morning.

GETTING THERE AND AROUND
Bus

Pisté's small **bus terminal** (8:30am-5:30pm daily, cash only) is just southeast of the Palacio Municipal, and about 2.5 kilometers (1.5 miles) from the entrance to Chichén Itzá. There is also a **ticket office** in the gift shop at the ruins (tel. 985/851-0377, 9am-5pm daily). (The visitors center at Chichén Itzá also has **free luggage storage,** which makes it easy to catch a bus right after visiting the ruins.) **All first-class departures leave from Chichén Itzá only.** Second-class departure times listed here are for the terminal in Pisté. Second-class buses coming and going between 8am and 5:30pm stop at both the terminal and the parking lot at the ruins. If planning to catch a second-class bus at the ruins, keep in mind that buses headed toward Cancún stop at the ruins slightly after the listed times, while those bound for Mérida pass by slightly earlier. Most bus service to and from Pisté and Chichén Itzá is on Oriente, ADO's second-class line, but the few first-class buses are worth the extra cost.

• Cancún: One daily first-class bus (US$19.85, 3.5 hours) at 4:30pm; second-class buses (US$10.35, 4-4.5 hours) every 30-60 minutes 12:30am-9:30pm.

• Cobá: For the town and archaeological site (US$5.25, 2.5 hours), take the second-class Tulum bus at 12:25am, 7:30am, and 1pm; the first-class buses do not stop there.

• Mérida: One first-class bus (US$11.15, 2 hours) leaves at 4:15pm; second-class buses (US$5.75, 2.5 hours) every 30-60 minutes 6am-11:30pm.

• Playa del Carmen: One first-class bus (US$28.75, 3.5 hours) leaves at 4:30pm; second-class buses (US$10.75, 4 hours) leave at 12:25am, 7:35am, and 1:05pm.

• Tulum: First-class buses (US$14.75, 2.5 hours) leave at 8:25am and 4:30pm; second-class departures (US$7.50, 3.5 hours) at 12:25am, 7:30am, and 1pm.

• Valladolid: First-class buses (US$6.50, 50 minutes) leave at 8:25am, 11:10am, and 4:30pm; second-class service (US$2, 1 hour) every 30-60 minutes 12:25am-10:30pm.

White *colectivos* (US$2, 40 minutes) leave for Valladolid every 30 minutes 7am-6pm from in front of the bus terminal.

Car

Chichén Itzá lies adjacent to Highway 180, 45 kilometers (27 miles) west of Valladolid, 120 kilometers (75 miles) east of Mérida, 150 kilometers (90 miles) from Tulum, and 200 kilometers (124 miles) west of Cancún. For drivers, the quickest and most typical way to get there is via the *cuota,* a large modern freeway extending from Cancún most of the way to Mérida, with a well-marked exit for Chichén Itzá and Pisté. There's a price for speed and convenience, though: The toll from Mérida is US$6, and a whopping US$22.30 from Cancún. You can also take the old *carretera libre* (free highway) all or part of the way; it's in reasonably good condition but takes much longer, mainly because you pass through numerous small villages and seemingly innumerable *topes* (speed bumps). If driving from Tulum, take the road toward Cobá, continuing to Chemax, where the road meets the *carretera libre.* Head west on the *carretera libre* until you reach Valladolid (30 kilometers/18 miles); from there, you can either continue on the *carretera libre* to Chichén Itzá (45 kilometers/27 miles) or cut north to the *cuota* (57 kilometers/35 miles, US$4.50 toll).

Air

Aeropuerto Internacional Chichén Itzá (CZA) is 16 kilometers (9.9 miles) east of Pisté, between the towns of Xcalacot and Kaua. Inaugurated in April 2000, it is one of the most modern airports in the country, with a 1,800-meter (5,900-foot) runway capable of receiving 747 jets. Although it initially received dozens of regular and charter flights, its license was suspended in 2001. Today it stands virtually empty, receiving only a smattering of charters, mostly from Cancún, Cozumel, and Chetumal, though rumors of restarting service crop up from time to time.

Valladolid

Valladolid draws tourists because of its mellow colonial atmosphere and its central location: 30 minutes from the archaeological zones of Chichén Itzá and Ek' Balam, an hour from the ruins at Cobá and the flamingo reserve in Río Lagartos, and two hours from Mérida, Cancún, and Tulum. It's an easy bus or car ride to any of these destinations, restaurants and hotels are reasonably priced, and you have the advantage of staying in a colonial Mexican town. If you're en route to one of the regional sites or simply want to have a small-city experience, consider spending a night here—you're sure to be happily surprised.

HISTORY

The site of several Maya revolts against the Spanish, Valladolid was conquered in 1543 by Francisco de Montejo, cousin of the like-named Spaniard who founded Mérida. It was once the Maya city of Zací. Montejo brutalized its inhabitants and crushed their temples, building large churches and homes in their place. It is perhaps not surprising, then, that the Caste War started in Valladolid, and that

the city played an important role in the beginning of the Mexican Revolution. Today, Valladolid is a charming colonial town with a rich history and strong Maya presence.

ORIENTATION

Valladolid is easy to get around. It's laid out in a grid pattern with even-numbered streets running north to south, odd-numbered streets running east to west. The central plaza at the center of the city is bordered by Calles 39, 40, 41, and 42.

SIGHTS
★ Iglesia y Ex-Convento San Bernardino de Siena

Located at the end of the Calzada de los Frailes, the **Iglesia y Ex-Convento San Bernardino de Siena** (Calle 41-A, tel. 985/856-2160, 7am-1pm and 5pm-8pm daily) is one of Valladolid's most attractive structures. Built by Franciscan missionaries between 1552 and 1560, the church is entered through a series of arches, and the facade, covered in a checkerboard-like stucco

A cache of weapons, possibly from the Caste War, was found hidden inside the Iglesia y Ex-Convento San Bernardino de Siena.

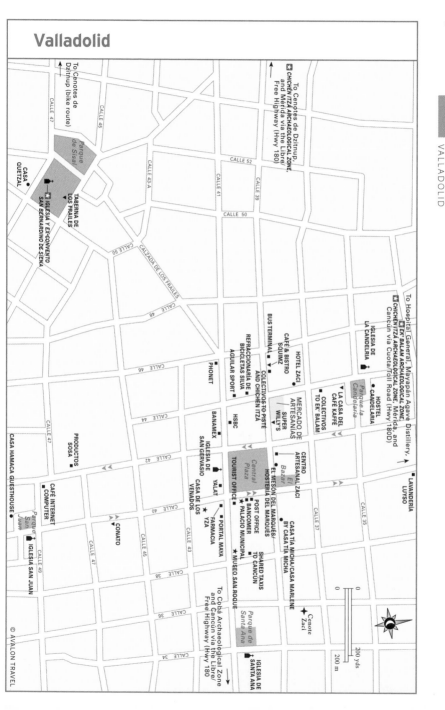

Valladolid

© AVALON TRAVEL

pattern, rises into a squat tower with turrets. Inside, there are original 16th-century frescoes, catacombs, and crypts. Annexed to it, the ex-monastery has rooms radiating from a center courtyard that features, uniquely, a cenote. Called Ziis-Há (Cold Water), the cenote helped the monks be self-reliant. In 2004, an Instituto Nacional de Antropología e Historia (INAH)-funded exploration of the cenote resulted in the discovery of 164 rifles and one cannon. Although neither the age nor the origin of the arms has been disclosed, it is speculated that they date from the mid-1800s, when the monastery was used as a fortress during the Maya uprisings. Mass is held at 7am and 7pm Monday-Friday; at 7am, 8:30am, and 7pm Saturday; and at 7am, 8am, 9am, 10am, 5pm, 6pm, 7pm, and 8:30pm Sunday. Special permission is required to visit the monastery; call ahead or ask in the church office.

Casa de los Venados

If you have even a passing interest in Mexican folk art—or an infatuation with exquisite colonial buildings—make sure to visit the House of the Deer (Calle 40 btwn Calles 41 and 43, tel. 985/856-2289, www.casadelosvenados.com, 10am tour daily, US$5 donation requested). After an architectural award-winning, eight-year remodel of this early 17th-century house, the American couple who own it had so many visitors stopping by to see their extensive art collection that they now welcome visitors for tours of their mansion home and their incredible 3,000-piece collection—the largest Mexican folk art collection not owned by a museum. The pieces span John and Dorianne Venator's 50 years of seeking out and commissioning catrinas, clay sculptures, wood carvings, paintings, and other decorative objects created by some of the most talented contemporary artisans from across Mexico, and the work usually incorporates religious, indigenous, or cultural themes. The museum is a labor of love, with all donations benefiting a local volunteer-run medical clinic and the Lions Club.

Iglesia de San Gervasio

Overlooking the central plaza, the San Gervasio Church (Calle 41 at Calle 42, no phone) has a sober Franciscan style. It was originally built in 1545 but in 1705 was deemed profaned and ordered demolished by the local bishop as the result of a political rivalry that involved the storming of the church, the desanctifying of its altar, and the death of four politicians. (The incident is now known as El Crimen de los Alcaldes, or The Mayors' Crime.) The church was rebuilt a year later, but its orientation changed so that the new altar would not be in the same position as the prior—indeed, the Iglesia de San Gervasio is one of the only colonial-era churches in the Yucatán whose facade faces north instead of west.

Museo San Roque

A long, high-ceilinged room—this used to be a church—the San Roque Museum (Calle 41 btwn Calles 38 and 40, no phone, 9am-9pm Mon.-Fri., 8am-6pm Sat.-Sun., free) is a worthwhile stop, with history exhibits on Valladolid, many focusing on the Caste War and the beginning of the Mexican Revolution. Displays of local handicrafts are also notable. Signage is in Spanish only.

Palacio Municipal

On the 2nd floor of the city hall (7am-7pm daily, free) is a large balcony overlooking the central plaza, with four large paintings by local artist Manuel Lizama. The paintings depict events in Valladolid's history: pre-Hispanic communities, the city's founding, the Caste War, and the Mexican Revolution. It's not spectacular, but still something to see.

Cenote Zaci

In the middle of town, Cenote Zaci (Calle 36 btwn Calles 37 and 39, no phone, 8am-6pm daily, US$2 adult, US$1.25 child under 13) is a dark natural pool at the bottom of a huge cavern, with a bank of trees on one side and a path looping down from the entrance above. It's often pooh-poohed as inferior to cenotes

Cenote Samula is a short bike—or cab—ride from Valladolid's central plaza.

at Dzitnup, but it's a perfectly peaceful and attractive spot, and a lot quicker and easier to get to. You may find leaves and pollen floating on the water's surface, but it's still great for swimming. To have the cenote to yourself, go midweek, or better yet, right after closing time, entering through the restaurant (you can use their bathroom to change) instead of the main gates.

Mayapán Agave Distillery

Along Valladolid's northern ring road, two kilometers (1.2 miles) south of the Cancún toll highway, the artisanal **Mayapán Agave Distillery** (Libremiento Nte., tel. 985/858-0246, www.mayapan.mx, 9am-6pm Mon.-Sat., US$3) leads visitors on half-hour tours that take in its agave fields and warehouse-size facility, detailing the traditional steps used to ferment, mash by horse-drawn mill, and distill the agave plant into liquor. They can't call it tequila because it's not made in Jalisco, but your taste buds might not be so finicky. Tours conclude with three different tastings and a

subtle nudge toward the gift shop. English tours are available.

Cenotes de Dzitnup

Four kilometers (2.5 miles) west of Valladolid on Highway 180 is the small community of Dzitnup, home to two appealing underground cenotes. Both make for a unique and refreshing swim—and on warm days you may find them somewhat crowded. Both share a ticket kiosk and a large parking lot. Many small *artesanía* stands sit at the entrance, and you'll be aggressively pursued by children offering to watch your car or sell you knickknacks.

Although the two are across the street from each other, **Cenote Xkeken** (no phone, 8am-7pm daily, US$4.50 adult, US$2 under 17, video cameras US$2.50) has been open longer and is better known; many postcards and travel guides call it "Cenote Dzitnup." After a reasonably easy descent underground (in a few places you must bend over because of a low ceiling; there's a hanging rope to help), you'll come to a circular pond of clear, cool water. It's a pretty, albeit damp, place, with a high dome ceiling that has one small opening at the top letting in a ray of sun and dangling green vines. Often an errant bird can be seen swooping low over the water before heading to the sun and sky through the tiny opening. Stalactites and at least one large stalagmite adorn the ceiling and cenote floor.

At **Cenote Samula** (no phone, 8:30am-5pm daily, US$5 adult, US$2 under 17, video cameras US$2.50), tree roots dangle impressively from the cavern roof all the way down to the water. You enter through a narrow tunnel, which opens onto a set of stairs that zigzag down to the water. Fearless kids jump from the stairs into the clear turquoise water below.

Many people ride bikes here, following a paved path that runs parallel to the highway. A cab to the cenotes runs about US$5.

Tours

For small group tours packing in local and regional attractions, **MexiGo Tours** (Calle 43 btwn Calles 40 and 42, tel. 985/856-0777, www.mexigotours.com, 8:30am-8pm) is highly recommended. Its "Flamingo" excursion (US$89 pp) visits Río Lagartos, Ek' Balam, and the cake-like 17th-century church in nearby Uayma; another popular outing visits Chichén Itzá and Izamal, with a stop for a dip at the dreamy Yokdzonot cenote (US$89). Both these tours include breakfast, lunch, and transportation, but not site entrance fees. There's a minimum of three people or it's an extra US$25 per person.

ENTERTAINMENT AND EVENTS

Taking the cue from Mérida's successful weekly celebrations, Sundays here now feature a year-round cultural event called **Domingo Vallisoletano.** From 10am until about 8:30pm, the city closes the streets around the central plaza for artisan expositions, *trova* balladeers, folkloric dancing, and programs for kids. The tourist office also leads free hour-long tours of the area around the plaza at 11am, 1pm, and 4pm, though you may want to confirm these times.

Every January 27-February 2, Valladolid celebrates its patron saint, La Vírgen de la Candelaria, in the **Expo-Feria Valladolid.** It's a blowout outdoor festival, where you'll see bullfights, rodeos, musical entertainment, and lots of food stands selling local delicacies and heart-stopping goodies. Venues vary; ask at the tourist office or your hotel for details.

SHOPPING

A tranquil courtyard of workshops and stores, the **Centro Artesanal Zaci** (Calle 39 btwn Calles 40 and 42, no phone, 7am-10pm daily) showcases local Maya women who make and sell their *huipiles* and hand-stitched blouses on-site. For a wider number of offerings, the **Mercado de Artesanías** (Calle 39 at Calle 44, no phone, 8am-8pm Mon.-Sat., 8am-2pm Sun.) has a decent variety of *guayaberas,* embroidered *huipiles,* hammocks, and other popular handicrafts. The selection isn't very large—there are only about a dozen shops here—so be sure to bargain.

If you're interested in high-end Mexican handicrafts and art, **Yalat** (Calle 41 btwn Calles 40 and 42, tel. 985/856-1969, 9am-8pm Mon.-Fri., 9am-7pm Sat.-Sun.) is worth a stop. It's pricey, but the quality and variety of the items sold is excellent.

A family-owned business still chugging away after more than 100 years, the unassuming shop of distiller **Productos Sosa** (Calle 42 btwn Calles 47 and 49, tel. 985/856-2142,

Artisan stands, like this one of jipi hats, are set up for Valladolid's weekly Domingo Vallisoletano.

8:30am-1:30pm and 4pm-7:30pm Mon.-Fri., 8:30am-2:30pm Sat.) sells smooth sugar cane liquors infused with ingredients like mint or anise with honey.

ACCOMMODATIONS

Valladolid offers a good selection of simple and mid-range hotels. Most are convenient to the central plaza. All have free Wi-Fi and, except for the hostel, provide parking.

Under US$50

Cozy, fan-cooled dormitories at ★ Hostel Candelaria (Parque la Candelaria, Calle 35 btwn Calles 42 and 44, tel. 985/856-2267, www.hostelvalladolidyucatan.com, US$10.50 dorm, US$24 s/d with shared bathroom, US$28 s/d with private bathroom) have 10-14 beds sharing one bathroom, with a low-ceilinged women-only dorm and a roomier mixed dorm. What the dorms lack in space is more than made up for by a sprawling back garden thick with papaya trees and hibiscus, shading an al fresco kitchen and eating area and hammocks tucked in nooks with personal reading lights. Inside the colonial building, you'll find another kitchen, free computers, lockers—including some for charging electronics—and a TV room. Socialize with other travelers over the free breakfast, then rent a bicycle to tour the local cenotes.

Set around a grassy courtyard, Hotel Zaci (Calle 44 btwn Calles 37 and 39, tel. 985/856-2167, www.hotelzaci.com.mx, US$37-41 s with a/c, US$46-55 d with a/c) offers well-kempt ground-floor rooms with decorative details like stenciling and ironwork furnishings. The top two floors contain remodeled "premier" rooms, which boast flat-screen TVs and newer decor. But the difference between the two levels of rooms is pretty minimal—there's just better light on the upper floors. A small, clean pool is a nice plus.

US$50-100

A converted 17th-century home, El Mesón del Marqués (central plaza, Calle 39 btwn Calles 40 and 42, tel. 985/856-2073, www. mesondelmarques.com, US$70 s/d standard with a/c, US$84 s/d superior with a/c, US$130-192 suite with a/c) boasts lush courtyards, a gurgling fountain, arches upon arches, and a verdant garden with an egg-shaped pool. Rooms are divided into three categories: standard, superior, and suite. The first two are decorated similarly with rustic wood furnishings and ironwork headboards—the difference is that standards are smaller and aren't updated with new-school air conditioners and TVs. Suites are spacious and modern, almost sleek, with lots of natural light as well as private terraces. All have Wi-Fi and cable TV.

Casa Quetzal (Calle 51 btwn Calles 50 and 52, tel. 985/856-4796, www.casa-quetzal. com, US$88-105 s/d with a/c, US$111 suite with a/c) is a charming, well-run bed-and-breakfast a half block from the pretty San Bernardino de Siena church. Large, attractive, high-ceilinged rooms surround a pretty garden and swimming pool, while a community kitchen and lovely reading room—with high-quality Mexican artwork, especially from Oaxaca and Jalisco—lend a homey feel. All rooms have hammocks, air-conditioning, Wi-Fi, and cable TV; ask for a room away from the street for less traffic noise. Free yoga classes take place in its dedicated salon twice daily. The hotel is somewhat removed from the central plaza, but the 10-minute walk there—along Valladolid's iconic Calzada de los Frailes—is a pleasure itself.

Over US$100

Steps from the plaza yet still very quiet, the combined hotels of ★ Casa Tía Micha and Casa Marlene by Casa Tía Micha (Calle 39 btwn Calles 38 and 40, tel. 985/856-0499, www.casatiamicha.wix.com, US$112-130 s/d with a/c) is run by the great-grandchildren of the former owner. Stately wooden doors, rainforest showerheads, wrought-iron or carved headboards, and vintage furniture can be found throughout, and one of the more luxurious upstairs rooms boasts a decadent Jacuzzi tub. There's also a new, refreshing pool on-site. A full breakfast is served in the tranquil fruit tree garden, near the old *pozo* (well). **Casa Hamaca Guesthouse** (Parque San Juan, Calle 49 at Calle 40, tel. 985/100-4270, www.casahamaca.com, US$110-135 s/d with a/c) has a convenient and peaceful location, facing a quiet church plaza about five blocks south of the main square. A lush garden and small pool add to the tranquility, and the guesthouse is spacious and bright. The eight rooms vary in size and decor: The Tree Suite has rattan furnishings, the Earth Suite has ochre highlights, and all rooms have dramatic hand-painted murals. A hearty breakfast is included, and massages, facials, Maya cleansings, and other treatments can be arranged. With advance notice the proprietor can also help set up rewarding volunteer opportunities or Spanish classes. Casa Hamaca is wheelchair accessible.

FOOD

Located next to the bus station, ★ **Café & Bistro Squimz** (Calle 39 near Calle 46, tel. 985/856-4156, www.squimz.com.mx, 7am-11pm Mon.-Sat., 8am-4pm Sun., US$3-9) is well worth a stop even if you're not on your way out of town. Big breakfasts and sandwiches are the specialties, though the coffee drinks and to-die-for milkshakes shouldn't be overlooked. If you've got a sweet tooth, try the homemade flan napolitano.

Adjacent to the Iglesia y Ex-Convento San Bernardino de Siena, the low lighting, attentive service, and open-air *palapa* dining room at **Taberna de los Frailes** (Calle 49 at Calle 41A, tel. 985/856-0689, www.tabernadelosfrailes.com, noon-11pm daily, US$7-16) set an elegant backdrop for a crowd-pleasing menu of creative Yucatecan mainstays, seafood cocktails, and a few vegetarian entrées. Its upscale bar has some sofa seating and a terrace area shaded by a profuse canopy of passion fruit. The restaurant's proximity to the monastery cenote can draw the odd mosquito; ask the staff for repellent if you need it.

Bohemia is alive and well at **Conato** (Calle 40 btwn Calles 45 and 47, tel. 985/856-2586,

5:30pm-2:30am Wed.-Mon., US$4.25-7), where religious iconography and images of Frida Kahlo clutter a dining room of family-style wooden tables set off by a colonial tile floor. Yucatecan-influenced chicken dishes, fresh salads, and serviceable pasta dishes have creative visual flourishes, and the go-vinda dessert crepes laced with cream and chocolate are almost too pretty to eat. Open until late, it's also a sociable place for drinks or coffee.

With tables on Parque Candelaria, **La Casa del Café Kaffé** (Calle 35 at Calle 44, tel. 985/856-2879, 9am-1pm and 7pm-10:30pm daily, US$2-3.50) is a fantastic place to get breakfast or a late-night snack. It's owned and run by a welcoming Chilean couple, and the menu features empanadas, quesadillas, sandwiches, fruit shakes, and a nice variety of coffee drinks. If you don't see what you crave on the menu, be sure to ask for it—meals often are made to order.

A gorgeous place to enjoy a meal, **Hostería del Marqués** (El Mesón del Marqués, Calle 39 btwn Calles 40 and 42, tel. 985/856-2073, 7am-11pm daily, US$8-13) is set in the interior courtyard of a 17th-century home turned hotel, with a colonial-style fountain and masses of fuchsia-colored bougainvillea draped over the balconies. The menu is predominantly Yucatecan, though there are a variety of international options. Good choices include scrambled eggs with *chaya, sopa de lima,* and *poc-chuc.*

El Bazar (parque central, Calle 39 at Calle 40, US$1.50-5) is a local food court with a dozen or so inexpensive eateries selling mostly premade Yucatecan specialties. Hours are variable, but all are open for breakfast and lunch. Food is hit or miss—take a look at the offerings and decide which looks the freshest. (If anything, avoid the tamales.) Better yet, order something off the menu that hasn't been sitting around, like scrambled eggs or *salbutes.*

For groceries, **Super Willy's** (Calle 39 btwn Calles 42 and 44, 7am-10pm daily) has a decent selection of fresh and canned foods.

INFORMATION AND SERVICES

Tourist Information

Try your best at prying some useful information from Valladolid's **tourist office** (Palacio Municipal, Calle 40 at Calle 41, tel. 985/856-2529, ext. 114, 9am-9pm daily). At the very least, you should be able to get a map or two, and English is spoken.

Emergency Services

If you need medical assistance, the modern new **Hospital General** (Av. Chan Yokdzonot, tel. 985/856-2883, 24 hours) is located 4.5 kilometers (2.8 miles) south of the *cuota* highway; for meds only, **Farmacia Yza** (Calle 41 near Calle 40, tel. 985/856-4018), just off the central plaza, is open 24 hours. The **police** (Parque Bacalar, Calle 41 s/n, 24 hours) can be reached at 985/856-2100 or toll-free at 066.

Money

On or near the central plaza, **HSBC** (Calle 41 btwn Calles 42 and 44, 9am-5pm Mon.-Fri., 9am-3pm Sat.), **Banamex** (Calle 41 btwn Calles 42 and 44, 9am-4pm Mon.-Fri.), and **Bancomer** (Calle 40 btwn Calles 39 and 41, 8:30am-4pm Mon.-Fri.) all have ATMs.

Media and Communications

A tiny **post office** (Calle 40 btwn Calles 39 and 41, 8am-4:30pm Mon.-Fri., 8am-1pm Sat.) sits on the central plaza. There's free Wi-Fi in the central plaza, and we assume that the signal's strongest where the laptop-toting teens congregate in front of the Palacio Municipal. For computer access, try **Café Internet Computer** (Calle 49 at Calle 42, 8am-11pm daily, US$0.75/hour) or **Phonet** (Calle 46 at Calle 41, 7am-midnight daily, US$0.70/hour), which also offers long-distance telephone service (US$0.50/minute to the United States and Canada, US$0.70/minute to the rest of the world).

Laundry

The bustling **Lavandería Luyso** (Calle 40 at Calle 33, no phone, 8am-8pm Mon.-Sat.,

8am-3pm Sun.) charges US$0.90 per kilo (2.2 pounds) and offers next-day service only.

GETTING THERE AND AROUND

Bus

Valladolid's **bus terminal** (Calle 39 at Calle 46, tel. 985/856-3448) is an easy walk from the central plaza, or if you have a lot of bags, a cheap taxi ride.

Taxi

Taxis are relatively easy to flag down, especially around the central plaza, and typically cost US$1.50-2 around town.

Colectivos (shared vans) to Pisté and Chichén Itzá (US$2, 40 minutes) depart approximately every 30 minutes from Calle 39 near the ADO bus terminal, and those for Mérida (US$11.25, 2.5 hours) leave from the terminal. Shared taxis for Cancún (US$11, 2.5 hours) congregate at Calle 38 between Calles 39 and 41.

Car

If you arrive from the toll highway (*cuota*), you'll enter town via Calle 42 (and return on Calle 40). It's a sobering US$18 toll driving in from Cancún (155 kilometers/93 miles), US$10.50 from Mérida (160 kilometers/96 miles), and US$4.50 to Chichén Itzá (57 kilometers/35 miles). In the center, eastbound Calle 41 and westbound Calle 39 access the *carretera libre* (free highway). If driving from Tulum (100 kilometers/60 miles), take the road toward Cobá, continuing to Chemax, where the road meets the *carretera libre*. Head west on the *carretera libre* for approximately 30 kilometers (18 miles) to arrive in Valladolid.

To rent a car in town, **Portal Maya** (Calle 41 btwn Calles 38 and 40, tel. 985/856-2513, 9am-1:30pm and 4pm-8pm Mon.-Sat.) is your lone option; it also organizes tours.

Bicycle

Bikes can be rented at both **Refraccionaría de Bicicletas Silva** (Calle 44 btwn Calles 39

Valladolid Bus Schedule

Departures from Valladolid's bus station (Calle 39 at Calle 46, tel. 985/856-3448) include:

Destination	Price	Duration	Schedule
Cancún	US$8-14.50	2-3.5 hrs	every 30-90 mins 12:35am-10:30pm
Chetumal	US$15.50	5 hrs	5:30am, 7:30am, 2:30pm, and 8:30pm
Chichén Itzá	US$2-6.50	50 mins	every 30-60 mins 5am-3:30pm
Chiquilá	US$7.75	3 hrs	2:45am
Cobá	US$2-6.50	1 hr	every 30-90 mins 5am-3:30pm
Mérida	US$12-13.75	2.5 hrs	every 30-90 mins 12:10am-9:10pm
Playa del Carmen	US$9.25-14.50	3 hrs	every 30-90 mins 12:50am-10:40pm
Tulum	US$6.50-8.50	2 hrs	13 departures 12:50am-10:40pm

and 41, tel. 985/856-3667, 9am-6pm daily) and neighboring Aguilar Sport (Calle 44 No. 195 btwn Calles 39 and 41, tel. 985/856-2125, 8am-2pm and 4pm-7pm daily) for US$1 per hour or US$5 per day, and from Hostel Candelaria (Parque la Candelaria, Calle 35 btwn Calles 42 and 44, tel. 985/856-2267) for US$1.25 per hour or US$7 per day.

Ek' Balam

Ek' Balam, Maya for Black Jaguar, is a unique and fascinating archaeological site whose significance has only recently been revealed and appreciated. Serious restoration of Ek' Balam didn't begin until the mid-1990s, and it was then that an incredibly well-preserved stucco frieze was discovered, hidden under an innocuous stone facade near the top of the site's main pyramid. The discovery rocketed Ek' Balam into preeminence, first among Maya scholars and more slowly among travelers in the Yucatán, once the frieze was excavated and opened to the public. Much remains a mystery about Ek' Balam, but archaeologists believe it was founded around 300 BC and became an important commercial center, its influence peaking in AD 700-1100.

Ek' Balam sees a fraction of the tourists that visit other Maya sites, despite being just 30 kilometers (19 miles) north of Valladolid and in close proximity to both Cancún and Mérida. Though the one-lane access road is riddled with potholes, the ruins and the adjacent cenote are an easy jaunt from Valladolid. Ek' Balam is small enough that even an hour is enough to appreciate its treasures, and it's a tranquil place that doesn't get besieged by mammoth tour groups.

The village of Ek' Balam is two kilometers (1.2 miles) from the ruins, with two good options for accommodations and food; for more

Ek' Balam Archaeological Zone

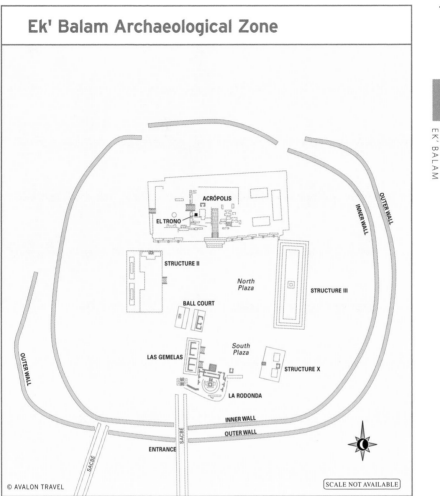

ACRÓPOLIS

EL TRONO

STRUCTURE II

North
Plaza

BALL COURT

STRUCTURE III

LAS GEMELAS

South
Plaza

STRUCTURE X

LA RODONDA

INNER WALL

OUTER WALL

ENTRANCE

INNER WALL

OUTER WALL

SACBÉ

SACBÉ

OUTER WALL

© AVALON TRAVEL

SCALE NOT AVAILABLE

options and other traveler services, head to Valladolid.

★ EK' BALAM ARCHAEOLOGICAL ZONE

Entering **Ek' Balam** (8am-5pm daily, US$9.50), you'll pass through a low thick wall and an elegant corbeled arch. Walls are rare in Maya cities, and were most commonly used for defense, as in the cases of Becán and Tulum. Ek' Balam's low thick walls would not have slowed marauding rivals, however, and so they most likely served to enforce social divisions, with some areas off-limits (but not out of view!) to all but the elite. They may also have been decorative—the city possessed great aesthetic flair, as the entry arch and the famous stucco frieze demonstrate.

Acrópolis and El Trono

The highlight of Ek' Balam is an artful and remarkably pristine stucco frieze known as **El Trono** (The Throne), located under a protective *palapa* roof two-thirds of the way up Ek' Balam's main pyramid, the **Acrópolis**. A steep stairway leads up the center of the pyramid, and a platform to the left of the stairs provides visitors a close-up view of El Trono.

About 85 percent of El Trono is the original stucco. Often structures like this would have been painted blue or red, but not so here. In fact, shortly after it was built, El Trono was sealed behind a stone wall 50-60 centimeters (19-24 inches) thick. It remained there untouched until the 1990s, when restoration workers accidentally—and fortuitously—dislodged one of the protective stones, revealing the hidden chamber beneath.

The tall, winged figures immediately catch your eye, as they appear so much like angels. In fact, they are high priests. Notice that one is deformed—his left arm is longer than the right, and has only four fingers. The Maya considered birth defects to be a sign of divinity, and the priest depicted here may have risen to his position precisely because of his deformation.

Directly over the door is a seated figure (unfortunately, the head is missing). This represents Ukit Kan Le'k Tok', one of Ek' Balam's former rulers, described in inscriptions as the "king of kings," and the person for whom El Trono was built and dedicated. A tomb was discovered in the chamber behind the frieze, containing thousands of jade, gold, obsidian, and ceramic artifacts left as offerings to this powerful leader. The small face at the king-figure's navel represents a rival whom he defeated in war.

Viewed as a whole, the frieze is unmistakably a Chenes-style monster mouth: a huge stylized mask in which the doorway represents the gaping mouth of a high god. The pointed upper and lower teeth are easy to spot, as are the spiral eyes. Monster mouths are never mundane, but this one is especially elaborate: Notice how two beautifully crafted figures straddle the lower eyelids, while hoisting the upper lids with their shoulders. At least five more figures, plus lattice patterns and other designs, adorn the rest of the mask.

Ek' Balam's remarkable stucco frieze, known as El Trono (The Throne)

Before heading down, climb the rest of the way to the top of the Acrópolis for a panoramic vista. At 32 meters (105 feet) high and 158 meters (515 feet) wide, the Acrópolis is bigger than Chichén Itzá's main pyramid, and in fact is one of the largest Maya pyramids ever built, a detail that's often overlooked amid the excitement surrounding El Trono. The scene from atop is memorable; with the exception of the odd telephone and radio tower, and the site's visitors center, the view of the broad Yucatecan landscape is probably not all that different than the one Maya priests and kings enjoyed from this very same vantage point more than a thousand years ago.

South Plaza

Descending the pyramid, you can see that Ek' Balam is a fairly small site, with two mid-size plazas (north and south), a ball court in the middle, and its main structures crowded together.

On the south side of the south plaza stands **La Rodonda,** or the Oval Palace. A squat midsize structure, La Rodonda has an eclectic array of overlapping lines and curves, stairs, and terraces. It underwent numerous iterations, as did virtually all Maya temples, but the result here was especially eclectic. Archaeologists suspect La Rodonda was used for astronomical observations, and the discovery of several richly adorned tombs suggest it had a ceremonial purpose as well.

Flanking La Redonda are **Las Gemelas** (The Twins), known as Structure 17. As the plaque indicates, these identical structures are perhaps the best example of Ek' Balam's particular architectural style. Having perfected the use of stucco, Ek' Balam's builders did not concern themselves with precise masonry, as the stones would be covered in a thick stucco cap. However, stucco proved much less resilient to erosion, and centuries later the structures here appear shabbier than even much older ones, like in Campeche's Río Bec region, where stucco was less common and stone blocks were more carefully cut and fitted. Recent excavations have focused on these two buildings, where intriguing freehand marks and paintings—perhaps akin to graffiti today—have been discovered.

Practicalities

Guides can be hired at the entrance to the ruins (US$50, 1-1.5 hours, available in Spanish or English). French- and Italian-speaking guides are sometimes available.

CENOTE X'CANCHÉ

A short distance from the Ek' Balam archaeological site, **Cenote X'Canché** (cell tel. 985/100-9815, www.ekbalam.com.mx, 9am-5pm daily, US$5) is an excellent community-run ecotourism project, and a must-do add-on to a ruins visit. From Ek' Balam's parking area, a dirt road winds 1.5 kilometers (0.9 mile) through low, dense forest to the cenote, which is 14 meters (46 feet) deep and nearly circular, with sheer walls and tree roots descending picturesquely to cool, clean water. A wooden staircase leads to the water's edge, great for swimming. It's a pleasant

shaded walk in, though many visitors rent bikes (US$6 for 3 hours) or take advantage of the on-site bike taxis (US$4 pp round-trip). Facilities include restrooms, shower and changing areas, a restaurant, *palapa*-shaded hammocks for reading and hanging out, and comfortable overnight accommodations. Rappelling from the cenote edge or ziplining across it can each be arranged for an additional fee (US$8-30, half price child under 12); there are also admission packages (US$25) that includes those activities plus bicycle rental.

ACCOMMODATIONS

In the Maya village near the ruins, ★ **Genesis Retreat Ek' Balam** (cell tel. 985/101-0277, www.genesisretreat.com, US$44 s/d with shared bathroom, US$44 with shared bathroom and a/c, US$60-68 s/d, US$75 s/d/t/q) has nine rooms and *cabañas* set on a leafy enclosed property, all different in style and decor. Each faces a natural bio-filtered pool in the middle of the property. Morning pastries and coffee are included in the rate; full breakfasts (US$8.50) and three-course dinners (US$12) are available to guests, too. There's true environmental commitment at work here: Recycled materials were used in its construction, its 101-hectare (250-acre) organic farm provides most of the produce for its meals, and there's a solar hot-water system and extensive greywater reuse on the property. The hardworking Canadian owner also offers tours of the village and local artisan workshops, and is involved in a number of educational projects around town. Be aware that a number of friendly pooches lounge about the property—fine if you like dogs, but not everyone's thing.

Dolcemente Ek' Balam (cell tel. 985/106-8083, US$46-52 s/d with a/c) doesn't compete with Genesis for Zen or eco-ambience; it's simply a nice, comfortable hotel. Spacious rooms have tile floors, okay beds, private hot-water bathrooms, and fans (except for two rooms with air-conditioning). Upstairs units have higher ceilings and better ventilation—making them worth requesting—and all look onto the hotel's peaceful garden.

Cenote X'Canché (cell tel. 985/100-9815, www.ekbalam.com.mx, US$38 s/d/t) rents three well-built and solar-powered *palapa cabañas* near the cenote, each with queen bed and a hammock (plus mosquito nets). The windows have good screens, and there's hot water and a fan. A three-course lunch or dinner at its restaurant costs US$8; breakfast is US$7.

FOOD

Dolcemente Ek' Balam (cell tel. 985/106-8083, noon-11pm Tues.-Sun., US$8-14) specializes in Italian food, including fresh handmade ravioli, fettuccini, and other pasta. Its products are 100 percent natural and organic. Meals are served in a large, tasteful dining room.

Restaurante Xcatiik (tel. 985/856-1146, 8am-10pm daily, US$9-20) With a swimming pool, kids' play area, and hammocks in the shade, this spotless restaurant is a sight for sore eyes after a day of ruin-hopping. Meals are fresh and flavorful, if somewhat predictable. You may encounter tour groups, but service remains friendly and prompt.

GETTING THERE AND AROUND
Car

From Valladolid, drive north on Highway 295 toward Tizimín for about 17 kilometers (10.5 miles), past the town of Temozón, to a well-marked right-hand turnoff to Ek' Balam. From there, drive another 11 kilometers (6.8 miles) to an intersection: Turn left to reach the village and accommodations, or continue straight to reach the archaeological site.

Taxi

Colectivo (shared) taxis from Valladolid to the village of Ek' Balam leave from a stop on Calle 44 between Calles 35 and 37 (US$3.25); mornings have the most frequent departures. Otherwise, a private taxi costs about US$15 for up to four people. If you're planning on visiting the ruins only, you can often negotiate with the driver to wait there for a couple of hours and bring you back for around US$25.

Background

The Landscape

The history of the Yucatán Peninsula is deeply intertwined with its unique geology and ecology. From the ancient Maya to modern-day tourism, the land and its resources have shaped the course of Yucatecan events. And the Yucatán, in turn, has helped shape the course of Mexican history, from being the stage upon which the early Spanish conquest was conducted to helping rescue a moribund Mexican economy in the 1980s. An understanding of the Yucatán Peninsula's land, ecology, culture, and politics is vital to understanding the region today.

GEOGRAPHY

The Yucatán Peninsula spans some 113,000 square kilometers (70,215 square miles) in southeastern Mexico, and is made up of three states: Yucatán, Campeche, and Quintana Roo. It has more than 1,600 kilometers (994 miles) of shoreline, with the Caribbean Sea to the east and the Gulf of Mexico to the north and west. To the southwest are the Mexican states of Tabasco and Chiapas, and directly south are the countries of Belize and Guatemala.

Geologically, the Yucatán Peninsula is a flat shelf of limestone, a porous rock that acts like a huge sponge. Rainfall is absorbed into the ground and delivered to natural stone-lined sinks and underground rivers. The result is that the Yucatán has virtually no surface water, neither rivers nor lakes. It also has very few hills. The geology changes as you move south, and the first sizable river—the Río Hondo—forms a natural boundary between Belize and Mexico.

The Coast

The northern and western coasts are bordered by the emerald waters of the Gulf of Mexico. Just inland, the land is dotted with lagoons, sandbars, and swamps. The east coast is edged by the turquoise Caribbean, and the glorious islands of Isla Cozumel, Isla Mujeres, and Isla Contoy lie just offshore. Along the coast runs the Mesoamerican Reef, the second-longest coral reef in the world.

Cenotes

Over the course of millennia, water that seeped below the Yucatán's porous limestone shelf eroded a vast network of underground rivers and caves. When a cave's ceiling wears thin, it may eventually cave in, exposing the water below. The Maya called such sinkholes *dzo'not,* which Spanish explorers recorded as *cenotes.* Most cenotes are extremely deep, and interconnected by way of underground channels. A cenote's surface may be near ground level, but more often it is much farther down, as much as 90 meters (295 feet) below ground level. In those cases, the Maya gathered water by carving stairs into the slick limestone walls or by hanging long ladders into abysmal hollows that led to underground lakes.

CLIMATE

The weather in the Yucatán falls into a rainy season (May-October) and a dry season (November-April). Travelers to the region in the dry season will experience warm days, occasional brief storms called *nortes,* and plenty of tourists. In the rainy season, expect spectacular storms and hot, muggy days. The region is infamous for its heat and humidity in May and June, which hovers around 90°F *and* 90 percent humidity.

Hurricane season runs July-November, with most activity occurring mid-August to mid-October. Cloudy conditions and scattered showers are common during this period, occasionally developing into tropical storms. Hurricanes are still relatively rare, but their effects are wide-reaching—even if a storm isn't predicted to hit the Yucatán, it may send plenty of heavy rain and surf that direction. If a hurricane *is* bearing down, don't try to tough it out; cut short your trip or head inland immediately.

ENVIRONMENTAL ISSUES
Hurricanes

Evidence that global warming may cause an increase in the number and/or intensity of Atlantic hurricanes has serious implications for the Yucatán Peninsula, already known to be within Hurricane Alley. The region has weathered countless storms, but something was different about Hurricanes Wilma (2005) and Dean (2007)—both storms broke records for intensity and caused major structural damage, but they also reshaped the shoreline in a way not seen before. Cancún's beaches were especially hard hit, the sand stripped away in many places to expose the hardened limestone beneath. Elsewhere, unusually thick deposits of sand on the coral reef and inland mangroves wiped out large portions of both important ecosystems.

Overdevelopment

Runaway construction along the Riviera Maya has a host of interconnected environmental impacts, some well-known, others poorly understood (and surely many that have yet to be identified). An obvious impact is the destruction of mangrove swamps, which extend along much of the coast a short distance inland from the beach. Well-known for supporting wildlife, mangroves also help buffer the effects of hurricane-related surge and currents, and are an important source of nutrients for coral and other sealife, as water from the wetlands drains into the ocean. Although protected by federal law, mangroves have been a primary victim of massive development projects.

Mangroves are emblematic of a more general characteristic of the Riviera Maya: highly porous earth and a weblike underground watershed. Contamination is extremely difficult to clean up or even contain, as it spreads quickly in multiple directions via underground currents, including into the ocean. This is damaging not only to the environment but also to local communities—and the resorts themselves—which draw drinking water from the same system.

And those local communities are growing even faster than the resorts—by some estimates, resorts require an average of five employees for every guest room. Multiply that by the number of resorts operating and being built, and it's no surprise that the region's population is booming. In that sense, development is doubly dangerous: increasing the risk of contamination while simultaneously spurring demand for the very resource it most threatens.

Deforestation

Among the top concerns of environmentalists in Mexico is deforestation, which has accelerated with Mexico's burgeoning population. Slash-and-burn farming is still widely practiced in remote areas, with or without regulation. In an effort to protect the land, environmentalists are searching for alternative sources of income for locals. One is to train them to become guides by teaching them about the flora and fauna of the region as well as how to speak English. While not solving the problem, it does place an economic value on the forest itself and provides an incentive for preserving it.

Another focus is the plight of the palm tree. The palm is an important part of the cultural and practical lifestyle of the indigenous people of Quintana Roo—it is used for thatch roofing and to construct lobster traps. However, the palms used—*Thrinax radiata* and *Coccothrinax readii*—are becoming increasingly rare. Amigos de Sian Ka'an together with the World Wildlife Fund are studying the palms' growth patterns and rates; they are anticipating a management plan that will encourage future growth. Other environmental projects include limiting commercial fishing, halting tourist development where it endangers the ecology, and studying the lobster industry and its future. A number of other worthwhile projects are still waiting in line.

Plants and Animals

Quintana Roo's forests are home to mangroves, bamboo, and swamp cypresses. Ferns, vines, and flowers creep from tree to tree and create a dense growth. The southern part of the Yucatán Peninsula, with its classic tropical rainforest, hosts tall mahoganies, *campeche zapote,* and *kapok*—all covered with wild jungle vines. On topmost limbs, orchids and air ferns reach for the sun.

Many animals found nowhere else in Mexico inhabit the Yucatán Peninsula's expansive flatlands and thick jungles. Spotting them can be difficult, though with patience and a skilled guide, not impossible.

TREES
Palms
A wide variety of palm trees and their relatives grow on the peninsula—tall, short, fruited, and even oil-producing varieties. Though similar, palms have distinct characteristics:

- Queen palms are often used for landscaping and bear a sweet fruit.
- Thatch palms are called *chit* by Maya, who use the fronds extensively for roof thatch.
- Coconut palms—the ones often seen on the beach—produce oil, food, drink, and shelter and are valued by locals as a nutritious food source and cash crop.
- Royal palms are tall with smooth trunks.
- Henequen is a cousin to the palm tree; from its fiber come twine, rope, matting, and other products. Because of its abundance, new uses for it are constantly sought.

Fruit Trees
Quintana Roo grows sweet and sour oranges, limes, and grapefruit. Avocado is abundant, and the papaya tree is practically a weed. The *mamey* tree grows full and tall (15-20 meters/49-65 feet), providing not only welcome shade but also an avocado-shaped fruit, brown on the outside with a vivid, salmon-pink flesh that tastes like a sweet yam. The *guaya* is another unusual fruit tree and a member of the lychee nut family. This rangy evergreen thrives on sea air and is commonly seen along the coast. Its small, green, leathery pods grow in clumps like grapes and contain a sweet, yellowish, jellylike flesh—tasty! The calabash tree provides gourds used for containers by Maya.

Other Trees
The ceiba (also called *kapok*) is a sacred tree for the Maya. Considered the link between the underworld, the material world, and the heavens, this huge tree is revered and left undisturbed—even if it sprouts in the middle of a fertile cornfield.

When visiting in the summer, you can't miss the beautiful *framboyanes* (royal poinciana). When in bloom, its wide-spreading branches become covered in clusters of brilliant orange-red flowers. These trees often line sidewalks and plazas, and when clustered together present a dazzling show.

FLOWERS
While wandering through jungle regions, you'll see numerous flowering plants. Here in their natural environment, these plants thrive in a way unknown to windowsills at home: Crotons exhibit wild colors, pothos grow 30-centimeter (11.8-inch) leaves, the philodendron splits every leaf in gargantuan

glory, and common morning glory creeps and climbs effortlessly over bushes and trees. You'll also be introduced to less well-known residents of this semi-tropical world: the exotic white and red ginger, plumeria (sometimes called frangipani) with its wonderful fragrance and myriad colors, and hibiscus and bougainvillea, which bloom in an array of bright hues.

Orchids

Orchids can be found on the highest limbs of the tallest trees, especially in the state of Quintana Roo. Of the 71 species reported in the Yucatán Peninsula, 80 percent are epiphytic, attached to host trees and deriving moisture and nutrients from the air and rain. Orchids grow in myriad sizes and shapes: tiny buttons spanning the length of a half-meter-long (two-foot) branch, large-petaled blossoms with ruffled edges, or intense tiger-striped miniatures.

MAMMALS
Nine-Banded Armadillos

The size of a small dog and sporting a thick coat of armor, this peculiar creature gets its name from the nine bands (or external "joints") that circle its midsection and give the little tank some flexibility. The armadillo's keen sense of smell can detect insects and grubs—its primary food source—up to 15 centimeters (6 inches) underground, and its sharp claws make digging for them easy. An armadillo also digs underground burrows, into which it may carry a full bushel of grass to make its nest, where it will sleep through the hot day and emerge at night. Unlike armadillos that roll up into a tight ball when threatened, this species will race to its burrow, arch its back, and wedge in so that it cannot be pulled out. The Yucatán Peninsula is a favored habitat for its scant rainfall; too much rain floods the burrow and can drown young armadillos.

Giant Anteaters

A cousin of the armadillo, this extraordinary animal measures two meters (6.6 feet) from the tip of its tubular snout to the end of its bushy tail. Its coarse coat is colored shades of brown-gray; the hindquarters are darker in tone, while a contrasting wedge-shaped pattern of black and white decorates the throat and shoulders. Characterized by an elongated head, long tubular mouth, and extended tongue (but no teeth), it can weigh up to 39 kilograms (86 pounds). The anteater walks on the knuckles of its paws, allowing its claws to remain tucked under while it looks for food.

Giant anteaters are found in forests and swampy areas in Mexico and throughout Central and South America. It is mainly diurnal in areas where there are few people but nocturnal in densely populated places. Its razor-sharp claws allow it to rip open the leathery mud walls of termite and ant nests, the contents of which are a main food source. After opening the nest, the anteater rapidly flicks its viscous tongue in and out of its small mouth opening. Few ants escape.

Tapirs

South American tapirs are found from the southern part of Mexico to southern Brazil. A stout-bodied animal, it has short legs and a tail, small eyes, and rounded ears. The nose and upper lip extend into a short but very mobile proboscis. Tapirs usually live near streams or rivers, which they use for daily bathing and as an escape from predators, especially jaguars and humans. Shy and placid, these nocturnal animals have a definite home range, wearing a path between the jungle and their feeding area. If attacked, the tapir lowers its head and blindly crashes off through the forest; they've been known to collide with trees and knock themselves out in their chaotic attempt to flee.

Peccaries

Next to deer, peccaries are the most widely hunted game on the Yucatán Peninsula. Two species of peccaries are found here: the collared javelina peccary and the white-lipped peccary. The feisty collared javelina stands 50 centimeters (20 inches) at the shoulder and can be one meter (3.3 feet) long, weighing as much as 30 kilograms (66 pounds). It is black and white with a narrow, semicircular collar of white hair on the shoulders. The name javelina (which means spear in Spanish) comes from the two tusks that protrude from its mouth. A related species, the white-lipped peccary, is reddish brown to black and has an area of white around its mouth. Larger than the javelina, it can grow to 105 centimeters (41 inches) long, and is found deep in tropical rainforests living in herds of 100 or more. Peccaries often are compared to the wild pigs found in Europe, but in fact they belong to entirely different families.

Felines

Seven species of cats are found in North America, four in the tropics. One of them—the jaguar—is heavy chested with sturdy, muscled forelegs. It has small, rounded ears and its tail is relatively short. Its color varies from tan and white to pure black. The male can weigh 65-115 kilograms (143-254 pounds), females 45-85 kilograms (99-187 pounds). The largest of the cats on the peninsula, the jaguar is about the same size as a leopard. Other cats found here are the ocelot and puma. In tropical forests of the past, the large cats were the only predators capable of controlling the populations of hoofed game such as deer, peccaries, and tapirs. If hunting is poor and times are tough, the jaguar will go into rivers and scoop up fish with its large paws. The river is also one of the jaguar's favorite spots for hunting tapirs, when the latter come to drink.

Monkeys

The jungles of Mexico are home to three species of monkeys: spider, howler, and black howler. Intelligent and endearing, these creatures are prime targets for the pet trade. They have been so hunted, in fact, that today all three are in danger of extinction. Experts estimate that for every monkey sold, three die during transportation and distribution. In an effort to protect these creatures, the Mexican government has prohibited their capture or trade. Tropical monkeys are most active at sunrise and sundown. If you go to Cobá or Punta Laguna Spider Monkey Reserve, keep your ears perked and your eyes peeled. You may see—or at least hear—a few monkeys. If possible, consider waking early or staying late to increase your chances of spotting a few.

SEALIFE
Coral Reefs

The spectacular coral reefs that grace the peninsula's east coast are made up of millions of tiny carnivorous organisms called polyps. Individual polyps can be less than a centimeter (0.4 inch) long or up to 15 centimeters (6 inches) in diameter. Related to the jellyfish and sea anemone, coral polyps capture prey with tiny tentacles that deliver a deadly sting.

Reef-building polyps have limestone exoskeletons, which they create by extracting calcium from the seawater. Reefs are formed as generation after generation of polyps attach themselves to and atop each other. Different species attach in different ways, resulting in the many shapes and sizes of ocean reefs: delicate lace, trees with reaching branches, pleated mushrooms, stovepipes, petaled flowers, fans, domes, heads of cabbage, and stalks of broccoli. Though made up of individual polyps, coral structures function like a single organism, sharing nutrients through a central gastro-vascular system. Even in ideal conditions, most coral grows no more than five centimeters (two inches) per year.

Reefs are divided into three types: barrier, atoll, and fringing. A barrier reef runs parallel to the coast, with long stretches separated by narrow channels. The Mesoamerican Reef extends 250 kilometers (155 miles) from the tip of Isla Mujeres to Sapodilla Cay in the Gulf of Honduras—only the Great Barrier Reef in Australia is longer. An atoll typically forms around the crater of a submerged volcano. The polyps begin building their colonies along the lip of the crater, forming a circular coral island with a lagoon in the center. The Chinchorro Bank, off the southern coast of Quintana Roo, is the largest coral atoll in the northern hemisphere, measuring 48 kilometers long and 14 kilometers wide (30 miles by 9 miles). A fringing reef is coral living on a shallow shelf that extends outward from shore into the sea.

Fish

The Yucatán's barrier reef is home to myriad fish species, including parrot fish, candy bass, moray eels, spotted scorpion fish, turquoise angelfish, fairy basslets, flame fish, and gargantuan manta rays. Several species of shark also thrive in the waters off Quintana Roo, though they're not considered a serious threat to swimmers and divers. Sport fish—sailfish, marlin, and bluefin tuna—also inhabit the outer Caribbean waters.

Inland, anglers will find hard-fighting bonefish and pompano in the area's lagoons, and snorkelers and divers will find several species of blind fish in the crystal-clear waters of cenotes. These fish live out their existence in dark underground rivers and lakes and have no use for eyes.

Sea Turtles

Tens of thousands of sea turtles of various species once nested on the coastal beaches of Quintana Roo. As the coast became populated, turtles were severely overhunted for their eggs, meat, and shell, and their numbers began to fall. Hotel and resort developments have hastened the decline, as there are fewer and fewer patches of untrammeled sand in which turtles can dig nests and lay their eggs. The Mexican government and various ecological organizations are trying hard to save the dwindling turtle population. Turtle eggs are dug up and reburied in sand on safe beaches; or when the hatchlings break through their shells, they are brought to a beach and allowed to rush toward the sea in hopes of imprinting a sense of belonging there so that they will later return to the spot. In some cases the hatchlings are scooped up and placed in tanks to grow larger before being released into the open sea. The government is also enforcing tough penalties for people who take turtle eggs or capture, kill, or sell these creatures once they hatch.

Manatees

The manatee—sometimes called the sea cow—is a gentle, inquisitive giant. They are closely related to dugongs, and more distantly to elephants, aardvarks, and hyraxes. Newborns weigh 30-35 kilograms (66-77 pounds), while adults can measure four

sea turtle

meters (13 feet) in length and weigh nearly 1,600 kilograms (3,500 pounds). Shaped like an Idaho potato, manatees have coarse pinkish-gray skin, tiny sunken eyes, a flattened tail and flipper-like forelimbs (including toenails), and prehensile lips covered in sensitive whiskers. The manatee is the only aquatic mammal that's completely vegetarian, eating an astounding 10 percent of its body weight every day in aquatic grass and vegetation; it's unique among all mammals for constantly growing new teeth to replace those worn down by its voracious feeding.

Large numbers of them once roamed the shallow inlets, bays, and estuaries of the Caribbean; their images are frequently seen in the art of the ancient Maya, who hunted them for food. Today, though posing no threat to humans or other animals, and ecologically important for their ability to clear waterways of oxygen-choking vegetation, manatees are endangered in the Yucatán and elsewhere. The population has been reduced by the encroachment of people in their habitats along the river ways and shorelines. Ever-growing numbers of motorboats also inflict deadly gashes on these surface-feeding creatures. Nowadays it is very rare to spot one; the most sightings are reported in Punta Allen and Bahía de la Ascensión.

BIRDS

Since a major part of the Yucatán Peninsula is still undeveloped and covered with trees and brush, it isn't surprising to find exotic, rarely seen birds across the landscape. The Mexican government is beginning to realize the great value in this and is making efforts to protect nesting grounds. In addition to the growing number of nature reserves, some of the best bird-watching locales are the archaeological zones. At dawn and dusk, when most of the visitors are absent, the trees that surround the ancient structures come alive with birdsong. Of all the ruins, Cobá—with its marsh-rimmed lakes, nearby cornfields, and relatively tall, humid forest—is a particularly good site for bird-watching. One of the more impressive birds to look for here is the keel-billed toucan, often seen perched high on a bare limb in the early hours of the morning. Others include *chachalacas* (held in reverence by the Maya), screeching parrots, and, occasionally, the ocellated turkey.

Quetzals

Though the ancient Maya made abundant use of the dazzling quetzal feathers for ceremonial costumes and headdresses, they hunted other fowl for food; nevertheless, the quetzal is the only known bird from the pre-Columbian era and is now almost extinct. Today, they are still found (though rarely) in the high cloud forests of Chiapas and Central America, where they thrive on the constant moisture.

Estuaries

The Yucatán's countless estuaries, or *rías,* play host to hundreds of bird species; a boat ride into one of them will give you an opportunity to see American flamingos, a variety of wintering ducks from North America, blue-winged teals, northern shovelers, and lesser scaups. You'll also see a variety of wading birds feeding in the shallow waters, including numerous types of heron, snowy egret, and, in the summer, white ibis. There are 14 species of birds endemic to the Yucatán Peninsula, including the ocellated turkey, Yucatán whippoorwill, Yucatán flycatcher, orange oriole, black catbird, and the yellow-lored parrot. Río Lagartos and Celestún are the Yucatán's best-known and most-visited estuaries, but those in Sian Ka'an Biosphere Reserve and Xcalak are also vibrant and accessible.

REPTILES

Although reptiles thrive in Yucatán's warm, sunny environment, humans are their worst enemy. In the past, some species were greatly reduced in number—hunted for their unusual skin. Although hunting them is now illegal, black marketers still take their toll on the species.

Caymans

The cayman is a member of the crocodilian order. Its habits and appearance are similar to those of crocodiles, with the main difference being in its underskin: The cayman's skin is reinforced with bony plates on the belly, making it useless for the leather market. (Alligators and crocodiles, with smooth belly skin and sides, have been hunted almost to extinction in some parts of the world because of the value of their skin.)

Several species of cayman frequent the brackish inlet waters near the estuaries of Río Lagartos (literally, River of Lizards); though seen less frequently, they also inhabit mangroves on the Caribbean coast. A large cayman can be 2.5 meters (8.2 feet) long and very dark gray-green and broad-snouted with eyelids that look swollen and wrinkled. Some cayman species have eyelids that look like a pair of blunt horns. They are quicker than alligators and have longer, sharper teeth. Skilled hunters, cayman are quick in water and on land, and will attack a person if cornered. The best advice is to give caymans a wide berth if spotted.

Iguanas

This group of American lizards—Iguanidae family—includes various large plant-eaters seen frequently in Quintana Roo. Iguanas grow to be one meter (3.3 feet) long and have a blunt head and long flat tail. Bands of black and gray circle its body, and a serrated column reaches down the middle of its back almost to the tail. The young iguana is bright emerald-green and often supplements its diet by eating insects and larvae.

The lizard's forelimbs hold the front half of its body up off the ground while its two back limbs are kept relaxed and splayed alongside its hindquarters. When the iguana is frightened, however, its hind legs do everything they're supposed to, and the iguana crashes quickly (though clumsily) into the brush searching for its burrow and safety. This reptile is not aggressive—it mostly enjoys basking in the bright sunshine along the Caribbean—but if cornered it will bite and use its tail in self-defense.

From centuries past, recorded references attest to the iguana's medicinal value, which partly explains the active trade of live iguana in the marketplaces. Iguana stew is believed to cure or relieve various human ailments.

Other Lizards

You'll see a great variety of other lizards on

caymans

the peninsula; some are brightly striped in various shades of green and yellow, while others are earth-toned and blend in with the gray and beige limestone that dots the landscape. Skinny as wisps of thread running on hind legs, or chunky and waddling with armor-like skin, the range is endless and fascinating.

Be sure to look for the black anole, which changes colors to match its environment, either when danger is imminent or as subterfuge to fool the insects on which it feeds. At mating time, the male anole puffs out its bright-red throat-fan so that all female lizards will see it.

Coral Snakes

Two species of coral snakes, which are related to the cobra, are found in the southern part of the Yucatán Peninsula. They have prominent rings around their bodies in the same sequence of red, black, yellow, or white and grow to 1-1.5 meters (3.3-4.9 feet). Their bodies are slender, with no pronounced distinction between the head and neck.

Coral snakes spend the day in mossy clumps under rocks or logs, emerging only at night. Though the bite of a coral snake can kill within 24 hours, chances of the average tourist being bitten by a coral (or any other) snake are slim.

Tropical Rattlesnakes

The tropical rattlesnake (*cascabel* in Spanish) is the deadliest and most treacherous species of rattler. It differs slightly from other species by having vividly contrasting neckbands. It grows 2-2.5 meters (6.6-8.2 feet) long and is found mainly in the higher and drier areas of the tropics. Contrary to popular myth, this serpent doesn't always rattle a warning of its impending strike.

INSECTS AND ARACHNIDS

Air-breathing invertebrates are unavoidable in any tropical locale. Some are annoying (gnats and no-see-ums), some are dangerous (black widows, bird spiders, and scorpions), and others can cause pain when they bite (red ants); but many are beautiful (butterflies and moths), and *all* are fascinating.

Butterflies and Moths

The Yucatán has an incredible abundance of beautiful moths and butterflies, some 40,000 species in all. Hikers might see the magnificent blue morpho, orange-barred sulphur,

butterfly spotting in the Yucatán

copperhead, cloudless sulphur, malachite, admiral, calico, ruddy dagger-wing, tropical buckeye, and emperor. The famous monarch is also a visitor during its annual migration from the northeastern United States. It usually makes a stopover on Quintana Roo's east coast on its way south to the Central American mountains where it spends the winter. The huge black witch moth—males can have a wingspan of seven inches and are sometimes mistaken for bats—is called *mariposa de la muerte* ("butterfly of death" in Spanish) or *ma ha na* (Yucatec Maya for "enter the home"), stemming from a common belief that if the moth enters the home of a sick person, that person will soon die.

Spiders and Scorpions

The Yucatán has some scary-looking spiders and scorpions (*arañas* and *alacranes*), but none is particularly dangerous. The Yucatán rust rump tarantula is surely the most striking, a hairy medium-size tarantula with long legs and a distinctive orange or rust-colored rear. Like most tarantulas, they are nocturnal and fairly timid, with females spending much of their time in burrows in the ground, and males roaming around incessantly looking for them. Its bite is harmless, but that doesn't

mean you should handle one: When threatened, tarantulas can shake off a cloud of tiny hairs, which are highly irritating if inhaled.

The Yucatán's long black scorpions—up to 10 centimeters (4 inches)!—have a painful sting that can cause swelling, and for some people shortness of breath, but is not deadly. Like tarantulas, scorpions avoid human contact and are therefore rare to see; that said, it's always a good idea to shake out shoes and beach towels before using them, just in case.

Bees

The Yucatán's most famous bee—of numerous species found here—is the aptly named Yucatán bee, also known as the Maya bee. The small stingless insect produces a particularly sweet honey that was prized by the ancient Maya, and was one of the most widely traded commodities in the Maya world. (Some researchers say the Descending God figure at Tulum and other archaeological sites is the god of bees.) The ancient Maya were expert beekeepers, a tradition that lives on today, albeit much reduced thanks in part to the availability of cheap standard honey. Yucatán honey (harvested using more modern methods) is still sold in Mexico and abroad, mostly online and in organic and specialty stores.

History

ACROSS THE BERING LAND BRIDGE

People and animals from Asia crossed the Bering land bridge into North America in the Pleistocene epoch about 50,000 years ago, when sea levels were much lower. As early as 10,000 BC, Ice Age humans hunted woolly mammoth and other large animals roaming the cool, moist landscape of central Mexico. The earliest traces of humans in the Yucatán Peninsula are obsidian spear points and stone tools dating to 9,000 BC. The Loltún caves in the state of Yucatán contained a cache of mammoth bones, which are thought to have

been dragged there by a roving band of hunters. As the region dried out and large game disappeared in the next millennia, tools of a more settled way of life appeared, such as grinding stones for preparing seeds and plant fibers.

ANCIENT CIVILIZATION

Between 7,000 and 2,000 BC, society evolved from hunting and gathering to farming; corn, squash, and beans were independently cultivated in widely separated areas in Mexico. Archaeologists believe that the earliest people who we can call Maya, or proto-Maya,

inhabited the Pacific coast of Chiapas and Guatemala. These tribes lived in villages that held more than 1,000 inhabitants apiece; beautiful painted and incised ceramic jars for food storage have been found from this region and time period. After 1,000 BC this way of life spread south to the highlands site of Kaminaljuyú (now part of Guatemala City) and, through the next millennium, to the rest of the Maya world. Meanwhile, in what are now the Mexican states of Veracruz and Tabasco, another culture, the Olmecs, was developing what is now considered Mesoamerica's first civilization. Its influence was felt throughout Mexico and Central America. Archaeologists believe that before the Olmecs disappeared around 300 BC, they contributed two crucial cultural advances to the Maya: the Long Count calendar and the hieroglyphic writing system.

LATE PRECLASSIC PERIOD

intricately decorated pottery at the Museo Maya de Cancún

During the Late Preclassic era (300 BC-AD 250), the Pacific coastal plain saw the rise of a Maya culture in Izapa near Tapachula, Chiapas. The Izapans worshipped gods that were precursors of the Classic Maya pantheon and commemorated religious and historical events in bas-relief carvings that emphasized costume and finery.

During the same period, the northern Guatemalan highlands were booming with construction; this was the heyday of Kaminaljuyú, which grew to enormous size, with more than 120 temple-mounds and numerous stelae. The earliest calendar inscription that researchers are able to read comes from a monument found at El Baúl to the southwest of Kaminaljuyú; it has been translated as AD 36.

In the Petén jungle region just north of the highlands, the dominant culture was the Chicanel, whose hallmarks are elaborate temple-pyramids lined with enormous stucco god-masks (as in Kohunlich). The recently excavated Petén sites of Nakbé and El Mirador are the most spectacular Chicanel cities yet found. El Mirador contains a 70-meter-tall (230-foot) temple-pyramid complex that is the tallest ancient structure in Mesoamerica. Despite the obvious prosperity of this region, there is almost no evidence of Long Count dates or writing systems in either the Petén jungle or the Yucatán Peninsula just to the north.

EARLY CLASSIC PERIOD

The great efflorescence of the southern Maya world stopped at the end of the Early Classic period (AD 250-600). Kaminaljuyú and other cities were abandoned; researchers believe that the area was invaded by Teotihuacano warriors extending the reach of their Valley of Mexico-based empire. On the Yucatán Peninsula, there is evidence of Teotihuacano occupation at the Río Bec site of Becán and at Acanceh near Mérida. You can see Teotihuacano-style costumes and gods in carvings at the great Petén city of Tikal and at Copán in Honduras. By AD 600, the Teotihuacano empire had

Early Civilizations and Maya Timeline

- **Paleoindian:** before 7000 BC
- **Archaic:** 7000-2500 BC
- **Early Preclassic:** 2500-1000 BC
- **Middle Preclassic:** 1000-400 BC
- **Late Preclassic:** 400 BC-AD 250
- **Early Classic:** AD 250-600
- **Late Classic:** AD 600-800
- **Terminal Classic:** AD 800-1000
- **Early Postclassic:** AD 1000-1250
- **Late Postclassic:** AD 1250-1519

contained 50,000 inhabitants, and there was vigorous intercity trade. Each Classic city-state reached its apogee at a different time; the southern cities peaked first, with the northern Puuc region cities following close behind.

By AD 925, nearly all of the city-states had collapsed and were left in a state of near-abandonment. The Classic Maya decline is one of the great enigmas of Mesoamerican archaeology. There are a myriad of theories—disease, invasion, peasant revolt—but many researchers now believe the collapse was caused by a combination of factors, including overpopulation, environmental degradation, and a series of devastating droughts. With the abandonment of the cities, the cultural advances disappeared as well. The last Long Count date was recorded in AD 909, and many religious customs and beliefs were never seen again.

collapsed, and the stage was set for the Classic Maya eras.

LATE CLASSIC PERIOD

The Maya heartland of the Late Classic period (AD 600-900) extended from Copán in Honduras through Tikal in Guatemala and ended at Palenque in Chiapas. The development of these city-states, which also included Yaxchilán and Bonampak, almost always followed the same pattern. Early in this era, a new and vigorous breed of rulers founded a series of dynasties bent on deifying themselves and their ancestors. All the arts and sciences of the Maya world, from architecture to astronomy, were focused on this goal. The Long Count calendar and the hieroglyphic writing system were the most crucial tools in this effort, as the rulers needed to recount the stories of their dynasties and of their own glorious careers.

During the Late Classic era, painting, sculpture, and carving reached their climax; objects such as Lord Pakal's sarcophagus lid from Palenque are now recognized as among the finest pieces of world art. Royal monuments stood at the center of large and bustling cities. Cobá and Dzibilchaltún each probably

EARLY POSTCLASSIC PERIOD

After the Puuc region was abandoned—almost certainly because of a foreign invasion—the center of Maya power moved east to Chichén. During this Early Postclassic era (AD 925-1200), the Toltec influence took hold, marking the end of the most artistic era and the birth of a new militaristic society built around a blend of ceremonialism, civic and social organization, and conquest. Chichén was the great power of northern Yucatán. Competing city-states either submitted to its warriors or, like the Puuc cities and Cobá, were destroyed.

LATE POSTCLASSIC PERIOD

After Chichén's fall in AD 1224—probably due to an invasion—a heretofore lowly tribe calling themselves the Itzá became the Late Postclassic (AD 1200-1530) masters of Yucatecan power politics. Kukulcán II of Chichén founded Mayapán in AD 1263-1283. After his death and the abandonment of Chichén, an aggressive Itzá lineage named the Cocom seized power and used Mayapán as a base to take over northern Yucatán. They succeeded through wars using Tabascan mercenaries and intermarrying with other powerful lineages. Foreign lineage heads were forced to live in Mayapán where they could easily be controlled. At its height, the city covered 6.5 square kilometers (4 square miles) within a defensive wall that contained more than 15,000 inhabitants. Architecturally, Mayapán leaves much to be desired; the city plan was haphazard, and its greatest monument was a sloppy, smaller copy of Chichén's Pyramid of Kukulcán.

The Cocom ruled for 250 years until AD 1441-1461, when an upstart Uxmal-based lineage named the Xiu rebelled and slaughtered the Cocom. Mayapán was abandoned and Yucatán's city-states were weakened in a series of bloody intramural wars that left them hopelessly divided when the conquistadors arrived. By the time of that conquest, culture was once again being imported from outside the Maya world. Putún Maya seafaring traders brought new styles of art and religious beliefs back from their trips to central Mexico. Their influence can be seen in the Mixtec-style frescoes at Tulum on the Quintana Roo coast.

SPANISH ARRIVAL AND CONQUEST

After Columbus's arrival in the New World, other adventurers traveling the same seas soon found the Yucatán Peninsula. In 1519, 34-year-old Hernán Cortés set out from Cuba—against the wishes of the Spanish governor—with 11 ships, 120 sailors, and 550 soldiers to search for slaves, a lucrative business. His search began on the Yucatán coast but eventually encompassed most of present-day Mexico. However, it took many decades and many lives for Spanish conquistadors to quell the Maya's resistance and cunning, despite a major advantage in military technology, including horses, gunpowder, and metal swords and armor. Francisco de Montejo, who took part in Cortés's earlier expedition into central Mexico, spent 1528-1535 trying to conquer the Yucatán, first from the east at Tulum and later from the west near Campeche and Tabasco,

but was driven out each time. Montejo's son, also named Francisco de Montejo "El Mozo" (The Younger), took up the effort and eventually founded the city of Mérida in 1542 and Campeche in 1546. From those strongholds, the Spanish conquest slowly spread across the peninsula.

Economic and religious oppression were central to the conquest, too. The Xiu indigenous group proved an important ally to the Spanish after its leader converted to Christianity. And in 1562, a friar named Diego de Landa, upon learning his converts still practiced certain Maya ceremonies, became enraged and ordered the torture and imprisonment of numerous Maya spiritual leaders. He also gathered all the religious artifacts and Maya texts—which he said contained "superstitions and the devil's lies"—and had them burned. It was a staggering loss—at least 27 codices—and one that Landa later seemed to regret and attempted to reconcile by writing a detailed record of Maya customs, mathematics, and writing.

The Caste War

By the 1840s, the brutalized and subjugated Maya organized a revolt against Euro-Mexican colonizers. Called the Caste War, this savage war saw Maya taking revenge on every white man, woman, and child by means of murder and rape. European survivors made their way to the last Spanish strongholds of Mérida and Campeche. The governments of the two cities appealed for help to Spain, France, and the United States. No one answered the call. It was soon apparent that the remaining two cities would be wiped out.

But just as Mérida's leaders were preparing to evacuate the city, the Maya abruptly picked up their weapons and left. The reason was an unusually early appearance of flying ants, a sign of coming rain and to the Maya an all-important signal to begin planting corn. Despite the suffering visited upon them over three centuries of Spanish conquest, the Maya warriors, who were also farmers, simply could not risk missing the planting season. They turned

Fray Diego de Landa

Just north of Oxkutzcab, the town of Maní has a quiet, peaceful atmosphere that belies a wrenching history. It was here, in 1562, that Friar Diego de Landa conducted a now-infamous *auto de fé*, in which he burned at least two dozen irreplaceable Maya codices and thousands of painted vases and other items, because he deemed them works of the devil. He accused numerous Maya religious leaders and laypeople of idolatry, and ordered them tortured, publicly humiliated, and imprisoned. The act was outrageous, even by Spanish colonial standards, and Landa was shipped back to Spain to face the Council of the Indies, the colonial authority, for conducting an illegal inquisition. He was eventually absolved—a panel of inspectors found he had broken no laws—but not before Landa came to regret his act, at least somewhat. Confined to a convent awaiting judgment, he set about writing down all he could remember about the Maya.

It was no minor undertaking: Landa spoke Yucatec Maya fluently, and had lived, traveled, and preached throughout the Yucatán for 13 years before his expulsion. In all, Landa spent close to a decade completing *An Account of the Things of Yucatán*. He returned to Mérida in 1571 as the newly appointed bishop of Yucatán, and died there in 1579. Landa's manuscript was largely forgotten until being rediscovered in 1863. Among other things, the manuscript contains a crude alphabet (or more precisely, a syllabary), which has proved invaluable to the modern-day decoding of the Maya hieroglyphics. Ironically, the very man who destroyed so much of the Maya's written history also provided the key for future researchers to unlock what remained.

their backs on certain victory and returned to their villages to tend their fields.

The unexpected reprieve allowed time for thousands of troops to arrive from Cuba, Mexico City, and the United States, and vengeance was merciless. Maya were killed indiscriminately. Some were taken prisoner and sold to Cuba as slaves; others left their villages and hid in the jungles—in some cases, for decades. Between 1846 and 1850, the population of the Yucatán Peninsula was reduced from 500,000 to 300,000. Quintana Roo along the Caribbean coast was considered a dangerous no-man's-land for almost another 100 years.

Growing Maya Power

Many Maya Indians escaped slaughter during the Caste War by fleeing to the isolated coastal forests of present-day Quintana Roo. A large number regrouped under the cult of the "Talking Cross"—an actual wooden cross that, with the help of a priest and a ventriloquist, spoke to the beleaguered indigenous fighters, urging them to continue fighting. Followers called themselves *Cruzob* (People of the Cross) and made a stronghold in the town of Chan Santa Cruz, today Carrillo Puerto.

Research (and common sense) suggests the Maya knew full well that a human voice was responsible for the "talking," but that many believed it was inspired by God.

Close to the border with British Honduras (now Belize), the leaders of Chan Santa Cruz began selling timber to the British and were given weapons in return. Simultaneously (roughly 1855-1857), internal strife weakened the relations between Campeche and Mérida, and their mutual defense as well. Maya leaders took advantage of the conflict and attacked Fort Bacalar, eventually gaining control of the entire southern Caribbean coast.

Up until that time, indigenous soldiers simply killed the people they captured, but starting in 1858 they took lessons from the colonials and began to keep whites for slave labor. Women were put to work doing household chores and some became concubines, while men were forced to work the fields and build new constructions. (The main church in Carrillo Puerto was built largely by white slaves.)

For the next 40 years, the Maya people and soldiers based in and around Chan Santa Cruz kept the east coast of the Yucatán for themselves, and a shaky truce with the Mexican government endured. The native people were economically independent, self-governing, and, with no roads in or out of the region, almost totally isolated. They were not at war as long as everyone left them alone.

The Last Stand

Only when President Porfirio Díaz took power in 1877 did the Mexican federal government begin to think seriously about the Yucatán Peninsula. Through the years, Quintana Roo's isolation and the strength of the Maya in their treacherous jungle had foiled repeated efforts by Mexican soldiers to capture the region. The army's expeditions were infrequent, but it rankled Díaz that a relatively small and modestly armed Maya force had been able to keep the Mexican army at bay for so long. An assault in 1901, under the command of General Ignacio Bravo, broke the government's losing streak. The general captured a village, laid railroad tracks, and built a walled fort. Supplies arriving by rail kept the fort stocked, but the indigenous defenders responded by holding the fort under siege for an entire year. Reinforcements finally came from the capital and the Maya were forced to retreat, first from the fort and then from many of their villages and strongholds. A period of brutal Mexican occupation followed, lasting until 1915, yet Maya partisans still didn't give up. They conducted guerrilla raids from the tangled coastal forest until the Mexican army, frustrated and demoralized, pulled out and returned Quintana Roo to the Maya.

Beginning in 1917 and lasting to 1920, however, influenza and smallpox swept through the Maya-held territories, killing hundreds of thousands of Maya. In 1920, with the last of their army severely diminished and foreign gum-tappers creeping into former Maya territories, indigenous leaders entered into a negotiated settlement with the Mexican federal government. The final treaties were signed in 1936, erasing the last vestiges of Maya national sovereignty in the region.

LAND REFORMS

Beginning in 1875, international demand for twine and rope made from henequen, a type of agave cactus that thrives in northern Yucatán, brought prosperity to Mérida, the state capital. Beautiful mansions were built by entrepreneurs who led the good life, sending their children to school in Europe and cruising with their wives to New Orleans in search of new luxuries and entertainment. Port towns were

The banner on this mural, located in the Plaza Central of Carrillo Puerto, reads "The Maya region is not an ethnographic museum, it is a people on the move."

developed on the Gulf coast, and a two-kilo-meter (1.2-mile) wharf in Progreso was built to accommodate the large ships that came for sisal (hemp from the henequen plant).

The only thing that didn't change was the lifestyle of indigenous people, who provided most of the labor on colonial haciendas. Henequen plants have incredibly hard, sharp spines and at certain times emit a horrendous stench. Maya workers labored long, hard hours, living in constant debt to the hacienda store.

Prosperity helped bring the Yucatán to the attention of the world. But in 1908, an American journalist named John Kenneth Turner stirred things up when he documented the difficult lives of the indigenous plantation workers and the accompanying opulence enjoyed by the owners. The report set a series of reforms into motion. Carrillo Puerto, the first socialist governor of Mérida, helped native workers set up a labor union, educational center, and political club that served to organize and focus resistance to the powerful hacienda system. Carrillo made numerous agrarian reforms, including decreeing that abandoned haciendas could be appropriated by the government. With his power and popularity growing, conservatives saw only one way to stop him. In 1923, Carrillo Puerto was assassinated.

By then, though, the Mexican Revolution had been won and reforms were being made throughout the country, including redistribution of land and mandatory education. Mexico entered its golden years, a 40-year period of sustained and substantial growth dubbed The Mexican Miracle, all the more miraculous because it took place in defiance of the worldwide Great Depression. In the late 1930s, President Lázaro Cárdenas undertook a massive nationalization program, claiming the major electricity, oil, and other companies for the state, and created state-run companies like PEMEX, the oil conglomerate still in existence today. In the Yucatán, Cárdenas usurped large parts of hacienda lands—as much as half of the Yucatán's total arable land, by some accounts, most dedicated to the growing of henequen—and redistributed it to poor farmers.

THE PRI YEARS

The economic prosperity allowed the ruling Institutional Revolutionary Party (PRI) to consolidate power, and before long it held every major office in the federal government, and most state governments as well. The Mexican Miracle had not ameliorated all

henequen, a type of agave cactus that thrives in northern Yucatán

social inequalities—and in fact had exacerbated some—but the PRI grew increasingly intolerant of dissent. Deeply corrupt, the party—and by extension the state—resorted to brutal and increasingly blatant repression to silence detractors. The most notorious example was the gunning down of scores of student demonstrators—some say up to 250—by security forces in 1968 in Mexico City's Tlatelolco Plaza. The massacre took place at night; by morning the plaza was cleared of bodies and scrubbed of blood, and the government simply denied that it ever happened.

The oil crisis that struck the United States in the early 1970s was at first a boon for Mexico, whose coffers were filled with money from pricey oil exports. But a failure to diversify the economy left Mexico vulnerable; as oil prices stabilized, the peso began to devalue. It had fallen as much as 500 percent by 1982, prompting then-president López Portillo to nationalize Mexico's banks. Foreign investment quickly dried up, and the 1980s were dubbed La Década Perdida (The Lost Decade) for Mexico and much of Latin America, a time of severe economic stagnation and crisis. In September 1985, a magnitude-8.1 earthquake struck Mexico City, killing 9,000 people and leaving 100,000 more homeless. It seemed Mexico had hit its nadir.

Yet it was during this same period that Cancún began to take off as a major vacation destination, drawing tourism and much-needed foreign dollars into the Mexican economy. The crises were not over—the implementation of the North American Free Trade Agreement (NAFTA) in 1994 was met simultaneously by a massive devaluation of the peso and an armed uprising by a peasant army called the Zapatistas in the state of Chiapas—but Mexico's economy regained some of its footing. A series of electoral reforms implemented in the late 1980s and through the 1990s paved the way for the historic 2000 presidential election, in which an opposition candidate—former Coca-Cola executive Vicente Fox of the right-of-center Partido de Acción Nacional (PAN)—defeated the PRI, ending the latter's 70-year reign of power. Fox was succeeded in 2006 by another PAN member, Felipe Calderón Hinojosa, in an election in which the PRI finished a distant third.

President Calderón campaigned on a promise to expand Mexico's job market and encourage foreign investment, including for new tourism projects in the Yucatán and elsewhere. But it was another pledge—to break up the drug trade and the cartels that controlled it—that consumed his entire presidency and plunged parts of Mexico into a spasm of violence unlike any since the revolution.

THE DRUG WARS

"The Drug War," as it is generally called, has its roots in the insatiable demand for drugs in the United States. Mexican drug cartels gained strength as operations in Colombia and the Caribbean were choked off in the 1990s; drug production in Mexico itself has also grown, especially methamphetamines. Mexican cartels traditionally operated within strictly defined territories—such as the Gulf cartel, the Sinaloa cartel, the Juárez cartel—and did so largely with impunity, thanks to corruption in the police and PRI-controlled local governments. The arrangement, though illicit, kept violence to a minimum as cartels kept to themselves and politicians and police turned a blind eye.

In 2006, encouraged by the United States, President Calderón dispatched the Mexican military to various northern cities to break up the cartels and their distribution networks. They achieved some initial success, but the broader effect was to disrupt the longtime balance of power. As control of routes and territories wavered, violence between rival cartels erupted with shocking speed and ferocity, with frequent shoot-outs and a gruesome cycle of attacks and reprisals. The official death toll is a staggering 60,000 people, though some estimates put it at double that. The vast majority of victims were gang-affiliated, though at least 2,000 police, soldiers, journalists, politicians, and even children were killed; 27,000 people are still classified as "missing." It's notable that virtually all the weapons used in the drug war were smuggled there from the United States.

MEXICO TODAY

In 2012, Mexico's national soccer team won its first Olympic gold medal, defeating heavily favored Brazil at the London games. It was a small blessing perhaps, but one that lifted the country's collective spirit. The election in 2012 of PRI candidate Enrique Peña Nieto seemed to signal an end to the drug war; Peña Nieto has focused on addressing drug abuse, unemployment, and corruption on a local level, and drug-related violence has diminished markedly. The Mexican military made several high-profile arrests, including the notorious cartel leader Joaquin "El Chapo" Guzmán Loera in Mazatlán in February 2014. The relative calm was shaken, however, with the kidnapping and murder of 43 student-teachers in the state of Guerrero in September 2014. They were traveling to the city of Iguala to protest a conference hosted by the mayor's wife; the mayor reportedly ordered police to intercept the students and turn them over to a local drug gang to be killed. The crime sparked nationwide protests. The mayor and his wife were arrested after fleeing the state, the governor resigned, and over 40 police officers were arrested; the police chief remains a fugitive. Peña Nieto, already at odds with the country's powerful teacher unions, was roundly criticized for a too-tepid reaction.

The trauma of "Los 43" notwithstanding, Mexico has mostly disappeared from the front page and reappeared in the travel section. Tourism has bounced back stronger than ever, with record numbers of visitors, especially to Cancún and the Riviera Maya. Low world oil prices and a downward creep of the peso's value during 2014 and 2015 have left Mexico with less buying power than expected, though plans to invest over US$1 billion in infrastructure remain mostly on track. Visitors will notice new roads, bridges, and bus and ferry terminals; alas, plans to construct high-speed trains between Playa del Carmen and Mérida were scuttled.

Government and Economy

GOVERNMENT

Mexico enjoys a constitutional democracy modeled after that of the United States, including a president (who serves one six-year term), a two-house legislature, and a judiciary branch. For 66 years (until the year 2000), Mexico was controlled by one party, the so-called moderate Partido Revolucionario Institucional (PRI). A few cities and states elected candidates from the main opposition parties—the conservative Partido de Acción Nacional (PAN) and leftist Partido de la Revolución Democrática (PRD)—but the presidency and most of the important government positions were passed from one hand-picked PRI candidate to the next, amid rampant electoral fraud.

Indeed, fraud and corruption have been ugly mainstays of Mexican government for generations. In the 1988 presidential election, PRI candidate Carlos Salinas Gortari officially garnered 51 percent of the vote, a dubious result judging from polls leading up to the election, and rendered laughable after a mysterious "breakdown" in the election tallying system delayed the results for several days.

Salinas Gortari ended his term under the same heavy clouds of corruption and fraud that ushered him in, accused of having stolen millions of dollars from the federal government during his term. That said, Salinas pushed through changes such as increasing the number of Senate seats and reorganizing the federal electoral commission that helped usher in freer and fairer elections. He also oversaw the adoption of NAFTA in 1993, which has sped up Mexico's manufacturing industry but seriously damaged other sectors, especially small farmers, many of whom are indigenous.

The 1994 presidential election was marred by the assassination in Tijuana of the PRI candidate Luis Donaldo Colosio, the country's first major political assassination since 1928. Colosio's campaign manager, technocrat Ernesto Zedillo, was nominated to fill the candidacy and eventually elected. Zedillo continued with reforms, and in 2000, for the first time in almost seven decades, the opposition candidate officially won. PAN candidate Vicente Fox, a businessman and former Coca-Cola executive from Guanajuato, took the reins, promising continued electoral reforms, a stronger private sector, and closer relations with the United States. He knew U.S. president-elect George W. Bush personally, having worked with him on border issues during Bush's term as governor of Texas. Progress was being made until the terrorist attacks of September 11, 2001, pushed Mexico far down on the U.S. administration's priority list. With Mexico serving a term on the U.N. Security Council, Fox came under intense pressure from the United States to support an invasion of Iraq. He ultimately refused—Mexican people were overwhelmingly opposed to the idea—but it cost Fox dearly in his relationship with Bush. The reforms he once seemed so ideally poised to achieve were largely incomplete by the time Fox's term ended.

The presidential elections of 2006 were bitterly contested and created—or exposed—a deep schism in the country. The eventual winner was PAN candidate Felipe Calderón Hinojosa, a former secretary of energy under Fox. His main opponent, Andrés Manuel López Obrador, was a former mayor of Mexico City and member of the left-leaning PRD. Though fraught with accusations and low blows, the campaign also was a classic clash of ideals, with Calderón advocating increased foreign investment and free trade, and López Obrador assailing the neo-liberal model and calling for government action to reduce poverty and strengthen social services. Both men claimed victory after Election Day; when Calderón was declared the winner, López Obrador alleged widespread fraud and called for a total recount. His supporters blocked major thoroughfares throughout the country for weeks. The Mexican Electoral Commission did a selective recount and affirmed a Calderón victory; the official figures set the margin at under 244,000 votes out of 41 million cast, a difference of just 0.5 percent. Calderón's inauguration was further marred by legislators fist-fighting in the chamber and the new president shouting his oath over jeers and general ruckus.

Calderón was confronted with a number of thorny problems upon inauguration, including a protest in Oaxaca that had turned violent, and spiraling corn prices that in turn drove up the cost of tortillas, the most basic of Mexican foods. While addressing those and other issues, he pressed forward with promised law-and-order reforms, raising police officers' wages and dispatching the Mexican military to staunch rampant gang- and drug-related crime in cities like Tijuana and Juárez. The latter sparked an all-out war between cartels, police, and the military.

In 2012, Mexicans elected Enrique Peña Nieto, the PRI candidate, as president. The results may be less a sign that Mexicans have forgiven the PRI its misdeeds of the not-so-distant past, and rather that they're simply exhausted by the violence that's taken place under the PAN (whose candidate finished a distant third). Peña Nieto has quietly shifted the federal government's focus to addressing drug abuse, unemployment, and corruption on a local level, while still pursuing arrests of high-profile cartel leaders. His term runs until 2018.

ECONOMY
Oil

Oil is a leading industry on the Yucatán Peninsula and throughout the Gulf coast, from Campeche to the Texas border. Mexico has long been one of the largest oil producers in the Western Hemisphere and the world, and for years it was a net exporter of crude oil and natural gas to the United States and elsewhere. However, declining crude oil production in the Gulf of Mexico, a lack of refining capacity in Mexico, and the rapid expansion of U.S. natural gas production (and high Mexican demand for natural gas) has turned the relationship on its head. Mexico still exports crude oil to the United States, but is one of the main importers of American refined products like gasoline. Mexico also imports natural gas and liquified natural gas from the United States, spurring plans for cross-border pipelines. Cities in the Yucatán Peninsula have long benefitted from Mexico's strong energy sector, but the effects of the worldwide decline in oil prices, coupled with a shifting relationship with the United States, may change spell changes for the future.

Fishing

Yucatecan fisheries also are abundant along the Gulf coast. At one time fishing was not much more than a family business, but today fleets of large purse seiners with their adjacent processing plants can be seen on the Gulf of Mexico. With the renewed interest in preserving fishing grounds for the future, the industry could continue to thrive for many years.

Tourism

Until the 1970s, Quintana Roo's economy amounted to very little. For a few years the chicle boom brought a flurry of activity up and down the state—it was shipped from the harbor of Isla Cozumel. Native and hardwood trees have always been in demand; coconuts and fishing were the only other natural resources that added to the economy, but neither on a large scale.

With the development of an offshore sandbar—Cancún—into a multimillion-dollar resort town, tourism became the region's number-one moneymaker. The development of the Riviera Maya (extending from Cancún to Tulum)—and now, the Costa Maya (south of Sian Ka'an to the border of Belize)—only guaranteed the continued success of the economy. New roads now give access to previously unknown beaches and Maya structures. Extra attention is going to archaeological zones ignored for hundreds of years. All but the smallest have restrooms, ticket offices, and gift shops.

Fishing remains a major source of income for locals.

People and Culture

DEMOGRAPHICS

Today, 75-80 percent of the Mexican population is estimated to be mestizo (a combination of the indigenous and Spanish-Caucasian races). Only 10-15 percent are considered to be indigenous peoples. For comparison, as recently as 1870, the indigenous made up more than 50 percent of the population. While there are important native communities throughout Mexico, the majority of the country's indigenous peoples live in the Yucatán Peninsula, Oaxaca, and Chiapas.

RELIGION

The vast majority of Mexicans are Roman Catholic, especially in the generally conservative Yucatán Peninsula. However, a vigorous evangelical movement gains more and more converts every year.

Regional Holidays and Celebrations

- Jan. 1: **New Year's Day**

- Jan. 6: **Día de los Reyes Magos:** Three Kings Day—Christmas gifts exchanged

- Feb. 2: **Virgen de la Candelaria:** Religious candlelight processions light up several towns

- Feb./Mar.: **Carnaval:** Seven-day celebration before Ash Wednesday

- Mar. 21: **Birthday of Benito Juárez:** President of Mexico for five terms; born in 1806

- Mar. 21: **Vernal Equinox in Chichén Itzá:** A phenomenon of light and shadow displays a serpent slithering down the steps of El Castillo

- May 1: **Día del Trabajador:** Labor Day

- May 3: **Day of the Holy Cross:** Dance of the Pigs' Head performed in Carrillo Puerto

- May 5: **Cinco de Mayo:** Commemoration of the Mexican army's 1862 defeat of the French at the Battle of Puebla

- Sept. 16: **Independence Day:** Celebrated on the night of the 15th

- Oct. 12: **Día de la Raza:** Indigenous Peoples Day; celebrated instead of Columbus Day

- Nov. 1-2: **All Souls' Day and Day of the Dead:** Church ceremonies and graveside celebrations in honor of the deceased

- Nov. 20: **Día de la Revolución:** Celebration of the beginning of the Mexican Revolution in 1910

- Dec. 12: **Virgen de Guadalupe:** Religious celebration in honor of Mexico's patron saint

- Dec. 25: **Christmas:** Celebrated on the night of the 24th

Papel Picado

Mexicans are famous for their celebrations—whether it's to honor a patron saint or to celebrate a neighbor's birthday, partying is part of the culture. Typically, fiestas feature live music, lots of food, fireworks, and brightly colored decorations, often including *papel picado* (literally, diced paper).

Papel picado is tissue paper cut or stamped with a design that reflects the occasion in some way: a manger scene at Christmas, church bells for a wedding, skeletons in swooping hats for Day of the Dead. Once cut, row upon row of *papel picado* is strung across city streets, in front of churches, or in people's backyards. It typically stays up until wind or rain leaves just a thin cord and a few bits of torn paper as a reminder of the celebration that was.

LANGUAGE

The farther away you are from a city in the Yucatán—and Mexico in general—the less Spanish you'll hear and the more dialects of indigenous languages you'll encounter. The government estimates that of the 10 million indigenous people in the country, about 25 percent do not speak Spanish. Of the original 125 native languages, 70 are still spoken, 20 of which are classified as Maya languages, including Tzeltal, Tzotzil, Chol, and Yucatec.

Although education was made compulsory for children in 1917, this law was not enforced in the Yucatán Peninsula until recently. Today, schools throughout the peninsula use Spanish-language books, even though many children do not speak the language. In some of the rural schools, bilingual teachers are recruited to help children make the transition.

ART

Mexico has an incredibly rich colonial and folk-art tradition. While not considered art to the people who make and use it, traditional indigenous clothing is beautiful, and travelers and collectors are increasingly able to buy it in local shops and markets. Prices for these items can be high, for the simple fact that they are hand-woven and can literally take months to complete. Valladolid is an especially good place to purchase pottery, carving, and textiles from around the Yucatán and beyond.

HOLIDAYS AND FESTIVALS

Mexicans take celebrations and holidays seriously—of their country, their saints, and their families. You'll be hard-pressed to find a two-week period when something or someone isn't being celebrated. On major holidays—Christmas, New Year's Eve, and Easter—be prepared for crowds at the beaches and ruins. Be sure to book your hotel and buy your airline and bus tickets well in advance; during holidays, the travel industry is saturated with Mexican travelers.

In addition to officially recognized holidays, villages and cities hold numerous festivals and celebrations: for patron saints, birthdays of officials, a good crop, a birth of a child. You name it, it's probably been celebrated. Festivals typically take place in and around the central plaza of a town with dancing, live music, colorful decorations, and fireworks. Temporary food booths are set up around the plaza and typically sell tamales (both sweet and meat), *buñuelos* (sweet rolls), tacos, *churros* (fried dough dusted with sugar), *carne asada* (barbecued meat), and plenty of regional drinks.

Essentials

Transportation

GETTING THERE

For centuries, getting to the Yucatán Peninsula required a major sea voyage to one of the few ports on the Gulf of Mexico, only to be followed by harrowing and uncertain land treks limited to mule trains and narrow paths through the tangled jungle. Today, the peninsula is easily accessible. Visitors arrive every day via modern airports, a network of good highways, excellent bus service, or by cruise ship. From just about anywhere in the world, the Yucatán is only hours away.

Air

The main international airports on the Yucatán Peninsula are in Cancún and Mérida. The **Cancún** airport is by far the busiest, with dozens of daily domestic and international flights. There are smaller airports in **Cozumel** and **Chetumal,** and another reportedly being built in **Tulum,** though it remains far from completion. There also is an airport near **Chichén Itzá,** but currently it only receives chartered flights. In addition, there are small airports in **Playa del Carmen** and **Mahahual** for private planes and air taxis.

Most travelers use the Cancún airport—it's well located for those vacationing in the Caribbean as well as for those traveling inland. Fares typically are cheaper to Cancún than to any other airport in the region.

Travelers who are planning to spend their entire time inland often choose to fly to Mérida instead—the city itself is an important destination, and it's close to many of the area's key sights and archaeological ruins.

There also is an airport in Chetumal, which is typically used for domestic travel. However, for travelers planning to spend most of their time in the Costa Maya, this may be more convenient.

DEPARTURE TAX

There is a departure tax to fly out of any Mexican airport—the cost varies depending on the location (US$48 at the Cancún International Airport). Most airlines incorporate the tax into their tickets, but it's worth setting aside some cash just in case.

Bus

The Yucatán's main interstate bus hubs are Mérida and Cancún, with service to and from Mexico City, Veracruz, Oaxaca, and other major destinations in the country. There also are buses between Chetumal and cities in Belize and Guatemala.

Car

Foreigners driving into Mexico are required to show a valid driver's license, title, registration, and proof of insurance for their vehicle. Mexican authorities do not recognize foreign-issued insurance; Mexican vehicle insurance is available at most border towns 24 hours a day, and several companies also sell policies over the Internet. Do not cross the border with your car until you have obtained the proper papers.

Cruise Ship

Increasing numbers of cruise ships stop along Mexico's Caribbean coast every year, some carrying as many as 5,000 people. Many sail out of Miami and Fort Lauderdale, stopping at Key West before continuing to Punta Venado (Riviera Maya), Isla Cozumel, and Mahahual.

Prices are competitive, and ships vary in services, amenities, activities, and

---

Previous: Some agencies still have old-school VW bugs for rent; Chacchoben ruins in the Costa Maya.

entertainment. Pools, restaurants, nightclubs, and cinemas are commonplace. Fitness centers and shops also make ship life convenient. To hone in on the type of cruise you'd like to go on, research options on the Internet, in the travel section of your local newspaper, and by contacting your travel agent.

If your budget is tight, consider traveling standby. Ships want to sail full and are willing to cut their prices—sometimes up to 50 percent—to do so. Airfare usually is not included. **Note:** Once you're on the standby list, you likely will have no choice of cabin location or size.

Neighboring Countries

Cancún is an important international hub, not only for tourists from North America and Europe but also for regional flights to Central America and the Caribbean. In southern Quintana Roo, Chetumal is the gateway to Belize, and there's a direct bus to Flores, Guatemala. Most travel to Guatemala, however, is through Chiapas, from the towns of Palenque and San Cristóbal de las Casas. Travel agencies can book tours to Belize and Guatemala, though it's relatively easy to arrange a trip yourself. Most travelers do not need prearranged visas to enter either country, but they may have to pay an entrance fee at the airport or border.

Cancún has long been a major gateway to Cuba, especially for Americans circumventing U.S. travel restrictions to the island. The historic shift in U.S.-Cuba relations announced by President Obama in 2014 makes it significantly easier for Americans to visit Cuba without going through a third country, though Cancún will surely remain a popular and convenient portal.

GETTING AROUND
Air

Although budget airlines like Interjet are starting to appear on the Mexican airline scene, flying domestically is still relatively expensive, and the Yucatán is no exception. Once you factor in the check-in process,

Navigating the Cancún Airport

Some travelers find Cancún's airport somewhat daunting to navigate. The key is to not get drawn into any of the many sales pitches you'll encounter. Leaving the plane, simply follow the crowd, queueing first for immigration, then retrieving your luggage, then queueing again for customs, where you're asked to press a button: Green means go, red means stop and have your bags searched. Once through customs, you'll enter a large, busy foyer packed with vendor booths, salespeople, and tourist office folks ranging from peppy to pushy, virtually all of whom you can ignore or politely rebuff. If you're renting a car, look for the booth of the company you've reserved with and let the attendant know you've arrived; he or she will direct you to a shuttle to take you to the rental center. If you need a taxi, look for one of three "Yellow Transfers" booths, the official airport taxi service. To catch a bus, walk out of the terminal—ignoring the hagglers and taxi drivers clustered in front—and look for the large ADO buses parked a few steps to your right; you can buy your ticket at the mobile desk set up there. If your resort has arranged transport for you, look for a driver outside the terminal with your name or the name of the resort on a sign. None of the options requires much walking so you don't really need a porter; if you do use one, a couple dollars per bag is the customary tip.

security, and baggage claim, there are very few flights within the region that make sense travel-wise, unless your time is incredibly tight. And if that is the case, you may as well see what you can do by car or bus and start planning a return trip.

Bus

Mexico's bus and public transportation system is one of the best in Latin America, if not the Western Hemisphere. In the Yucatán Peninsula, ADO and its affiliate bus lines practically have a monopoly, but that has not made bus travel any less efficient or less affordable. Dozens of buses cover every major route many times per day, and even smaller towns have frequent and reliable service.

Buses come in three main categories:

First Class: Known as *primera clase* or sometimes *ejecutivo,* first class is the most common and the one travelers use most often. Buses have reclining seats and TVs where movies are played on long trips. First-class buses make some intermediate stops but only in large towns. The main first-class lines in the Yucatán are ADO.

Deluxe Class: Usually called *lujo* (luxury), deluxe class is a step up; they often are slightly faster since they're typically nonstop. The main deluxe line is ADO-GL, which costs 10-25 percent more than regular ADO. ADO-GL buses have nicer seats and better televisions (and even more recent movies!). Sometimes there are even free bottles of water in a cooler at the back. Even nicer are ADO-Platino buses, which often charge twice as much as regular ADO. Platino offers cushy, extra-wide seats (only three across instead of four), headphones, and sometimes a light meal like a sandwich and soda.

Second Class: *Segunda clase,* or second class, is significantly slower and less comfortable than first class, and they're not all that much cheaper. Whenever possible, pay the dollar or two extra for first class. Second-class buses are handy in that you can flag them down anywhere on the roadside, but that is also precisely the reason they're so slow. In smaller towns, second class may be the only service available, and it's fine for shorter trips. The main second-class lines in the Yucatán are Mayab, Oriente, Noreste, and ATS.

For overnight trips, definitely take first-class or deluxe. Not only will you be much more comfortable, second-class buses are sometimes targeted by roadside thieves since they drive on secondary roads and stop frequently.

Wherever bus service is thin, you can count on there being frequent *colectivos* or *combis*—vans or minibuses—that cover local routes. They can be flagged down anywhere along the road.

Car

As great as Mexico's bus system is, a car is the best way to tour the Yucatán Peninsula. Most of the sights—ruins, deserted beaches, haciendas, caves, cenotes, wildlife—are well outside of the region's cities, down long access roads, or on the way from one town to

First-class buses have air-conditioning, reclining seats, and even movies.

Driving Distances in Kilometers

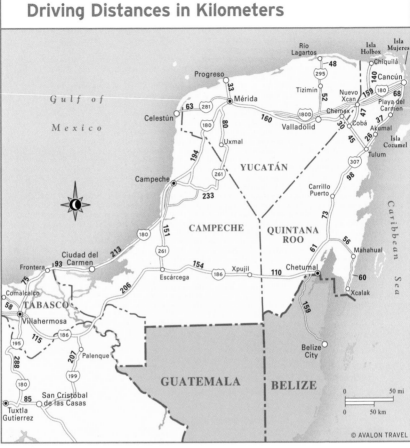

the next. Having a car also saves you the time and effort of walking or the cost of cabbing to all those "missing links"; it also allows you to enjoy the sights for as much or as little time as you choose.

If you're here for a short time—a week or less—and want to sightsee, definitely get a car for the simple reason that you'll have the option of seeing and doing twice as much. If renting for your entire vacation isn't feasible moneywise, consider getting a car for just a couple of days to explore a bit: Chichén Itzá and other nearby archaeological zones, DIY cenotes, and the less-accessible parts of

Quintana Roo like the Sian Ka'an Biosphere Reserve and the Costa Maya.

CAR RENTAL

The best rates (and best vehicles) are typically found online with the major international rental chains like Hertz, Thrifty, Budget, and Avis. That said, there are many local agencies in cities like Cancún, however, and they occasionally have good walk-in deals.

• It's best to book on the car rental company's own website rather than a travel website. The prices are virtually the same, and

Driving in Mexico

Having a car can make exploring the Yucatán Peninsula quicker and easier, and there are many places you can only reach with your own wheels. Here are some tips to make your driving experience a bit smoother:

Off the highways, the biggest hazard are *topes* (speed bumps). They are common on all roads and highways, save the toll roads. They vary in size, but many are big and burly, and hitting them at even a slow speed can do a number on you, your passengers, and your car. As soon as you see a sign announcing an upcoming town or village, be ready to slow down.

Narrow one-way streets are common in many cities in the Yucatán. Fortunately, the **stop signs** in those areas usually have smaller plaques (beneath the big red one) indicating direction and right of way. A **black rectangle** means you have the right of way, a **red one** means you don't.

If you break down or run out of gas on a main road during daylight hours, stay with your car. **Los Ángeles Verdes** (The Green Angels, toll-free Mex. tel. 078 or 800/903-9200), a government-sponsored tow-truck and repair service, cruise these roads on the lookout for drivers in trouble 8am-6pm daily. They carry a CB radio, gas, and small parts, and are prepared to fix tires. If you have a cell phone—or happen to be near a pay phone—call your car rental agency first; the Ángeles Verdes are a great backup.

if there are any problems, the rental office can't blame it on the other website.

- Ask your credit card company if your card provides free collision (liability) insurance on rental cars abroad. (Most do.) Unlike ordinary insurance, you'll have to pay any charges upfront and then file for reimbursement once you return. The coverage is usually better, though, with zero deductible and coverage even on dirt roads. Remember you have to actually use the card to pay for the rental in order to get the benefit!

- Car rental agencies make most of their money off the insurance, not the vehicle. That's why they push so hard for you to buy coverage. They'll warn you that with credit card insurance you'll have to pay 100 percent of any damages upfront; this is true, but it will be reimbursed when you file a claim back home. They may require you to authorize a larger "hold" on your card, as much as US$5,000, for potential damages. This is no big deal—it's not an actual charge—but that amount will be unavailable for other purchases. Consider bringing two or more credit cards, especially if your credit limit is low.

- Third-party insurance is required by law, and rental agencies are technically required to provide it. Lately, however, rental agencies say third-party coverage is free for anyone who also purchases collision insurance. But if you decline their collision insurance (because you get it through your credit card), suddenly there's a charge for third-party coverage. Credit cards typically do not offer third-party coverage, so you end up having to pay it. It's less expensive than collision insurance, but still a bummer to pay.

Before driving off, the attendant will review the car for existing damage—definitely accompany him or her on this part and don't be shy about pointing out every nick, scratch, and ding. Other things to confirm before driving off include:

- There is a spare tire (preferably a full-size, not temporary, one) and a working jack and tire iron.

- All doors lock and unlock, including the trunk.

- The headlights, brake lights, and turn signals work.

- All the windows roll up and down properly.
- The proper—and current—car registration is in the car. In some cases, your car rental contract serves as the registration.
- The amount of gas in the tank—you'll have to return it with the same amount.
- There is a 24-hour telephone number for the rental agency in case of an emergency.

HIGHWAYS AND ROAD CONDITIONS

Driving in the Yucatán isn't as nerve-racking as you might think. The highways are in excellent condition, and even secondary roads are well maintained. There are a few dirt and sand roads—mostly along the Costa Maya and in the Sian Ka'an Biosphere Reserve. If anything, frequent—and sometimes unexpected—*topes* (speed bumps) in small towns are the biggest driving hazard.

The main highways in the region are Highway 307, which runs the length of Mexico's Caribbean coast; Highway 180, the thoroughfare that links Cancún, Mérida, and Campeche City; and Highway 186, which crosses the southern portion of the Yucatán Peninsula and leads travelers to Campeche's Río Bec region and Comalcalco in Tabasco.

In the entire region, there are only two toll roads, both sections of Highway 180: between Mérida and Cancún (a whopping US$32—US$20 from Cancún to Valladolid, US$12 from Pisté to Mérida) and between Campeche City and the town of Champotón (US$4.75). Although far from cheap, they can save a significant amount of time driving, and are safer for driving at night. Secondary roads are free and pass through picturesque countryside and indigenous villages; they are slower and have more obstacles like pedestrians, bicycles, and speed bumps, but can be a rewarding way to go.

DRIVING SCAMS

Most travelers have heard horror stories about Mexican police and worry about being taken for all their money or trundled off to jail without reason. While it is true that there is

Taxi Scam

Beware of any taxi driver who tries to convince you that the hotel you're going to is closed, roach infested, flooded, burned down, has no running water, was destroyed by a hurricane (add your disaster of choice). As sincere as the driver might seem, he is more often than not retaliating against hotels that refuse to pay a finder's fee. Taxi drivers in Cancún and throughout the Riviera Maya earn significant commissions—as much as US$10 per person *per night*—for bringing guests to certain establishments. Some hotels refuse to pay the fee, and taxi drivers, in turn, try to take their clients to "cooperative" hotels instead. Don't fall for it. You may have to be firm, but insist that your driver take you to the hotel of your choice. Your best option is to call ahead for a room reservation, which also serves to confirm that the hotel actually is open and operational.

corruption among the police, they don't target tourists; foreigners are, after all, the economic lifeblood of the region—the police don't want to scare them away.

As long as you are a careful and defensive driver, it is very unlikely you'll have any interaction with the police. Most travelers who are pulled over actually have done something wrong—speeding, running a stop sign, turning on red. In those situations, remain calm and polite. If you have an explanation, definitely give it; it is not uncommon to discuss a given situation with an officer. Who knows, you may even convince him you're right—it's happened to us!

Of greater concern are gas station attendants. Full service is the norm here—you pull up, tell the person how much you want, and he or she does the rest. A common scam is for one attendant to distract you with questions about wiper fluid or gas additives while another starts the pump at 50 or 100 pesos. Before you answer any questions, be sure the attendant resets, or "zeroes," the pump before starting to pump.

Hitchhiking

Hitchhiking is not recommended for either men or women. That said, it sometimes can be hard to know what is a private vehicle and what is a *colectivo* (shared van). If there's no bus terminal nearby, your best bet is to look for locals who are waiting for public transportation and see which vans they take. If you have no choice but to hitch a ride, opt for a pickup truck, where you can sit in the back.

Tours

Regional travel agents and tour operators offer a vast range of organized trips. You pay extra, of course, but all arrangements and reservations are made for you: from guides and transportation to hotels and meals. Special-interest trips also are common—archaeological tours, hacienda and convent routes, bird-watching and dive trips. Ask around and surf the Internet—you'll find a world of organized adventure.

Visas and Officialdom

PASSPORTS

Gone are the days you could zip down to Mexico with just your driver's license and birth certificate. All nationalities must have a valid passport to enter Mexico by air, land, or sea. (Since January 2007 and March 2010, respectively, U.S. and Canadian citizens are required to have a passport to enter the country.)

VISAS AND TOURIST CARDS

Citizens of most countries, including the United States, Canada, and members of the E.U., do not need to obtain a visa to enter Mexico. All foreigners, however, are issued a white tourist card when they enter, with the number of days that they are permitted to stay in the country written at the bottom, typically 30-60 days. If you plan to stay for more than a month, politely ask the official to give you the amount of time you need; the maximum stay is 180 days.

Hold onto your tourist card! It must be returned to immigration officials when you leave Mexico. If you lose it, you'll be fined and may not be permitted to leave the country (much less the immigration office) until you pay.

To extend your stay up to 180 days, head to the nearest immigration office a week *before* your tourist card expires. Be sure to bring it along with your passport. There, you'll fill out several forms, go to a bank to pay the US$25 processing fee, make photocopies of all the paperwork (including your passport, entry stamp, tourist card, and credit card), and then return to the office to get the extension. For every extra 30 days requested, foreigners must prove that they have US$1,000 available, either in cash or travelers checks, or simply by showing a current credit card. The process can take anywhere from a couple of hours to a week, depending on the office.

CUSTOMS

Plants and fresh foods are not allowed into Mexico, and there are special limits on alcohol, tobacco, and electronic products. Archaeological artifacts, certain antiques, and colonial art cannot be exported from Mexico without special permission.

Above all, do not attempt to bring marijuana or any other narcotic into or out of Mexico. Jail is one place your trusty guidebook won't come in handy.

Returning home, you will be required to declare all items you bought in Mexico. Citizens of the United States are allowed to reenter with US$800 worth of purchases duty-free; the figure for other travelers varies by country.

CONSULATES

The consulates in Cancún handle passport issues (replacing a lost one, adding pages, etc.) and can help their citizens if they are in a serious or emergency situation, including hospitalization, assault, arrest, lawsuits, or death. They usually do not help resolve common disputes—with tour operators or hotels, for example.

Foreign consulates and consular agencies in the region include:

AUSTRIA
Cancún: Calle Punta Conoco No. 36, tel. 998/884-1598, konsul_a@yahoo.com.mx, 9am-1pm Monday-Friday

BELGIUM
Cancún: Plaza Tropical, Av. Tulum 192, tel. 998/892-2512, www.diplomatie.be, 10am-2pm Monday-Friday

BELIZE
Cancún: Av. Nader 34, tel. 998/887-8415, 9am-5pm Monday-Friday
Chetumal: Av. Genova 369, tel. 983/285-3511, conbelizeqroo@gmail.com, 9am-1pm Monday-Friday

CANADA
Cancún: Centro Empresarial, Blvd. Kukulcán Km. 12, tel. 998/883-3360, www.canada.org.mx, 9am-1pm Monday-Friday

CUBA
Cancún: Pecari 17, tel. 998/884-3423, www.cubadiplomatica.cu/mexico, 9am-1pm Monday-Friday

DENMARK
Cancún: Omni Hotel, Blvd. Kukulcán Km. 16.5, tel. 998/881-0600, apresidencia@grupo-cancun.net, 9am-1pm Monday-Friday

FINLAND
Cancún: Edificio Popolnah, Av. Nader 28, tel. 998/884-1600, notariacancun@prodigy.net.mx, 9am-2pm and 5pm-8pm Monday-Friday

FRANCE
Cancún: Colegio Británico, Calle Pargo 24, tel. 998/883-9816, consulatcancun@aol.com, by appointment only
Mérida: Calle 60 btwn Calles 41 and 43, tel. 999/930-1500, consuladofrancia@sipse.com.mx, 9am-5pm Monday-Friday

GERMANY
Cancún: Calle Punta Conocó 36, tel. 998/884-1598, konsul_d@yahoo.com.mx, 9am-noon Monday-Friday

GUATEMALA
Cancún: Edificio Barcelona, Av. Nader 148, 998/884-8296, 9am-1pm Monday-Friday
Chetumal: Avenida Héroes de Chapultepec 356, tel. 983/832-3045, 9am-1pm Monday-Friday

IRELAND
Cancún: Av. Cobá 15, tel. 998/112-5436, consul@gruporoyale.com, 9am-1pm Monday-Friday

ITALY
Cancún: Parque Las Palapas, Alcatraces 39, tel. 998/884-1261, conitaca@prodigy.net.mx, 9am-2pm Monday-Friday

NETHERLANDS
Cancún: Pabellón Caribe, Av. Nichupté s/n, tel. 998/884-8672, nlconsulcancun@prodigy.net.mx, 9am-1pm Monday-Friday

NORWAY
Cancún: Calle Venado 30, tel. 998/887-4412, noruega@aviomar.com.mx, 9am-1pm Monday-Friday

SPAIN
Cancún: Blvd. Kukulcán at Calle Cenzontle, tel. 998/848-9918, consules@sercc.com.mx, 10am-1pm Monday-Friday

SWEDEN
Cancún: Omni Cancún Hotel & Villas, Blvd. Kukulcán Km. 16.5, tel. 998/881-0600,

msalinas@omnicancun.com.mx, tel. 998/881-0600, 9am-6pm Monday-Friday

SWITZERLAND
Cancún: above Rolandi's restaurant, Av. Cobá 12, tel. 998/884-8486, 9am-2pm Monday-Friday

UNITED KINGDOM
Cancún: The Royal Sands Resort & Spa, Blvd. Kukulcán Km. 13.5, tel. 998/881-0100, www.ukinmexico.fco.gov.uk/en, 9am-3pm Monday-Friday

UNITED STATES
Cancún: Torre La Europea, Blvd. Kukulcán Km. 13, tel. 998/883-0272, conagencycancun@state.gov, 8am-1pm Monday-Friday, appointment required for some services

Mérida: Calle 60 No. 338-K btwn Calles 29 and 31, tel. 999/942-5700, http://merida.usconsulate.gov, 7:30am-4:30pm Monday-Friday, appointment required for some services

Playa del Carmen: La Palapa, Calle 1 btwn Avs. 15 and 20, tel. 984/873-0303, conagencycancun@state.gov, 9am-1pm Monday-Friday

UNDERAGE TRAVELERS
In the United States, anyone under 18 traveling internationally without *both* parents or legal guardians must present a signed, notarized letter from the parent(s) or guardian(s) granting the minor permission to leave the country. This requirement is aimed at preventing international abductions, but it causes frequent and major disruptions for vacationers.

Accommodations and Food

ACCOMMODATIONS
Lodging in the Yucatán Peninsula truly runs the gamut: campgrounds, hostels, small hotels, bed-and-breakfasts, boutique hotels, large modern hotels, and all-inclusive resorts. There are a handful of fishing lodges in places like the Sian Ka'an Biosphere Reserve.

Taxes on your hotel bill, referred to generally as I.V.A. (value-added tax; pronounced EE-va in Spanish), are usually 12 percent but can be as high as 17-22 percent. Be sure to ask if the rate you're quoted includes taxes (*¿Incluye impuestos?*); in many cases, especially at smaller hotels, the taxes are applied only if you pay by credit card.

You may be required to make a deposit in order to reserve a room, especially in popular areas during high season. However, in Mexico credit cards cannot be charged without a physical signature, so they aren't much help as a deposit. Many hotels utilize PayPal or a similar service; those that do not will give you the name of their bank and account number, and you must stop by a branch and make the deposit with the teller. Be sure to get a receipt, and notify the hotel after making the deposit.

Cancellation policies tend to be rather unforgiving, especially during high season; you may be required to give a month or more advance notice to receive even a partial refund. Trip insurance is a good idea if your plans are less than concrete.

FOOD
Considered among the most distinct cuisines of the country, Yucatecan food reflects the influences of its Maya, European, and Caribbean heritage. Some of the most popular menu items include:

- *Cochinita Pibil:* pork marinated in achiote, orange juice, and other spices then wrapped in banana leaves and baked.
- *Panucho:* small thick tortillas stuffed with refried beans and covered with shredded turkey, pickled onion, and avocado.
- *Poc-Chuc:* slices of pork marinated in orange juice and coated with a tangy sauce.

- *Salbute:* small handmade tortillas topped with shredded turkey, pickled onion, and slices of avocado.

- *Sopa de Lima:* turkey stock soup with shredded turkey, fried tortilla strips, and *lima* juice.

Conduct and Customs

CLOTHING

Perhaps the single most-abused social custom in Mexico is the use of shorts. Mexicans rarely wear them outside the home or off the beach, while many foreign travelers seem to have packed nothing but shorts. There is a bit more flexibility in beach areas, but it's worth getting in the habit of wearing long pants or skirts whenever going to dinner, attending performances, and especially when entering churches and government offices, where shorts and tank tops are considered inappropriate (and, in some cases, disrespectful).

Topless and nude sunbathing are not customary on Mexican beaches, and are rarely practiced in Cancún and other areas frequented by Americans and Canadians. However, on beaches popular with Europeans, especially Playa del Carmen and Tulum, it is more commonplace. Wherever you are, take a look around to help decide whether baring some or all is appropriate.

PHOTOGRAPHING LOCALS

No one enjoys having a stranger take his or her picture for no good reason, and Mexicans—indigenous or otherwise—are no different. The best policy is simply not to take these photographs unless you've first asked the person's permission and he or she has agreed. **Tip:** If the potential subject of your photo is a vendor, buy something and *then* ask if you can take a photo—you're more likely to get a positive response.

GREETINGS

Even a small amount of Spanish can go a long way in showing respect and consideration for people you encounter. Make a point of learning basic greetings like *buenos días* (good morning) and *buenas tardes* (good afternoon) and using them in passing, or as preface to a conversation; it is considered somewhat impolite to launch into a discussion without greeting the other person first.

Travel Tips

WHAT TO TAKE

Essentials for the Yucatán include sunscreen, sunglasses, and a billed hat. If you wear contacts or glasses, bring a replacement set. A good pair of shoes—or at least Teva-style sandals—is vital for exploring Maya ruins safely, and insect repellent definitely can come in handy. If you lose or forget something, Cancún, Playa del Carmen, Tulum, and Chetumal all have huge supermarkets, including Walmart.

ACCESS FOR TRAVELERS WITH DISABILITIES

Mexico has made many improvements for the blind and people in wheelchairs—many large stores and tourist centers have ramps or elevators. A growing number of hotels also have rooms designed for guests with disabilities, and museums occasionally create exhibits with, for example, replicas of Maya artifacts or folk art that visually impaired travelers can hold and touch. (None were currently on display at the time of research, however.) That said, Mexico is still a hard place to navigate if you have a disability. Smaller towns are the most problematic, as their sidewalks can be narrow, and even some main streets are not paved. Definitely ask for help—for what Mexico lacks in infrastructure, its people often make up for in graciousness.

TRAVELING WITH CHILDREN

The Yucatán Peninsula is a great place to take kids, whether youngsters or teenagers. The variety of activities and relative ease of transportation help keep everyone happy and engaged. Perhaps best of all, Mexico is a country where family is paramount, so kids—even fussy ones—are welcome just about everywhere.

WOMEN TRAVELING ALONE

Solo women should expect a certain amount of unwanted attention, mostly in the form of whistles and catcalls. It typically happens as they walk down the street and sometimes comes from the most unlikely sources—we saw a man dressed as a clown turn mid-balloon animal to whistle at a woman walking by. Two or more women walking together attract

much less unwanted attention, and a woman and man walking together will get none at all (at least of this sort—street vendors are a different story). While annoying and often unnerving, this sort of attention is almost always completely benign, and ignoring it is definitely the best response. Making eye contact or snapping a smart retort only will inspire more attention. Occasionally men will hustle alongside a woman and try to strike up a conversation—if you don't want to engage, a brief *no, gracias* should make that clear. To minimize unwanted attention, avoid revealing clothing, such as tight jeans, low-cut shirts, or bikini tops, as street wear. Carrying a notebook—or creating the appearance of working—also helps.

SENIOR TRAVELERS

Seniors should feel very welcome and safe visiting the Yucatán. Mexico is a country that affords great respect to *personas de la tercera edad* (literally, "people of the third age"), and especially in the tradition-minded Yucatán Peninsula. But as anywhere, older travelers should take certain precautions. The Yucatán, particularly inland areas, is known to be extremely hot and humid, especially May-July. Seniors should take extra care to stay cool and

Calm water and soft sand make for great family beaches.

hydrated. Exploring the Maya ruins also can be hot, not to mention exhausting. Bring water and snacks, especially to smaller sites where they may not be commonly sold. Travelers with balance or mobility concerns should think twice about climbing any of the pyramids or other structures. They can be deceptively treacherous, with steps that are steep, uneven, and slick.

Cancún and Playa del Carmen have state-of-the-art hospitals, staffed by skilled doctors, nurses, and technicians, many of whom speak English. Most prescription medications are available in Mexico, often at discount prices. However, pharmacists are woefully undertrained, and you should always double-check the active ingredients and dosage of any pills you buy here.

GAY AND LESBIAN TRAVELERS

While openly gay women are still rare in Mexico, gay men are increasingly visible in large cities and certain tourist areas. Cancún and Playa del Carmen both have a visible gay presence and a number of gay-friendly venues. Nevertheless, many locals—even in large cities—are not accustomed to open displays of homosexuality and may react openly and negatively. Many hotel attendants also simply don't understand that two travel companions of the same gender may prefer one bed—in some cases they will outright refuse to grant the request. Some couples find it easier to book a room with two queen-size beds and just sleep in one.

TRAVELING WITH IMPORTANT DOCUMENTS

Scan and/or make copies of your passport, tourist card, and airline tickets. Whether you're traveling solo or with others, leave a copy with someone you trust at home. Store another copy online (i.e., your email account or on the cloud) and if you have a travel companion, give a copy to him or her. Be sure to carry a *copy* of your passport and tourist card in your purse or wallet and leave the originals in the hotel safe or locked in your bag; they're a lot more likely to be lost or stolen on the street than taken by hotel staff. When you move from place to place, carry your passport and important documents in a travel pouch, always under your clothing. Write down your credit card and ATM numbers and the 24-hour service numbers and keep those in a safe place.

Health and Safety

SUNBURN

Common sense is the most important factor in avoiding sunburn. Use waterproof and sweatproof sunscreen with a high SPF. Reapply regularly—even the most heavy-duty waterproof sunscreen washes off faster than it claims to on the bottle (or gets rubbed off when you use your towel to dry off). Be extra careful to protect parts of your body that aren't normally exposed to the sun—a good way to cover every inch is to apply sunscreen *before* you get dressed—and give your skin a break from direct sun every few hours. Remember that redness from a sunburn takes several hours to appear—that is, you can be sunburned long before you *look* sunburned.

If you get sunburned, treat it like any other burn by running cool water over it for as long and as often as you can. Do not expose your skin to more sun. Re-burning the skin can result in painful blisters that can easily become infected. There are a number of products designed to relieve sunburns, most with aloe extracts. Finally, be sure to drink plenty of water to keep your skin hydrated.

HEAT EXHAUSTION AND HEAT STROKE

The symptoms of heat exhaustion are cool moist skin, profuse sweating, headache, fatigue, and drowsiness. It is associated with dehydration and commonly happens during or after a strenuous day in the sun, such as while visiting ruins. You should get out of the sun, remove any tight or restrictive clothing, and sip a sports drink such as Gatorade. Cool compresses and raising your feet and legs help too.

Heat exhaustion is not the same as heat stroke, and is distinguished by a high body temperature, a rapid pulse, and sometimes delirium or even unconsciousness. It is an extremely serious, potentially fatal condition, and victims should be taken to the hospital immediately. In the meantime, wrap the victim in wet sheets, massage the arms and legs to increase circulation, and do not administer large amounts of liquids. Never give liquids if the victim is unconscious.

DIARRHEA

Diarrhea is not an illness in itself, but your body's attempt to get rid of something bad in a hurry; that something can be any one of a number of strains of bacteria, parasites, or amoebae that are often passed from contaminated water. No fun, it is usually accompanied by cramping, dehydration, fever, and, of course, frequent trips to the bathroom.

If you get diarrhea, it should pass in a day or two. Anti-diarrheals such as Lomotil and Imodium A-D will plug you up but don't cure you—use them only if you can't be near a bathroom. The malaise you feel from diarrhea typically is from dehydration, not the actual infection, so be sure to drink plenty of fluids—a sports drink such as Gatorade is best. If it's especially bad, ask at your hotel for the nearest *laboratorio* (laboratory or clinic), where a stool sample can be analyzed for around US$5 to determine if you have a parasitic infection or a virus. If it's a common infection, the lab technician will tell you what medicine to take. Be aware that medicines for stomach infection are seriously potent, killing not only the bad stuff but the good stuff as well; they'll cure you but leave you vulnerable to another infection. Avoid alcohol and spicy foods for several days afterward.

A few tips for avoiding diarrhea include:

- Only drink bottled water. Avoid using tap water even for brushing your teeth.

- Avoid raw fruits or vegetables that you haven't disinfected and cut yourself. Lettuce is particularly dangerous since water is easily trapped in the leaves. Also, as tasty as they look, avoid the bags of sliced fruit sold from street carts.

- Order your meat dishes well done, even if it's an upscale restaurant. If you've been to a market, you'll see that meat is handled very differently here.

INSECTS

Insects are not of particular concern in the Yucatán, certainly not as they are in other parts of the tropics. Mosquitoes are common, but are not known to carry malaria. Dengue fever, also transmitted by mosquitoes, is present but still rare. Some remote beaches, like the Costa Maya, may have sand flies or horseflies, but they have been all but eliminated in the more touristed areas. Certain destinations are more likely to be buggy, like forested archaeological zones and coastal bird-watching areas, and travelers should bring and use insect repellent there, if only for extra comfort.

CRIME

The Yucatán Peninsula is generally quite safe, and few travelers report problems with crime of any kind. Cancún is the one area where particular care should be taken, however. You may find illicit drugs relatively easy to obtain, but bear in mind that drug crimes are prosecuted vigorously in Mexico (especially ones involving foreigners), and your country's embassy can do very little to help. Sexual assault and rape have been reported by women at nightclubs, sometimes after having been slipped a "date rape" drug. While the clubs are raucous and sexually charged by definition, women should be especially alert to the people around them and wary of accepting drinks from strangers. In all areas, commonsense precautions are always recommended, such as taking a taxi at night instead of walking (especially if you've been drinking) and avoiding flashing your money and valuables, or leaving them unattended on the beach or elsewhere. Utilize the safety deposit box in your hotel room, if one is available; if you rent a car, get one with a trunk so your bags will not be visible through the window.

Information and Services

MONEY
Currency and Exchange Rates

Mexico's official currency is the peso, divided into 100 centavos. It is typically designated with the symbol $, but you may also see MN$ (*moneda nacional,* or national currency). We've listed virtually all prices in their U.S. dollar equivalent, but occasionally use M$ to indicate the price is in Mexican pesos.

U.S. dollars and E.U. euros are accepted in a few highly touristed locations like the Zona Hotelera in Cancún and the shopping districts of Playa del Carmen. However, you'll want and need pesos everywhere else, as most shopkeepers appreciate visitors paying in the local currency. **Note:** Foreign bills only are accepted because coins can't be changed to pesos.

At the time of research, US$1 was equal to M$13, slightly less for Canadian dollars, and M$16.90 for euros.

ATMs

Almost every town in the Yucatán Peninsula has an ATM, and they are without question the easiest, fastest, and best way to manage your money. Be aware that you may be charged a transaction fee by the ATM (US$2-3 typically) as well as your home bank (as much as US$10). It's worth asking your bank if it partners with a Mexican bank, and whether transaction fees are lower if you use that bank's cash machines. Also, be sure to use ATMs that are affiliated with a recognizable bank, to avoid exorbitant service charges.

Travelers Checks

With the spread of ATMs, travelers checks have stopped being convenient for most travel, especially in a country as developed as Mexico. If you do bring them, you will have to exchange them at a bank or a *casa de cambio* (exchange booth).

Credit Cards

Visa and MasterCard are accepted at all large hotels and many medium and small ones, upscale restaurants, main bus terminals, travel agencies, and many shops throughout Mexico. American Express is accepted much less frequently. Some merchants tack on a 3-10 percent surcharge for any credit card purchase—ask before you pay.

Cash

It's a good idea to bring a small amount of U.S. cash, on the off chance that your ATM or credit cards suddenly stop working; a US$200 reserve should be more than enough for a two-week visit. Stow it away with your other important documents, to be used only if necessary.

Tax

A 12 percent value-added tax (*IVA* in Spanish) applies to hotel rates, restaurant and bar tabs, and gift purchases. When checking in or making reservations at a hotel, ask if tax has already been added. In some cases, the tax is 17 percent.

Bargaining

Bargaining is common and expected in street

and artisans' markets, but try not to be too aggressive. Some tourists derive immense and almost irrational pride from haggling over every last cent, and then turn around and spend several times that amount on beer or snacks. The fact is, most bargaining comes down to the difference of a few dollars or even less, and earning those extra dollars is a much bigger deal for most artisans than spending them is to most tourists.

Tipping

While tipping is always a choice, it is a key supplement to many workers' paychecks. In fact, for some—like baggers at the grocery store—the tip is the *only* pay they receive. And while dollars and euros are appreciated, pesos are preferred. **Note:** Foreign coins can't be changed to pesos, so are useless to workers. Average gratuities in the region include:

• Archaeological zone guides: 10-15 percent if you're satisfied with the service; for informal guides (typically boys who show you around the site), US$2-3 is customary.

• Gas station attendants: around US$0.50 if your windshield has been cleaned, tires have been filled, or the oil and water have

been checked; no tip is expected for simply pumping gas.

• Grocery store baggers: US$0.25-0.50.

• Housekeepers: US$1.50-2 per day; either left daily or as a lump sum at the end of your stay.

• Porters: about US$1-2 per bag.

• Taxi drivers: Tipping is not customary.

• Tour guides: 10-15 percent; don't forget the driver—US$1-2 is typical.

• Waiters: 10-15 percent; make sure the gratuity is not already included in the bill.

COMMUNICATIONS AND MEDIA
Postal Service

Mailing letters and postcards from Mexico is neither cheap nor necessarily reliable. Delivery times vary greatly, and letters get "lost" somewhat more than postcards. Letters (under 20 grams) and postcards cost US$1 to the United States and Canada, US$1.20 to Europe and South America, and US$1.35 to the rest of the world. Visit the **Correos de México** website (www.correosdemexico.com.mx) for pricing on larger packages and other services.

A little haggling is okay, but avoid going overboard.

Useful Telephone Numbers

TRAVELER ASSISTANCE

- Emergencies: 060 or 066
- Ángeles Verdes (Green Angels): 078 or 800/903-9200
- Directory Assistance: 044

LONG-DISTANCE DIRECT DIALING

- Domestic long-distance: 01 + area code + number
- International long-distance (United States only): 001 + area code + number
- International long-distance (rest of the world): 00 + country code + area code + number

LONG-DISTANCE COLLECT CALLS

- Domestic long-distance operator: 02
- International long-distance operator (English-speaking): 09

Telephone

Ladatel—Mexico's national phone company—maintains good public phones all over the peninsula and country. Plastic phone cards with little chips in them are sold at most mini-marts and supermarkets in 30-, 50-, 100-, and 200-peso denominations. Ask for a *tarjeta* Ladatel—they are the size and stiffness of a credit card, as opposed to the thin cards used for cell phones. Insert the card into any public pay phone, and the amount on the card will be displayed on the screen. Rates and dialing instructions (in Spanish and English) are inside the phone cabin. At the time of research, rates were roughly US$0.10 per minute for local calls, US$0.40 per minute for national calls, and US$0.50 per minute for calls to the United States and Canada.

A number of Internet cafés offer inexpensive **Web-based phone service,** especially in the larger cities where broadband connections are fastest. Rates tend to be significantly lower than those of Ladatel, and you don't have to worry about your card running out.

Beware of phones offering "free" collect or credit card calls; far from being free, their rates are outrageous.

If you've got an unlocked GSM cell phone, you can purchase a local SIM card for around US$15, including US$5 credit, for use during your trip. Calls are expensive, but text messaging is relatively cheap, including to the United States; having two local phones/chips can be especially useful for couples or families traveling together.

Internet Access

Internet cafés can be found in virtually every town in the region. Most charge around US$1 per hour, though prices can be much higher in malls and heavily touristed areas. Most places also will burn digital photos onto a CD or DVD—they typically sell blank discs, but travelers should bring their own USB cable.

Wireless Internet is also becoming popular at all levels of hotels; if you need to stay connected while you're on the road, and you're willing to travel with a laptop or tablet, it's easy—and free—to access the Internet.

Newspapers

The most popular daily newspapers in the Riviera Maya are *Novedades Quintana Roo* (www.sipse.com/novedades), *¡Por Esto!*

Cell Phone Calls

MEXICAN LANDLINE TO MEXICAN CELL PHONE:

- Within the same area code: 044 + 3-digit area code + 7-digit phone number
- Different area code: 045 + 3-digit area code + 7-digit phone number

MEXICAN CELL PHONE TO MEXICAN CELL PHONE:

- Within the same area code: 7-digit number only
- Different area code: 3-digit area code + 7-digit number

INTERNATIONAL LANDLINE/CELL PHONE TO A MEXICAN CELL PHONE:

- From U.S. or Canada: 011 + 52 + 1 + 3-digit area code + 7-digit number
- From other countries: international access code + 52 + 1 + 3-digit area code + 7-digit number

(www.poresto.net), and *El Diario de Yucatán* (www.yucatan.com.mx). The main national newspapers are also readily available, including *Reforma* (www.reforma.com), *La Prensa* (www.la-prensa.com.mx), and *La Jornada* (www.jornada.unam.mx). For news in English, you'll find the *Miami Herald Cancún Edition* in Cancún and occasionally in Playa del Carmen.

Radio and Television

Most large hotels and a number of midsize and small ones have cable or satellite TV, which usually includes CNN (though sometimes in Spanish only), MTV, and other U.S. channels. AM and FM radio options are surprisingly bland—you're more likely to find a good *rock en español* station in California than you are in the Yucatán.

MAPS AND TOURIST INFORMATION
Maps

A husband-and-wife team creates **MapChick** maps (www.cancunmap.com), outstanding and exhaustively detailed maps of Cancún, Playa del Carmen, the Riviera Maya, Isla Cozumel, Isla Mujeres, and inland archaeological zones. They're as much guidebooks as

maps, with virtually every building and business identified, many with short personal reviews, plus useful information like taxi rates, driving distances, ferry schedules, and more. Maps cost around US$15 and often come with a couple of smaller secondary maps; they're sold on the MapChick website as well as at www.amazon.com.

Most local tourist offices distribute maps to tourists free of charge, though quality varies considerably. Car rental agencies often have maps, and many hotels create maps for their guests of nearby restaurants and sights.

Tourist Offices

Most cities in the region have a tourist information office or kiosk. Some are staffed with friendly and knowledgeable people and have a good sense of what tourists are looking for. At others, you'll seriously wonder how the people there were hired. It is certainly worth stopping in if you have a question—you may well get it answered, but don't be surprised if you don't.

Photography and Video

Digital cameras are as ubiquitous in Mexico as they are everywhere else, but memory sticks and other paraphernalia can be prohibitively expensive; bring a spare chip in case your primary one gets lost or damaged. If your chip's capacity is relatively small, and you're not bringing your laptop along, pack a couple of blank DVDs and a USB cable to download and burn photos, which you can do at most Internet cafés.

Video is another great way to capture the color and movement of the region. Be aware that all archaeological sites charge an additional US$3.50 to bring in a video camera; tripods often are prohibited.

WEIGHTS AND MEASURES
Measurements

Mexico uses the metric system, so distances are in kilometers, weights are in kilograms, gasoline is sold by the liter, and temperatures are given in Celsius. See the chart at the back of this book for conversions from the imperial system.

Time Zone

The entire Yucatán Peninsula used to be part of the Central Standard Time zone (along with Mexico City and much of central Mexico), with a region-wide shift in fall and spring for daylight savings. However, beginning in 2015, the state of Quintana Roo (which includes Cancún, Playa del Carmen, Cozumel, Tulum, and the Costa Maya) will join the Eastern Standard Time zone October-April only. Put another way, while the rest of the Yucatán and Central Time Zone "fall back" in October, Quintana Roo will stay on daylight savings time, making it one hour ahead of its neighbors (and thus the same as the Eastern Time Zone). In April, the Central Time Zone will "catch up" and the entire region will be on the same hour again. The change is meant to give the Riviera Maya a longer-feeling day during the winter months and make travel from the U.S. East Coast easier. It's sure to make travel to and from the Yucatecan interior a bit more confusing, however; be sure to double-check your flight and bus times to avoid missed connections.

Electricity

Mexico uses the 60-cycle, 110-volt AC current common in the United States. Bring a surge protector if you plan to plug in a laptop.

Resources

Spanish Glossary

The form of Spanish spoken in the Yucatán Peninsula is quite clear and understandable, and far less clipped or colloquial than in other countries. That's good news for anyone new to the language, and hoping to use their trip to learn more.

abarrotería: small grocery store

alcalde: mayor or municipal judge

alfarería: pottery

alfarero, alfarera: potter

amigo, amiga: friend

andador: walkway or strolling path

antojitos: Mexican snacks, such as huaraches, flautas, and quesadillas

artesanías: handicrafts, as distinguished from *artesano, artesana,* the person who makes handicrafts

audiencia: one of the royal executive-judicial panels sent to rule areas of Latin America during the 16th century

ayuntamiento: either the town council or the building where it meets

bienes raices: literally "good roots," but popularly, real estate

boleto: ticket, boarding pass

bucear, buzo: to scuba dive, scuba diver

caballero: gentleman

cabecera: head town of a municipal district, or headquarters in general

cabrón: a bastard; sometimes used affectionately

cacique: chief or boss

calesa: early 1800s-style horse-drawn carriage; also called *calandria*

camionera central: central bus station; alternatively, *terminal camionera*

campesino: country person; farm worker

canasta: basket

cárcel: jail

casa de huéspedes: guesthouse, often operated in a family home

caudillo: dictator or political chief

charro, charra: cowboy, cowgirl

churrigueresque: Spanish baroque architectural style incorporated into many Mexican colonial churches, named after José Churriguera (1665-1725)

cofradía: Catholic fraternal service association, either male or female, mainly in charge of financing and organizing religious festivals

colectivo: a shared public taxi or minibus that picks up and drops off passengers along a designated route; alternatively, *combi*

colegio: preparatory school

colonia: city neighborhood or subdivision; similar to *fraccionamiento* or *barrio*

combi: a shared public minibus; alternatively, *colectivo*

comedor: small restaurant

correo: post office

criollo: person of all-Spanish descent born in the New World

cuadra: city block

Cuaresma: Lent

cuota: literally "toll," commonly refers to a toll highway

curandero, curandera: indigenous medicine man or woman

dama: lady

Domingo de Ramos: Palm Sunday

Don, Doña: title of respect, generally used for an older man or woman

158

ejido: a constitutional, government-sponsored form of community, with shared land ownership and cooperative decision-making

encomienda: colonial award of tribute from a designated indigenous district

farmacia: pharmacy or drugstore

finca: farm

fraccionamiento: city sector or subdivision; similar to *colonia* or *barrio*

gasolinera: gasoline station

gringo: term referring to North American Caucasians, sometimes derogatorily, sometimes not

grito: impassioned cry; *El Grito* commonly refers to Mexican Independence Day celebrations, from Hidalgo's *Grito de Dolores*

hacienda: large landed estate; also the government treasury

impuestos, I.V.A. (pronounced EE-va): taxes, value-added tax

indígena: indigenous person; commonly, but incorrectly, an indian (*indio*)

jardín: garden or small park

jejenes: "no-see-um" biting gnats

judiciales: the federal or state police, best known to motorists for their highway checkpoint inspections; alternatively, *federales*

lancha: small motorboat; alternatively, *panga*

larga distancia: long-distance telephone service, or the *caseta* (booth) where it's provided

licenciado: academic degree (abbr. Lic.) approximately equivalent to a bachelor's degree

lonchería: small lunch counter, usually serving juices, sandwiches, and *antojitos* (Mexican snacks)

machismo; macho: exaggerated sense of maleness; person who holds such a sense of himself

mescal: alcoholic beverage distilled from the fermented hearts of maguey (century plant)

mestizo: person of mixed European/indigenous descent

milpa: native farm plot, usually of corn, squash, and/or beans

mordida: slang for bribe; literally, "little bite"

palapa: thatched-roof structure, often open air

panga: small motorboat; alternatively, *lancha*

parque central: town plaza or central square; alternatively, *zócalo*

PEMEX: government gasoline station, acronym for "Petróleos Mexicanos," Mexico's national oil corporation

peninsulares: the Spanish-born ruling colonial elite

petate: a mat, traditionally woven of palm leaf

plan: political manifesto, usually by a leader or group consolidating or seeking power

plaza: shopping mall

policía: municipal police, alternatively *preventativa*

Porfiriato: the 34-year (1876-1910) ruling period of president-dictator Porfirio Díaz

pozole: popular stew of hominy in broth, usually topped by shredded pork, cabbage, and diced onion

presidencia municipal: the headquarters, like a U.S. city or county hall, of a Mexican *municipio,* a county-like local governmental unit

propina: tip, as at a restaurant or hotel; alternatively, *servicio*

pueblo: town or people

puta: whore

quinta: a villa or country house

retorno: highway turnaround

Semana Santa: literally Holy Week, the week before Easter, a popular travel period for Mexicans

temporada: season, as in *temporada alta/baja* (high/low season)

tenate: soft, pliable basket, without handle, woven of palm leaf

terminal camionera: central bus station; alternatively, *camionera central*

vecinidad: neighborhood, alternatively *barrio*

zócalo: town plaza or central square; alternatively, *parque central*

ABBREVIATIONS

Av.: *avenida* (avenue)

Blvd.: *bulevar* (boulevard)

Calz.: *calzada* (thoroughfare, main road)

Carr.: *carretera* (highway)

Col.: *colonia* (subdivision)

Nte.: *norte* (north)

Yucatec Maya Glossary

The Maya language family includes 30 distinct languages, together spoken by nearly six million people in Mexico, Guatemala, and Belize. Yucatec Maya is spoken by around 800,000 people, and is the most commonly spoken Maya language in the Yucatán Peninsula (and second overall, after K'iche in Guatemala). Most ancient glyphs were written in early forms of Yucatec Maya or another Maya language, Ch'ol.

MAYA GODS AND CEREMONIES

Acanum: protective deity of hunters
Ahau Can: serpent lord and highest priest
Ahau Chamehes: deity of medicine
Ah Cantzicnal: aquatic deity
Ah Chuy Kak: god of violent death and sacrifice
Ahcit Dzamalcum: protective god of fishermen
Ah Cup Cacap: god of the underworld who denies air
Ah Itzám: the water witch
Ah kines: priests that consult the oracles and preside over ceremonies and sacrifices
Ahpua: god of fishing
Ah Puch: god of death
Ak'Al: sacred marsh where water abounds
Bacaboob: supporters of the sky and guardians of the cardinal points, who form a single god, Ah Cantzicnal Becabs
Bolontiku: the nine lords of the night
Chaac: god of rain and agriculture
Chac Bolay Can: butcher serpent living in the underworld
Chaces: priests' assistants in agricultural and other ceremonies
Cihuateteo: women who become goddesses through death in childbirth
Cit Chac Coh: god of war

Hetzmek: ceremony when the child is first carried astride the hip
Hobnil Bacab: bee god, protector of beekeepers
Holcanes: warriors charged with obtaining slaves for sacrifice
Hunab Ku: giver of life, builder of the universe, and father of Itzámna
Ik: god of the wind
Itzámna: lord of the skies, creator of the beginning, god of time
Ixchel: goddess of birth, fertility, and medicine; credited with inventing spinning
Ixtab: goddess of the cord and of suicide by hanging
Kinich: face of the sun
Kukulcán: quetzal-serpent, plumed serpent
Metnal: the underworld, place of the dead
Nacom: warrior chief
Noh Ek: Venus
Pakat: god of violent death
Zec: spirit lords of beehives

FOOD AND DRINK

alche: inebriating drink, sweetened with honey and used for ceremonies and offerings
ic: chili
itz: sweet potato
kabaxbuul: heaviest meal of the day, eaten at dusk and containing cooked black beans
kah: pinole flour
kayem: ground maize
macal: a root
muxubbak: tamale
on: avocado
op: plum
p'ac: tomatoes
put: papaya
tzamna: black bean
uah: tortillas
za: maize drink

ANIMALS

acehpek: dog used for deer hunting
ah maax cal: prattling monkey
ah maycuy: chestnut deer
ah sac dziu: white thrush
ah xixteel ul: rugged land conch
bil: hairless dog reared for food
cutz: wild turkey
cutzha: duck
hoh: crow
icim: owl
jaleb: hairless dog
keh: deer
kitam: wild boar
muan: evil bird related to death
que: parrot
thul: rabbit
tzo: domestic turkey
utiu: coyote

MUSIC AND FESTIVALS

ah paxboob: musicians
bexelac: turtle shell used as percussion instrument
chohom: dance performed in ceremonies related to fishing
chul: flute
hom: trumpet
kayab: percussion instrument fashioned from turtle shell
Oc na: festival where old idols of a temple are broken and replaced with new ones
okot uil: dance performed during the Pocan ceremony
Pacum chac: festival in honor of the war gods
tunkul: drum
zacatan: drum made from a hollowed tree trunk; one opening is covered with hide

ELEMENTS OF TIME

baktun: 144,000-day Maya calendar
chumuc akab: midnight
chumuc kin: midday
emelkin: sunset
haab: solar calendar of 360 days plus five extra days of misfortune, which complete the final month
kaz akab: dusk
kin: the sun, the day, the unity of time
potakab: time before dawn
yalhalcab: dawn

NUMBERS

hun: one
ca: two
ox: three
can: four
ho: five
uac: six
uuc: seven
uacax: eight
bolon: nine
iahun: ten
buluc: eleven
iahca: twelve
oxlahum: thirteen
canlahum: fourteen
holahun: fifteen
uaclahun: sixteen
uuclahun: seventeen
uacaclahun: eighteen
bolontahun: nineteen
hunkal: twenty

PLANTS AND TREES

ha: cacao seed
kan ak: plant that produces a yellow dye
ki: sisal
kiixpaxhkum: chayote
kikche: tree trunk that is used to make canoes
kuche: red cedar tree
k'uxub: annatto tree
piim: fiber of the cotton tree
taman: cotton plant
tauch: black zapote tree
tazon te: moss

MISCELLANEOUS WORDS

ah kay kin bak: meat-seller
chaltun: water cistern
cha te: black vegetable dye
chi te: eugenia, plant for dyeing
ch'oh: indigo
ek: dye
hadzab: wooden swords

halach uinic: leader
mayacimil: smallpox epidemic
palapa: traditional Maya structure constructed without nails or tools
pic: underskirt
ploms: rich people

suyen: square blanket
xanab: sandals
xicul: sleeveless jacket decorated with feathers
xul: stake with a pointed, fire-hardened tip
yuntun: slings

Spanish Phrasebook

Spanish commonly uses 30 letters—the familiar English 26, plus four straightforward additions: ch, ll, ñ, and rr.

PRONUNCIATION

Once you learn them, Spanish pronunciation rules—in contrast to English and other languages—generally don't change. Spanish vowels generally sound softer than in English.

Vowels

a like ah, as in "hah": *agua* AH-gooah (water), *pan* PAHN (bread), and *casa* CAH-sah (house)

e like eh, as in "hem": *mesa* MEH-sah (table), *tela* TEH-lah (cloth), and *de* DEH (of, from)

i like ee, as in "need": *diez* dee-EHZ (ten), *comida* ko-MEE-dah (meal), and *fin* FEEN (end)

o like oh, as in "go": *peso* PEH-soh (weight), *ocho* OH-choh (eight), and *poco* POH-koh (a bit)

u like oo, as in "cool": *uno* OO-noh (one), *cuarto* KOOAHR-toh (room), and *usted* oos-TEHD (you); when it follows a "q" the u is silent: *quiero* ki-EH-ro (I want); when it follows an "h" or has an umlaut, it's pronounced like "w": *huevo* WEH-vo (egg)

Consonants

b, d, f, k, l, m, n, p, q, s, t, v, w, x, y, z, ch pronounced almost as in English; h is silent

c like k, as in "keep": *cuarto* KOOAR-toh (room), *Tepic* tay-PEEK (capital of Nayarit state); when it precedes "e" or "i," pronounce c like s, as in "sit": *cerveza* sehr-VEH-sah (beer), *encima* ehn-SEE-mah (atop)

g like g, as in "gift" when it precedes "a," "o," "u," or a consonant: *gato* GAH-toh (cat), *hago* AH-goh (I do, make); otherwise, pronounce g like h, as in "hat": *giro* HEE-roh (money order), *gente* HEN-tay (people)

j like h, as in "has": *Jueves* HOOEH-vehs (Thursday), *mejor* meh-HOR (better)

ll like y, as in "yes": *toalla* toh-AH-yah (towel), *ellos* EH-yohs (they, them)

ñ like ny, as in "canyon": *año* AH-nyo (year), *señor* SEH-nyor (mister, sir)

r is lightly trilled: *pero* PEH-roh (but), *tres* TREHS (three), *cuatro* KOOAH-troh (four)

rr like a Spanish r, but with much more emphasis and trill: *burro* (donkey), *carretera* (highway), *ferrocarril* (railroad)

Note: The single exception to the above is the pronunciation of y when it's being used as the Spanish word for "and," as in *Eva y Leo.* In such case, pronounce it like the English ee, as in "keep": Eva "ee" Leo (Eva and Leo).

Accent

The rule for accent, the relative stress given to syllables within a given word, is straightforward. If a word ends in a vowel, an "n," or an "s," accent the next-to-last syllable; if not, accent the last syllable.

Pronounce *gracias* GRAH-seeahs (thank you), *orden* OHR-dehn (order), and *carretera* kah-reh-TEH-rah (highway) with the stress on the next-to-last syllable.

Otherwise, accent the last syllable: *venir* vay-NEER (to come), *ferrocarril* feh-roh-cah-REEL (railroad), and *edad* eh-DAHD (age).

Exceptions to the accent rule are always marked with an accent sign: (á, é, í, ó, or ú), such as *teléfono* teh-LEH-foh-noh (telephone), *jabón* hah-BON (soap), and *rápido* RAH-pee-doh (rapid).

BASIC AND COURTEOUS EXPRESSIONS

Most Spanish-speakers consider formalities important. Whenever approaching anyone, try to say the appropriate salutation—good morning, good evening, etc. Standing alone, the greeting *hola* (hello) can sound brusque.

Hello. *Hola.*
Good morning. *Buenos días.*
Good afternoon. *Buenas tardes.*
Good evening. *Buenas noches.*
How are you? *¿Cómo está Usted?*
Very well, thank you. *Muy bien, gracias.*
Okay; good. *Bien.*
Not okay; bad. *No muy bien; mal.*
So-so. *Más o menos.*
And you? *¿Y usted?*
Thank you. *Gracias.*
Thank you very much. *Muchas gracias.*
You're very kind. *Muy amable.*
You're welcome. *De nada.*
Good-bye. *Adios.*
See you later. *Hasta luego.*
please *por favor*
yes *sí*
no *no*
I don't know. *No sé.*
Just a moment, please. *Un momento, por favor.*
Excuse me, please (when you're trying to get attention). *Disculpe* or *Con permiso.*
Excuse me (when you've made a mistake). *Lo siento.*
Pleased to meet you. *Mucho gusto.*
Do you speak English? *¿Habla Usted inglés?*
Is English spoken here? *¿Se habla inglés?*
I don't speak Spanish well. *No hablo bien el español.*
I don't understand. *No entiendo.*

How do you say . . . in Spanish? *¿Cómo se dice . . . en español?*
What is your name? *¿Cómo se llama Usted?*
My name is . . . *Me llamo . . .*
Would you like . . . *¿Quisiera Usted . . .*
Let's go to . . . *Vamos a . . .*

TERMS OF ADDRESS

When in doubt, use the formal *Usted* (you) as a form of address.

I *yo*
you (formal) *Usted*
you (familiar) *tu*
he/him *él*
she/her *ella*
we/us *nosotros*
you (plural) *ustedes*
they/them *ellos* (all males or mixed gender); *ellas* (all females)
mister, sir *señor*
missus, ma'am *señora*
miss, young lady *señorita*
wife *esposa*
husband *esposo*
friend *amigo* (male); *amiga* (female)
boyfriend; girlfriend *novio; novia*
son; daughter *hijo; hija*
brother; sister *hermano; hermana*
father; mother *padre; madre*
grandfather; grandmother *abuelo; abuela*

TRANSPORTATION

Where is . . . ? *¿Dónde está . . . ?*
How far is it to . . . ? *¿A cuánto está . . . ?*
from . . . to . . . *de . . . a . . .*
How many blocks? *¿Cuántas cuadras?*
Where (Which) is the way to . . . ? *¿Dónde está el camino a . . . ?*
the bus station *la terminal de autobuses*
the bus stop *la parada de autobuses*
Where is this bus going? *¿Adónde va este autobús?*
the taxi stand *la parada de taxis*
the train station *la estación de ferrocarril*
the boat *el barco* or *la lancha*
the airport *el aeropuerto*

I'd like a ticket to . . . *Quisiera un boleto a . . .*
first (second) class *primera (segunda) clase*
roundtrip *ida y vuelta*
reservation *reservación*
baggage *equipaje*
Stop here, please. *Pare aquí, por favor.*
the entrance *la entrada*
the exit *la salida*
the ticket office *la taquilla*
(very) near; far *(muy) cerca; lejos*
to; toward *a*
by; through *por*
from *de*
the right *la derecha*
the left *la izquierda*
straight ahead *derecho; directo*
in front *en frente*
beside *al lado*
behind *atrás*
the corner *la esquina*
the stoplight *el semáforo*
a turn *una vuelta*
here *aquí*
somewhere around here *por aquí*
right there *allí*
somewhere around there *por allá*
street; boulevard *calle; bulevar*
highway *carretera*
bridge *puente*
toll *cuota*
address *dirección*
north; south *norte; sur*
east; west *oriente (este); poniente (oeste)*

ACCOMMODATIONS

hotel *hotel*
Is there a room? *¿Hay cuarto?*
May I (may we) see it? *¿Podría (podríamos) verlo?*
What is the rate? *¿Cuál es la tarifa?*
Is that your best rate? *¿Es su mejor precio?*
Is there something cheaper? *¿Hay algo más económico?*
a single room *un cuarto sencillo*
a double room *un cuarto doble*

double bed *cama matrimonial*
twin bed *cama individual*
with private bath *con baño privado*
hot water *agua caliente*
shower *ducha; regadera*
towels *toallas*
soap *jabón*
toilet paper *papel higiénico*
blanket *cobija*
sheets *sábanas*
air-conditioned *aire acondicionado*
fan *abanico; ventilador*
key *llave*
manager *gerente*

FOOD

I'm hungry *Tengo hambre.*
I'm thirsty. *Tengo sed.*
menu *carta; menú*
order *orden*
glass *vaso*
fork *tenedor*
knife *cuchillo*
spoon *cuchara*
napkin *servilleta*
soft drink *refresco*
coffee *café*
tea *té*
drinking water *agua pura; agua potable*
carbonated water *agua mineral*
bottled uncarbonated water *agua sin gas*
beer *cerveza*
wine *vino*
milk *leche*
juice *jugo*
cream *crema*
sugar *azúcar*
cheese *queso*
snack *antojito; botana*
breakfast *desayuno*
lunch *almuerzo or comida*
daily lunch special *comida corrida*
dinner *cena*
the check *la cuenta*
eggs *huevos*
bread *pan*
salad *ensalada*

fruit *fruta*
mango *mango*
watermelon *sandía*
papaya *papaya*
banana *plátano*
apple *manzana*
orange *naranja*
lime *limón*
fish *pescado*
shellfish *mariscos*
shrimp *camarones*
meat (without) *(sin) carne*
chicken *pollo*
pork *puerco*
beef; steak *res; bistec*
bacon; ham *tocino; jamón*
fried *frito*
roasted *asado*
barbecue; barbecued *barbacoa; al carbón*
food to go *comida para llevar; para llevar*
delivery service *servicio a domicilio*

SHOPPING

money *dinero*
money-exchange bureau *casa de cambio*
I would like to exchange travelers checks. *Quisiera cambiar cheques de viajero.*
What is the exchange rate? *¿Cuál es el tipo de cambio?*
How much is the commission? *¿Cuánto cuesta la comisión?*
Do you accept credit cards? *¿Aceptan tarjetas de crédito?*
money order *giro*
How much does it cost? *¿Cuánto cuesta?*
What is your final price? *¿Cuál es su último precio?*
expensive *caro*
cheap *barato; económico*
more *más*
less *menos*
a little *un poco*
too much *demasiado*

HEALTH

Help me please. *Ayúdeme por favor.*
I am ill. *Estoy enfermo.*
Call a doctor. *Llame un doctor.*
Take me to... *Lléveme a...*
hospital *hospital; clinica medica*
drugstore *farmacia*
pain *dolor*
fever *fiebre*
headache *dolor de cabeza*
stomachache *dolor de estómago*
burn *quemadura*
cramp *calambre*
nausea *náusea*
vomiting *vomitar*
medicine *medicina*
antibiotic *antibiótico*
pill; tablet *pastilla*
aspirin *aspirina*
ointment; cream *pomada; crema*
bandage *venda*
cotton *algodón*
sanitary napkins *Kotex*
birth control pills *pastillas anticonceptivas*
contraceptive foam *espuma anticonceptiva*
condoms *preservativos; condones*
contact lenses *pupilentes*
glasses *lentes*
dental floss *hilo dental*
dentist *dentista*
toothbrush *cepillo de dientes*
toothpaste *pasta de dientes*
toothache *dolor de dientes*
delivery service *servicio a domicilio*

POST OFFICE AND COMMUNICATIONS

long-distance telephone *teléfono de larga distancia*
I would like to call... *Quisiera llamar a...*
collect *por cobrar*
person to person *persona a persona*
credit card *tarjeta de crédito*
post office *correo*
letter *carta*

stamp *estampilla, timbre*
postcard *tarjeta*
air mail *correo aereo*
registered *registrado*
money order *giro*
package; box *paquete; caja*
string; tape *cuerda; cinta*
Internet *internet*
Internet café *ciber café; ciber*
website *página web*
Web search *búsqueda*
link *enlace*
email *correo electrónico*
Skype *Skype*
Facebook *face*

AT THE BORDER

border *frontera*
customs *aduana*
immigration *migración*
tourist card *tarjeta de turista*
inspection *inspección; revisión*
passport *pasaporte*
profession *profesión*
marital status *estado civil*
single *soltero*
married; divorced *casado; divorciado*
widowed *viudado* (male); *viudada*
 (female)
insurance *seguro*
title *título*
driver's license *licencia de manejar*

AT THE GAS STATION

gas station *gasolinera*
gasoline *gasolina*
unleaded *sin plomo*
fill it up, please *lleno, por favor*
tire *llanta*
tire repair shop *vulcanizadora*
air *aire*
water *agua*
oil; oil change *aceite; cambio de aceite*
grease *grasa*
My ... doesn't work. *Mi ... no sirve.*
battery *batería*
radiator *radiador*
alternator *alternador*

generator *generador*
tow truck *grúa*
repair shop *taller mecánico*
tune-up *afinación*
auto parts store *refaccionería*

VERBS

In Spanish, verbs employ mostly predictable forms and come in three classes, which end in *ar, er,* and *ir*. Note that the first-person (*yo*) verb form is often irregular.

to buy *comprar*
I buy, you (he, she, it) buys *compro, compra*
we buy, you (they) buy *compramos, compran*

to eat *comer*
I eat, you (he, she, it) eats *como, come*
we eat, you (they) eat *comemos, comen*

to climb *subir*
I climb, you (he, she, it) climbs *subo, sube*
we climb, you (they) climb *subimos, suben*

Here are more (with irregularities indicated):

to do or make *hacer* (regular except for *hago,* I do or make)
to go *ir* (very irregular: *voy, va, vamos, van*)
to go (walk) *andar*
to love *amar*
to work *trabajar*
to want *desear, querer*
to need *necesitar*
to read *leer*
to write *escribir*
to repair *reparar*
to stop *parar*
to get off (the bus) *bajar*
to arrive *llegar*
to stay (remain) *quedar*
to stay (lodge) *hospedar*

to leave *salir* (regular except for *salgo,* I leave)
to look at *mirar*
to look for *buscar*
to give *dar* (regular except for *doy,* I give)
to carry *llevar*
to have *tener* (irregular but important: *tengo, tiene, tenemos, tienen*)
to come *venir* (similarly irregular: *vengo, viene, venimos, vienen*)

Spanish has two forms of "to be":

to be *estar* (regular except for *estoy,* I am)
to be *ser* (very irregular: *soy, es, somos, son*)

Use *estar* when speaking of location or a temporary state of being: "I am at home." *"Estoy en casa."* "I'm sick." *"Estoy enfermo."* Use *ser* for a permanent state of being: "I am a doctor." *"Soy doctora."*

NUMBERS

zero *cero*
one *uno*
two *dos*
three *tres*
four *cuatro*
five *cinco*
six *seis*
seven *siete*
eight *ocho*
nine *nueve*
10 *diez*
11 *once*
12 *doce*
13 *trece*
14 *catorce*
15 *quince*
16 *dieciseis*
17 *diecisiete*
18 *dieciocho*
19 *diecinueve*
20 *veinte*
21 *veintiuno*
30 *treinta*
40 *cuarenta*
50 *cincuenta*
60 *sesenta*
70 *setenta*
80 *ochenta*
90 *noventa*
100 *cien*
101 *cientiuno*
200 *doscientos*
500 *quinientos*
1,000 *mil*
10,000 *diez mil*
100,000 *cien mil*
1,000,000 *millón*
one half *medio*
one third *un tercio*
one fourth *un cuarto*

TIME

What time is it? *¿Qué hora es?*
It's one o'clock. *Es la una.*
It's three in the afternoon. *Son las tres de la tarde.*
It's 4am *Son las cuatro de la mañana.*
six-thirty *seis y media*
a quarter till eleven *un cuarto para las once*
a quarter past five *las cinco y cuarto*
an hour *una hora*

DAYS AND MONTHS

Monday *lunes*
Tuesday *martes*
Wednesday *miércoles*
Thursday *jueves*
Friday *viernes*
Saturday *sábado*
Sunday *domingo*
today *hoy*
tomorrow *mañana*
yesterday *ayer*
January *enero*
February *febrero*
March *marzo*
April *abril*
May *mayo*
June *junio*
July *julio*
August *agosto*

September *septiembre*	a week *una semana*
October *octubre*	a month *un mes*
November *noviembre*	after *después*
December *diciembre*	before *antes*

Suggested Reading

Beletsky, Les. *Travellers' Wildlife Guides: Southern Mexico*. Northampton, MA: Interlink Books, 2006. A perfect companion guide if you plan on bird-watching, diving/snorkeling, hiking, or canoeing your way through your vacation. Excellent illustrations.

Coe, Andrew. *Archaeological Mexico: A Guide to Ancient Cities and Sacred Sites*. Emeryville, CA: Avalon Travel Publishing, 2001.

Coe, Michael D. *Breaking the Maya Code*. New York: Thames and Hudson, 2012. A fascinating account of how epigraphers, linguists, and archaeologists succeeded in deciphering Maya hieroglyphics.

Coe, Michael D. *The Maya*. New York: Thames and Hudson, 2011. A well-illustrated, easy-to-read volume on the Maya people.

Cortés, Hernán. *Five Letters*. New York: Gordon Press, 1991. Cortés's letters to the king of Spain, telling of his accomplishments and justifying his actions in the New World.

Davies, Nigel. *The Ancient Kingdoms of Mexico*. New York: Penguin Books, 1991. An excellent study of the preconquest of the indigenous peoples of Mexico.

De Landa, Bishop Diego. *Yucatán Before and After the Conquest*. New York: Dover Publications, 2012. This book, translated by William Gates from the original 1566 volume,

has served as the basis for much of the research that has taken place since.

Díaz del Castillo, Bernal. *The Conquest of New Spain*. New York: Penguin Books, 1963. History straight from the adventurer's reminiscences, translated by J. M. Cohen.

Fehrenbach, T. R. *Fire and Blood: A History of Mexico*. New York: Collier Books, 1995. Over 3,000 years of Mexican history, related in a way that will keep you reading.

Ferguson, William M. *Maya Ruins of Mexico in Color*. Norman, OK: University of Oklahoma Press, 1985. Good reading before you go, but too bulky to carry along. Oversized with excellent drawings and illustrations of the archaeological structures of the Maya.

Franz, Carl, and Lorena Havens. *The People's Guide to Mexico*. Berkeley, CA: Avalon Travel, 2012. A humorous guide filled with witty anecdotes and helpful general information for visitors to Mexico. Don't expect any specific city information, just nuts-and-bolts hints for traveling south of the border.

Greene, Graham. *The Power and the Glory*. New York: Penguin Books, 2003. A novel that takes place in the 1920s about a priest and the antichurch movement that gripped Mexico.

Heffern, Richard. *Secrets of the Mind-Altering Plants of Mexico*. New York: Pyramid Books, 1974. A fascinating study of many substances, from ancient ritual hallucinogens to today's medicines that are found in Mexico.

Maya: Divine Kings of the Rain Forest. Cologne: Könemann, 2006. A beautifully compiled book of essays, photographs, and sketches relating to the Maya, past and present. Too heavy to take on the road but an excellent read.

McNay Brumfield, James. *A Tourist in the Yucatán.* Watsonville, CA: Tres Picos Press, 2004. A decent thriller that takes place in the Yucatán Peninsula; good for the beach or a long bus ride.

Meyer, Michael, and William Sherman. *The Course of Mexican History.* New York: Oxford University Press, 2013. A concise one-volume history of Mexico.

Nelson, Ralph. *Popul Vuh: The Great Mythological Book of the Ancient Maya.* Boston: Houghton Mifflin, 1974. An easy-to-read translation of myths handed down orally by the Quiche Maya, family to family, until written down after the Spanish conquest.

Perry, Richard, and Rosalind Perry. *Maya Missions: Exploring Colonial Yucatán.* Santa Barbara, CA: Espadaña Press, 2002. Detailed and informative guide, including excellent hand-drawn illustrations, about numerous colonial missions and structures in the Yucatán Peninsula.

Sodi, Demetrio M. (in collaboration with Adela Fernández). *The Mayas.* Mexico City: Panama Editorial S.A., 1987. This small book presents a fictionalized account of life among the Maya before the conquest. Easy reading for anyone who enjoys fantasizing about what life *might* have been like before recorded history in the Yucatán.

Stephens, John L. *Incidents of Travel in Central America, Chiapas, and Yucatán.* 2 vols. New York: Cosimo Classics, 2008. Good companions to refer to when traveling in the area. Stephens and illustrator Frederick Catherwood rediscovered many of the Maya ruins on their treks that took place in the mid-1800s. Easy reading.

Thompson, J. Eric. *Maya Archaeologist.* Norman, OK: University of Oklahoma Press, 1974. Thompson, a noted Maya scholar, traveled and worked at many of the Maya ruins in the 1930s.

Thompson, J. Eric. *The Rise and Fall of the Maya Civilization.* Norman, OK: University of Oklahoma Press, 1973. One man's story of the Maya. Excellent reading.

Webster, David. *The Fall of the Ancient Maya.* New York: Thames and Hudson, 2002. A careful and thorough examination of the possible causes of one of archaeology's great unsolved mysteries—the collapse of the Classic Maya in the 8th century.

Werner, David. *Where There Is No Doctor.* Palo Alto, CA: The Hesperian Foundation, 1992. This is an invaluable medical aid to anyone traveling not only to isolated parts of Mexico but to any place in the world where there's not a doctor (or the Internet).

Wolf, Eric. *Sons of the Shaking Earth.* Chicago: University of Chicago Press, 1962. An anthropological study of the indigenous and mestizo people of Mexico and Guatemala.

Wright, Ronald. *Time Among the Maya.* New York: Grove Press, 2000. A narrative that takes the reader through the Maya country of today, with historical comments that help put the puzzle together.

Internet Resources

www.bacalarmosaico.com
Laguna Bacalar's online resource for tourists and locals—a mishmash of information, in a good way.

www.backyardnature.net/yucatan
Notes and observations by an experienced naturalist about the major plants and animal species in the northern Yucatán Peninsula.

www.cancunmap.com
An excellent source of detailed maps of the Riviera Maya and some inland archaeological zones.

www.colonial-mexico.com
Photos and text on colonial Mexico by Richard and Rosalind Perry, authors of the *Maya Missions* handbook.

www.intheroo.com
Searchable listings of all kinds (housing, wedding planners, legal services, etc.) for all major Riviera Maya cities, plus maps, articles, and user forums.

www.locogringo.com
Website with extensive business listings for the Riviera Maya.

www.mesoweb.com
Website relating to Mesoamerican cultures, including detailed reports and photos of past and current archaeological digs.

www.mostlymaya.com
Eclectic but informative website on various Maya topics; especially useful for info on Maya languages.

www.qroo.gob.mx
Official website of Quintana Roo state, including information for tourists.

www.sac-be.com
Buggy online version of an English-language Riviera Maya newspaper, with longish articles and reviews of a wide smattering of area destinations, excursions, and restaurants.

www.todotulum.com
Great resource for Tulum—everything from nightlife to real estate.

www.travelyucatan.com
Detailed information and practical advice about traveling to and around the Yucatán Peninsula.

www.visitmahahual.com
Website with information on activities, hotels, and restaurants in Mahahual.

Index

INDEX

List of Maps

Photo Credits

Also Available

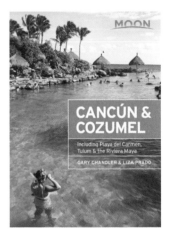

MAP SYMBOLS

═════	Expressway	○	City/Town	✗	Airport	⚲ Golf Course
────	Primary Road	◉	State Capital	✗	Airfield	🅿 Parking Area
────	Secondary Road	⊛	National Capital	▲	Mountain	▲ Archaeological Site
------	Unpaved Road	★	Point of Interest	✦	Unique Natural Feature	⚑ Church
────	Feature Trail	•	Accommodation			⛽ Gas Station
- - - -	Other Trail	▼	Restaurant/Bar	🗽	Waterfall	⬭ Glacier
············	Ferry	■	Other Location	▲	Park	▨ Mangrove
═════	Pedestrian Walkway	Λ	Campground	🚩	Trailhead	⬯ Reef
▥▥▥	Stairs			✗	Skiing Area	⬮ Swamp

CONVERSION TABLES

°C = (°F − 32) / 1.8
°F = (°C × 1.8) + 32
1 inch = 2.54 centimeters (cm)
1 foot = 0.304 meters (m)
1 yard = 0.914 meters
1 mile = 1.6093 kilometers (km)
1 km = 0.6214 miles
1 fathom = 1.8288 m
1 chain = 20.1168 m
1 furlong = 201.168 m
1 acre = 0.4047 hectares
1 sq km = 100 hectares
1 sq mile = 2.59 square km
1 ounce = 28.35 grams
1 pound = 0.4536 kilograms
1 short ton = 0.90718 metric ton
1 short ton = 2,000 pounds
1 long ton = 1.016 metric tons
1 long ton = 2,240 pounds
1 metric ton = 1,000 kilograms
1 quart = 0.94635 liters
1 US gallon = 3.7854 liters
1 Imperial gallon = 4.5459 liters
1 nautical mile = 1.852 km

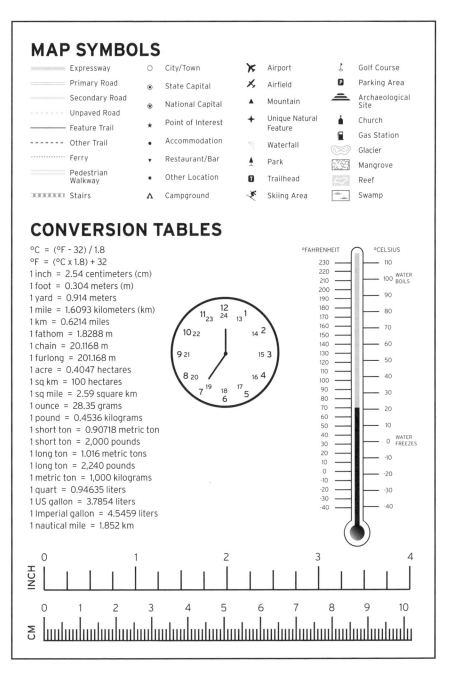

MOON TULUM
Avalon Travel
a member of the Perseus Books Group
1700 Fourth Street
Berkeley, CA 94710, USA
www.moon.com

Editor and Series Manager: Kathryn Ettinger
Copy Editor: Ann Seifert
Graphics Coordinator: Darren Alessi
Production Coordinator: Darren Alessi
Cover Design: Faceout Studios, Charles Brock
Interior Design: Domini Dragoone
Moon Logo: Tim McGrath
Map Editor: Kat Bennett
Cartographers: Brian Shotwell, Kaitlin Jaffe,
    Kat Bennett
Indexer: Greg Jewett

ISBN-13: 978-1-63121-233-8
ISSN: 2469-391X

Printing History
1st Edition — February 2016
5 4 3 2 1

Front cover photo: the Maya ruins of Tulum
    © LOOK Die Bildagentur der Fotografen GmbH /
    Alamy Stock Photo

Printed in Canada by Friesens